The Concept of Human Rights in Judaism, Christianity and Islam

Key Concepts in Interreligious Discourses

Edited by
Georges Tamer

Volume 2

The Concept of Human Rights in Judaism, Christianity and Islam

---

Edited by
Catharina Rachik and Georges Tamer

DE GRUYTER

Published with the friendly support of the Hanns-Seidel-Stifung.

**Hanns
Seidel
Stiftung**

ISBN 978-3-11-056053-4
e-ISBN (PDF) 978-3-11-056157-9
e-ISBN (EPUB) 978-3-11-056064-0
ISSN 2513-1117

Library of Congress Control Number: 2022943042

Bibliographic information published by the Deutsche Nationalbibliothek
The Deutsche Nationalbibliothek lists this publication in the Deutsche Nationalbibliografie;
detailed bibliographic data are available on the Internet at http://dnb.dnb.de.

The Concept of Human Rights in Judaism, Christianity and Islam

Edited by
Catharina Rachik and Georges Tamer

DE GRUYTER

Published with the friendly support of the Hanns-Seidel-Stifung.

**Hanns
Seidel
Stiftung**

ISBN 978-3-11-056053-4
e-ISBN (PDF) 978-3-11-056157-9
e-ISBN (EPUB) 978-3-11-056064-0
ISSN 2513-1117

Library of Congress Control Number: 2022943042

Bibliographic information published by the Deutsche Nationalbibliothek
The Deutsche Nationalbibliothek lists this publication in the Deutsche Nationalbibliografie;
detailed bibliographic data are available on the Internet at http://dnb.dnb.de.

© 2023 Walter de Gruyter GmbH, Berlin/Boston
Printing and binding: CPI books GmbH, Leck

www.degruyter.com

Preface

The present volume in the book series "Key Concepts in Interreligious Discourses" (KCID) contains the results of a conference on the concept of human rights in Judaism, Christianity and Islam held at the Friedrich-Alexander-Universität Erlangen-Nürnberg on December 15–16, 2016. The conference was generously funded by the Hanns Seidel Foundation, which I wish to thank for its manifold and continuous support of our investigation of interreligious discourses in the service of social cohesion and mutual understanding among people of different faith.

The conference and book series "Key Concepts in Interreligious Discourses" (KCID) belong to the main projects of the Bavarian Research Center for Interreligious Discourses (BaFID). The main aim of the Center is the study of the fundamental ideas and central concepts in Judaism, Christianity and Islam in order to uncover their reciprocal connections and reveal similarities and differences between these three religions. In this way, BaFID endeavors to deepen peaceful relationships between religious communities by communicating obtained research results. In addition to the published volumes, particularly salient selections from each volume are made available online in Arabic, English and German on BaFID's website.

In this fashion, BaFID fulfills its aspirations not only by reflecting on central religious ideas amongst a small group of academic specialists, but also by disseminating such ideas in a way appealing to the broader public. Academic research which puts itself at the service of society is vital in order to counteract powerful contemporary trends towards a form of segregation rooted in ignorance, and to strengthen mutual respect and acceptance amongst religions. Such a result is guaranteed due to the methodology deployed by the research center, namely the discursive investigation of the concepts, as documented in the present volume on the concept of human rights.

I wish to thank Dr. Albrecht Döhnert, Dr. Sophie Wagenhofer and their assistants at the publisher house De Gruyter for their competent caretaking of this volume and the entire book series. I would also like to thank Dr. Samuel Wilder for his language assistance in preparing the volume.

Georges Tamer
Erlangen, March 2022

https://doi.org/10.1515/9783110561579-001

Table of Contents

Heiner Bielefeldt

Introduction: Human Rights and Religion(s)

1 Exploring a Multifaceted Relationship

Since World War II, human rights have become the central reference of an international normative consensus.[1] Already the *UN Charter* demands "respect for human rights and for fundamental freedoms of all without distinction as to race, sex, language or religion" as one of the main aspirations of the newly constituted world community.[2] While this reference remains rather abstract, the *Universal Declaration of Human Rights* (UDHR), issued by the General Assembly on 10 December 1948 represents the historical and political breakthrough at the international level.[3] The preamble starts with the due "recognition of the inherent dignity and of the equal and inalienable rights of all members of the human family", thus setting the tone for the rest of the document. Article 1 summarizes the normative profile of human rights by proclaiming: "All human beings are born free and equal in dignity and rights. They are endowed with reason and conscience and should act towards one another in a spirit of brotherhood." The remaining articles spell out a broad range of specific rights, which include civil and political as well as economic, social and cultural rights. The right to freedom of religion or belief (article 18) is of particular significance for the present chapter. It reads as follows: "Everyone has the right to freedom of thought, conscience and religion; this right includes freedom to change his religion or belief, and freedom, either alone or in community with others and in public or private, to manifest his religion or belief in teaching, practice, worship and observance." In the subsequent decades UDHR served as the main reference document for the development of legally binding human rights conventions, including the 1966 *International Covenant on Civil and Political Rights*, which in article 18 confirms and further specifies the right to freedom of religion or belief.

---

1 This article follows in large parts chapter 9 by Bielefeldt, Heiner/Wiener, Michael, *Religious Freedom Under Scrutiny,* Philadelphia: University of Pennsylvania Press, 2020. I would like to express my profound gratitude to Penn Press for the permission to use the text for this introduction.
2 United Nations, *United Nations Charter,* article 1, para. 3, https://www.un.org/en/about-us/un-charter/full-text (accessed on 28.02.2022).
3 United Nations Dag Hammarskjöld Library (ed.), *General Assembly Resolution 217 A,* December 10, 1948, http://www.un.org/en/sections/documents/general-assembly-resolutions/ (accessed on 28.02.2022).

https://doi.org/10.1515/9783110561579-002

While human rights are immediately binding upon States, which under international law are supposed to function as formal guarantors of these rights, their underlying normative ethos permeates societal groups as well, including religious communities. In particular, if religious communities wish to exercise an impact on public political life, they must clarify their own attitude towards human rights. This presents a number of challenges, which religious communities have to face. As I will point out, the liberating spirit does not always fit easily with all elements of the traditional ethical teachings of many religions. The need for clarification, however, also rests on the side of human rights. Obviously, the normative consensus that human rights represent remains precarious. Apart from the proverbial cleavage between normative aspirations and stubborn realities, which has always existed, the very idea of human rights has recently come under renewed pressure. Whereas in the past, criticism of human rights often came from the political left, objections against human rights nowadays often manifest themselves in the language of "traditional religious values".[4] This is one of the reasons, why it is also in the interest of human rights to clarify the relationship towards religion.

In this introduction, I first describe some prima facie affinities and conflicts between the human rights approach and religions (sections 2 and 3). In order to explore that relationship more systematically, I then analyze one of the core functions that define the human rights approach, namely shaping peaceful co-existence of people of different religious or belief-related orientations by empowering human beings (section 4). This empowerment function explains the specific normative authority that human rights claim, including when dealing with religious communities, as well as certain limitations inherent in the human rights approach. The introduction concludes with describing freedom of religion or belief as a custodian right against the danger of turning human rights into an object of idolatry (section 5).

2 Affinities

Human rights language abounds with religious ideas, metaphors and concepts. The 1776 *Declaration of Independence* invokes God as the ultimate guarantor of fundamental rights: "We hold these truths to be self-evident, that all men are created equal, that they are endowed by their Creator with certain unalienable

---

4 See below, section 3 of this introduction.

rights [...]."[5] The French Revolution's *Déclaration de droits de l'homme et du citoyen* (1789), while not explicitly presupposing a divine authority, contains the notion of sacredness, which occurs twice in the text. According to the preamble, the authors "have resolved to set forth in a solemn declaration the natural, inalienable and sacred rights of man." Article 17 qualifies property as a "sacred and inviolable right".[6] Kant, otherwise known as the intellectual epitome of Prussian sobriety, venerates human rights as the "apple of God's eye".[7] In his essay on enlightenment, he warns that "to give up enlightenment altogether, either for oneself or for one's descendants, is to violate and to trample upon the sacred rights of man."[8] A century later, Émile Durkheim declares human rights to be part of a quasi-religious sacralization of the individual, which he thinks belongs to the most important moral achievements of the modern era.[9] Drawing on Durkheim's thoughts, Hans Joas recently published a book titled *The Sacredness of the Person*.[10]

The peculiar closeness to religious language is no coincidence. Notions like "inalienability" or "inviolability" illustrate that human rights exceed the usual pragmatic functions of law. They touch upon existential questions of human life: the inherent dignity of every person, the unconditioned conditions of any normative interaction, the self-understanding of human beings as responsible agents, the ultimate foundations of morality and law, i.e. issues that have also been a traditional domain of various religions. Human rights norms enjoy an elevated rank within the sphere of law. They are not rights like any rights, which people may possess or not possess, appreciate or ignore, acquire or abandon, because what is at stake in human rights is no less than the humanness of the human being. This warrants their qualification as "inalienable rights". Some human rights standards, like the ban on torture or the prohibition of infringements into the person's inner nucleus of faith-formation, command an apodictic

5 Cf. Ushistory.org (ed.), *US Declaration of Independence of 1776*, www.ushistory.org/declaration/document (accessed on 28.02.2022).
6 Cf. The History Guide (ed.), *French Declaration of the Rights of Man and the Citizen*, August 1789, http://historyguide.org/intellect/declaration.html (accessed on 28.02.2022).
7 Kant, Immanuel, "Toward Perpetual Peace," in: Mary Gregor (ed.), *The Cambridge Edition of the Works of Immanuel Kant. Practical Philosophy*, 311–52, Cambridge: Cambridge University Press, 1996, 325: footnote.
8 Kant, Immanuel, "What is Enlightenment?," in: Mary Gregor (ed.), *The Cambridge Edition of the Works of Immanuel Kant. Practical Philosophy*, 11–22, Cambridge: Cambridge University Press, 1996, 20.
9 Cf. Durkheim, Émile, *Les formes élémentaires de la vie religieuse*, Paris: Félix Alcan, 1912.
10 Joas, Hans, *The Sacredness of the Person. A New Genealogy of Human Rights*, Washington D.C.: Georgetown University Press, 2013.

respect without any justifiable exceptions or limitations, even in situations of emergency. These and other prohibitions demarcate the "red lines", which a State must never cross, regardless of the political circumstances. It is no coincidence that these prohibitions have been qualified as "absolute" norms, thus again carrying a predicate that seems to stem from the religious sphere.

One can describe the affinities between human rights and religion from the opposite angle. Some of the principles and concepts that define the human rights approach – human dignity, justice, liberation and equality – resonate profoundly within religious and philosophical traditions.[11] The most frequently cited Biblical metaphor accounting for the special rank of human beings is man's and woman's creation "in the image and likeness of God".[12] The book of Genesis concludes that shedding human blood is taboo.[13] In Psalm 8, the singer admires the sublime beauty of the nightly sky, which makes him simultaneously aware of his frailty and his special calling within the whole of creation. He turns to God wondering: "What is man that you are mindful of him, and the son of Adam that you care for him."[14] Psalm 8 in a way anticipates Kant's observation that "the starry heavens above me" and "the moral law within me" together "fill the mind with ever new and increasing admiration and reverence."[15] Another famous Biblical reference is Israel's escape from slavery. The exodus provides a powerful narrative, which already inspired the first generations of abolitionists in their fight against slave trade and slavery. "Let my people go" – this refrain of a famous gospel song has become the banner of numerous liberation movements to the present day.

Such motives are not a monopoly of the Biblical tradition. The Qur'ān acknowledges man's role as God's vicegerent (*khalīfa*) on earth,[16] which is the reason why even the angels have to bow before Adam.[17] According to sura 33, the human being has taken from God a trust (*amāna*), which the mountains and the heavens, representing the most powerful cosmic elements, had previously re-

---

11 For an overview cf. Swidler, Arlene (ed.), *Human Rights in Religious Traditions*, New York: The Pilgrim Press, 1982.
12 Gen 1:27.
13 Gen 9:6.
14 Pss 8:5 English standard version.
15 Kant, Immanuel, "Critique of Practical Reason," in: Mary Gregor (ed.), *The Cambridge Edition of the Works of Immanuel Kant. Practical Philosophy*, 133–272, Cambridge: Cambridge University Press, 1996, 269. This dictum, which sums up Kant's whole philosophy, has been carved in his tombstone.
16 Sura 2:30.
17 Sura 2:34.

jected.[18] This Qur'ānic verse describes the simultaneous awareness of human frailty and human calling, roughly analogous to Psalm 8. The Qur'ān furthermore warns that whoever kills a man acts as if he killed the whole of humanity,[19] thus ascribing to each individual human being a worth above any utilitarian calculation.

The possibilities to invoke substantial affinities between human rights and religions are manifold and accommodate a broad variety of religious traditions.[20] From this observation, it is only a small step to postulating that human rights and religions move in the same direction concerning their basic normative aspirations. It has been a popular assumption that the ethical principles underlying human rights stem from the Jewish-Christian tradition. Some commentators have defined human rights as "Christian values" in a modern guise.[21] The authors of the *Universal Islamic Human Rights Declaration* of 1981, in turn, contend that human rights directly stem from the Qur'ān.[22] Others take a more ecumenical approach by pointing to substantive overlaps between all the major religions and modern ideas of dignity and rights.[23] Incidentally, it is not only religiously interested people who wish to demonstrate similarities between the ethos of various religions and modern standards of human rights; many human rights advocates, too, strive to solidify human rights norms further by invoking a broad normative consensus traceable to the authoritative scriptures and traditions of the world religions.

---

18 Sura 33:72.

19 Sura 5:32.

20 I limit myself to a few examples from the Bible and the Qur'ān for the simple reason that I know these religious texts better than other scriptures or traditions.

21 Cf. Fikentscher, Wolfgang, "Die heutige Bedeutung des nicht-säkularen Ursprungs der Grundrechte," in: Ernst-Wolfgang Böckenförde/Robert Spaemann (eds.), *Menschenrechte und Menschenwürde. Historische Voraussetzungen – säkulare Gestalt – christliches Verständnis*, 43–73, Stuttgart: Klett-Cotta, 1987.

22 The Universal Islamic Declaration of Human Rights (1981) proclaims in its foreword: "Islam gave to mankind an ideal code of human rights fourteen centuries ago." Cf. http://www.alhewar.com/ISLAMDECL.html (accessed on 28.02.2022). See also Bielefeldt, Heiner, "'Western' versus 'Islamic' Human Rights Conceptions? A Critique of Cultural Essentialism in the Discussion on Human Rights," *Political Theory* 28 (2000), 90–121.

23 Cf. Little, David/Sachedina, Abdulaziz A./Kelsay, John, "Human Rights and World's Religions: Christianity, Islam and Religious Liberty," in: Nazila Ghanea (ed.), *Religion and Human Rights. Why Protect Freedom of Religion or Belief and Models for Protection of Freedom of Religion or Belief?*, 57–83, New York: Routledge, 2010.

3 Conflicts

Those who postulate a harmonious relationship between human rights and religious traditions have to face a number of serious challenges, however. Gender-related rights are the most obvious area of conflict. The equality of men and women is deeply anchored in numerous human rights documents, starting with the *UN Charta* and not ending with the 1979 *Convention on the Elimination of All Forms of Discrimination Against Women* (CEDAW). This collides with traditional gender roles, which are often justified in the name of religion. The potential for conflicts increases steeply once we add the more recent claims of non-discrimination based on sexual orientation and gender identity.

Freedom of religion or belief is another contentious issue. Owing to its universal nature, freedom of religion or belief necessarily provides space also for critics, dissenters, converts, the members of schismatic movements, sceptics, agnostics and various minorities. For some believers this is not easy to accept. Especially the right to change one's religion remains a provocation. Doesn't this mean to place the individual and his or her personal preferences above divine laws? If so, doesn't this illustrate the "Promethean" spirit of human rights, in the name of which man rebels against his creator? The significance of such fundamental objections for understanding ongoing reservations against human rights can hardly be overemphasized. Apart from the more specific areas of contestations, e.g. in the area of gender rights, it is *the human rights approach as such* that has frequently caused suspicion, anxiety and opposition, given its emancipatory thrust epitomized in notions of empowerment, liberation and equal respect for all.

In the case of the Catholic Church, the history of open resistance started as early as in 1791, when Pope Pius VI in his *Breve Quod Aliquantum* condemned the French Revolution's human rights declaration as a deviation from the right path as defined by the Church. The official polemics culminated in the notorious *Syllabus Errorum* (1864), in which Pius IX castigated human rights among other grave errors of modernity. The conflict gradually ebbed away towards the turn of the century and came to an official end in the encyclical *Pacem in terries* (1963) through which John XXIII acknowledged human rights among the hopeful "signs of the time".[24] The Protestant churches, too, had their complicated historical encounters with human rights. A century ago, church historian Ernst Troeltsch deconstructed the popular idea that human rights have their origins

---

24 Cf. Hilpert, Konrad, *Menschenrechte und Theologie: Forschungsbeiträge zur ethischen Dimension der Menschenrechte*, Freiburg: Herder, 2001, 390 ff.

in the Protestant Reformation. He pointed out that, unlike some of the marginalized "step children" of the Reformation, i.e. spiritualists, sectarians and free-churches, the mainstream Protestant churches only gradually overcame their initial reluctance towards the modern concept of equal rights of freedom for all.[25] Reservations against human rights continue to be strong within the family of Orthodox Churches. Representatives of the Russian Orthodox Church have repeatedly associated human rights with "Western" ideas, which they think should not spread on Russian soil.[26] Obviously, there are also numerous human rights conflicts in Islamic societies. Some Islamist intellectuals construe an antagonism between "rights of man" and "rights of God". Others oppose human rights as part of what they consider a "Westoxication", i.e. an alleged Western subversion aimed at undermining collective Islamic identities.[27] Those holding such views, frequently call for authoritarian policies against human rights orientated civil society organizations, which they stigmatize as fifth columns operating in the service of alien and hostile forces.

In the view of many traditionalist critics, human rights reflect an anthropocentric ideology centered on the idea that "man is the measure of all things".[28] In addition to this come concerns that individual freedom could erode communitarian loyalty. Others lament what they consider a one-sided emphasis on legal claims, to the detriment of duties and responsibilities. Such conservative reservations often manifest themselves in the language of "traditional religious values" which have been pitted against the emancipatory spirit of modern human rights. An example is the discussion on traditional values, which culminated in the adoption of two resolutions by the UN Human Right Council in 2009 and 2012. The resolution of September 2012 carries the title *Promoting Human Rights and Fundamental Freedoms through a Better Understanding of Traditional Values of Humankind.*[29] One of the problems of this resolution is that it fails to define the crucial term "traditional values", which remains entirely nebulous. Critics of the resolution fear that the amalgamation of human rights standards

---

25 Cf. Troeltsch, Ernst: *Die Soziallehren der christlichen Kirchen und Gruppen*, Tübingen: J. C. B. Mohr, 1912.

26 Cf. Willems, Joachim: "Die Russisch-Orthodoxe Kirche und die Menschenrechte," in: Heiner Bielefeldt (ed.), *Jahrbuch Menschenrechte 2009. Schwerpunkt: Religionsfreiheit*, 152–65, Wien: Böhlau, 2008.

27 Cf. Mayer, Ann E., *Islam and Human Rights: Tradition and Politics*, Boulder: Westview, [5]2012.

28 This motto has been ascribed to the Ancient Greek sophist Protagoras.

29 Cf. United Nations Human Rights Council (ed.), *Resolution 12/3*, October 1, 2009, www.ohchr.org/EN/HRBodies/HRC/RegularSessions/Session12/Pages/ResDecStat.aspx (accessed on 28.02.2022).

with undefined "traditional values" will cause a loss of normative clarity. They furthermore point to the fact that the Russian Federation, a State not known for a pro-human rights agenda, acted as the driving force pushing the "traditional values" agenda, with support of the Russian Orthodox Church.

In 2008, the Moscow Patriarchate issued a document on its understanding of human rights. While cautiously endorsing the notion of human rights, the document contains a number of far-reaching reservations. Even the idea of human dignity receives a surprising anti-egalitarian turn. While the Moscow Patriarchate generally acknowledges everyone's dignity as a divine gift, the document at the same time stresses the need for "restoring a person to his appropriate dignity".[30] Drawing on a terminological distinction established by the early Church Fathers, the Moscow Patriarchate differentiates between the being created "in the image of God", which includes all human beings, and the "likeness of God", which has been lost through man's fall and thus requires active efforts for restauration. This suggests that the dignity of the individual exists in different measures, depending on the degree of living in accordance with the moral teachings of the Church.

The *Cairo Declaration on Human Rights in Islam* adopted by the OIC in 1990 displays a similar ambiguity. After proclaiming that all humans are equal in their dignity, the document adds that "the true religion is the guarantee for enhancing such dignity along the path to human integrity."[31] Here again, dignity appears to be an attribute which can be increased by acts of piety and religious compliance. Instead of providing the normative basis for everyone's equal dignity and equal rights, the term dignity thus assumes a meritocratic, i.e. anti-egalitarian meaning. This is not the only stumbling block. The 1990 Cairo Declaration fails to recognize equal rights of men and women. Another striking feature is the absence of freedom of religion, which the Cairo Declaration replaces by a prohibition "to exploit the poverty and ignorance" of people with the intention to convert them to any religion or belief other than Islam.[32] This formulation does not merely fall short of article 18 of the UDHR and article 18 of the ICCPR; it actually turns their meaning upside down. Finally, the 1990 Cairo Declaration stipulates that all the

---

30 Cf. The Russian Orthodox Church. Department for External Church Relations (ed.), *The Russian Orthodox Church's Basic Teachings on Human Dignity, Freedom and Rights*, 2008, https://old. mospat.ru/en/documents/dignity-freedom-rights/ (accessed on 28.02.2022).
31 Article 1 of the Cairo Declaration of Human Rights in Islam. Cf. University of Minnesota Human Rights Library (ed.), *Cairo Declaration of Human Rights in Islam*, Aug. 5, 1990, U.N. GAOR, World Conf. on Hum. Rts., 4th Sess., Agenda Item 5, U.N. Doc. A/CONF.157/PC/62/ Add.18, 1993 [English translation], http://hrlibrary.umn.edu/instree/cairodeclaration.html (accessed on 28.02.2022).
32 Cf. article 10 of the Cairo Declaration.

rights enumerated in the document remain subject to the Islamic sharia.[33] It is therefore fair to say that the Cairo Declaration, in its version of 1990, is even further remote from the UN human rights standards than the document of the Moscow Patriarchate. What both have in common is a tendency to counter the emancipatory spirit of human rights by the primacy of traditional religious values and religious laws. One should take note, however, that the Organization for Islamic Cooperation (OIC) updated the Cairo Declaration in 2021. The new version differs substantially from the text of 1990 and is much more in line with international human rights standards.

In the face of ambiguous positions and ongoing religious opposition, sceptics have wondered whether human rights and religions could ever fully fit together. Such scepticism, which historically mainly came from religious traditionalists, has also become popular in humanist circles who consider the continued influence of religious communities as a main obstacle to a consistent implementation of human rights. The analysis of specific conflicts, for example around gender-related emancipation, culminates in the diagnosis of an allegedly unbridgeable gulf between human rights and religion(s) in general.

It is worth noting in this context that the term "humanism" carries very different connotations, depending on the context in which it is used. In the German context, there is still a strong tendency to associate "Humanismus" to Christian intellectuals like Erasmus of Rotterdam or Thomas Moore, who strived for a new synthesis of Christian theology and philanthropic classical philosophy. From this angle, there is no inherent contradiction between religious and humanistic positions.[34] In English, by contrast, the term "humanism" usually signifies a more critical attitude towards religion. Humanists in this understanding often subscribe to anti- or post-religious belief systems, at times based on a thoroughly scientific worldview. Julian Huxley, first president of the British Humanist Association and one of the founders of the International Ethical and Humanist Union, promoted an atheistic worldview, to which he contributed from his scientific background as an evolutionary biologist. Richard Dawkins, author of the bestseller *The God Delusion*,[35] likewise comes from evolutionary biology. Through his books, Dawkins exercises a strong influence among humanist circles, not only in Britain.

---

33 Cf. articles 24 and 25 of the Cairo Declaration (version of 1990).
34 Many of the "humanistic gymnasiums" in Germany are actually run by the Catholic Church. While in German language this observation holds no surprise, in English it sounds like a fully-fledged oxymoron.
35 Dawkins, Richard, *The God Delusion*, London: Bantam Press, 2006.

Now, it is obviously tempting to associate "human rights" with "humanism". For both terms have a common linguistic root, which at the same time points to a common interest to acknowledge the central place human beings occupy in ethical practice. Yet this common linguistic root can also cause confusion when leading to narrowly humanistic ownership-claims through which the human rights concept itself would take on a post-religious or anti-religious flavor. Some humanists actually claim that their own human rights commitment is from the outset more consistent than that of faith-based organizations, because the latter have to struggle with possible contradictions between their Holy Scriptures, on the one hand, and modern human rights documents, on the other. Obviously, non-religious humanists do not have this problem. However, to conclude that humanists are generally better suited for promoting human rights than the followers of the various religions would amount to a particularly "humanistic" superiority claim, which would be no less corrosive for a broad acceptance of human rights than exclusive Christian or other religious ownership claims on human rights.

4 Shaping Pluralism by Empowering Human Beings

The two complementary perspectives on the relationship between human rights and religions – the emphasis on affinities and the stress on conflicts – are based on correct observations from which they both draw problematic consequences. It is true that some of the basic ideas underlying human rights have existed in the ethical teaching of various religions, possibly since centuries or millennia. Human dignity may be the most obvious example. Moreover, many religious believers show strong commitment for the cause of human rights, without in the least feeling schizophrenic. This observation defies abstractly antagonistic constructions of the relationship between human rights and religions. On the other hand, those who assume that human rights and religions per se move in the same direction may fail to take differences and conflicts seriously enough. Even the normative affinities between human rights and religions, to which we have pointed above, cannot be taken for granted; they must be carved out actively, which requires embarking on reform projects towards innovative exegesis, hermeneutics and critical theology.

Critics who place all the emphasis on normative tensions between human rights and religions likewise capture an important aspect of that complicated relationship. They may base their scepticism on conflicts concerning gender-issues as well as different attitudes towards emancipation and equality in general. However, such conflicts do not necessarily display a zero-sum-logic such that one side could only win what the other side loses. Turning existing tensions into an abstract either-or-dichotomy would amount to denying, from the outset, any possibility of a meaningful normative rapprochement between the ethos of religions and the modern idea of human rights. As result of such dichotomized views, human rights commitment would remain reserved to a comparatively small circle of religiously distanced humanists.

In order to overcome both harmonious amalgamations and abstract dichotomizations, it is useful to reflect on the specific function that human rights have in facilitating fair coexistence among people living in pluralistic societies. Historically, human rights developed in response to experiences of structural injustice, often linked to conflict-driven pluralization processes. In Europe,[36] much of this happened in the wake of the Protestant Reformation, which had led to an irredeemable schism within Occidental Christendom. Instead of trying to restore confessional homogeneity of the territorial State, which had caused bloodshed for more than a century, human rights represent a paradigm shift towards the *recognition of pluralism*. This recognition goes way beyond the early modern politics of tolerance, because it no longer takes one predominant confession – Catholicism, Lutheran or Reformed Protestantism – as the standard against which to condone or "tolerate" others. Rather, human rights appreciate the pluralism of religions and beliefs as something inherently valuable. This is an innovative approach. Strictly speaking, however, the appreciation of pluralism is not due to the various religious or belief systems themselves; rather, it relates to *human beings*. The guiding idea underpinning the human rights approach is to empower human beings to find their own ways in the area of religion and belief, as long as this is compatible with the equal freedom of others.

The empowerment-function of human rights is more than just a procedural device for managing the existing diversity of convictions, positions, beliefs, ethos forms etc. It rests on a substantive normative insight, namely, the due respect for the *potential of responsible agency inherent in all human beings*. This constitutes the special rank of human dignity, which must be accorded to all human beings equally. Normative claims and obligations of any kind, ranging from personal promises or civil law contracts to constitutional norms and international conventions, necessarily presuppose that human beings have the potential of responsible agency. Even those individuals who actually fail to live up to the expectation

---

36 The reference to a particular history, namely European history, does not imply that Europe provides the binding model, which people from other parts of the world should merely emulate.

of responsible conduct are usually held "responsible" for their shortcomings.[37] This illustrates the indispensable nature of this presupposition; it has an axiomatic status as the point of departure of any normative interaction whatsoever. Accordingly, the recognition of the potential of responsible agency – and thus of human dignity – does not depend on empirical qualities or skills of this or that individual; it defines a fundamental status position, which is to be respected in all human beings equally, simply because they are "members of the human family", to cite from the preamble of the UDHR.[38] Human dignity can only be a universal and egalitarian concept – or it fails to make any sense.

5 Authority, Not Idolatry of Human Rights

What follows from these observations for understanding the relationship between human rights and religions? In order to be able to set the normative framework of free and equal coexistence under the condition of an irreversible pluralism, human rights cannot be just another belief-system – as if they were located at the same level as Christianity, Islam, Hinduism or atheism. If they were simply juxtaposed to the various religions or belief systems, e. g. as a new humanist quasi-religion or "civil religion", human rights would merely enlarge the existing pluralism instead of being able to *shape* pluralistic coexistence normatively by providing a binding framework for all. The predicament would get even worse, if human rights were thought to provide the mere smallest common denominator amidst the ethical teachings contained in various religious traditions. This would amount to reducing them to a dependent variable of the various existing religious and ethical teachings and strip them of any normative authority vis-à-vis religious communities. However, to place human rights "above" religions or beliefs would also lead to alternative impasses. Claiming an unqualified normative superiority for human rights would imply that religions and beliefs would end

---

37 We have to leave out a discussion of borderline cases, in which the potential of responsible agency may appear questionable. The axiomatic status of the ascription of human dignity requires that even such cases must be covered by respect for human dignity. Cf. Bielefeldt, Heiner, *Auslaufmodell Menschenwürde? Warum sie in Frage steht und warum wir sie verteidigen müssen*, Freiburg: Herder, 2011.
38 Cf. Waldron, Jeremy/Dan-Cohen, Meir (eds.), *Dignity, Rank, & Rights. With comments by Wai Chee Dimock, Don Herzog, & Michael Rosen*, Oxford: Oxford University Press, 2015, 33: "So that is my hypothesis: the modern notion of *human* dignity involves an upwards equalization of rank, so that we now try to accord to every human being something of the dignity, rank, and expectation of respect that was formerly accorded to nobility." (Emphasis in the original.)

up as mere "sub-confessions", as it were, under the allegedly all-encompassing and superior human rights framework. It is not likely that many religious believers worldwide would accept such a subordinated role of their faith and their ethos. In addition, such an abstract hierarchy with human rights being on top of the pyramid would undermine the appreciation of diversity, which, as pointed out before, is one of the core functions of human rights.

It is impossible to "locate" human rights one-dimensionally vis-à-vis religions or beliefs. Whatever place one might choose, the result appears fraught with a dilemma. Human rights can neither be located "besides" or "below" religions, nor do they throne "above" them. It does not make sense to reduce them to the smallest common denominator "amidst" various religious traditions and their ethical teachings, nor do human rights come from "outside", i.e. as an alternative belief system aimed at replacing the authority traditionally claimed by religions or beliefs. What all these one-dimensional attempts to define the relationship between human rights and religions have in common is that they fail to consider the place that *human beings* have within that equation. As already mentioned, the human person is the ultimate right's holder within the framework of human rights. When describing the relationship between human rights and religions, we thus must again insert human beings as the common focus of both.

By institutionalizing due respect for the dignity, freedom and equality of human beings, human rights claim a *specific authority*, which is reflected in their qualification as "inalienable rights". This authority manifests itself also vis-à-vis religious communities, which themselves cannot remain outside of the binding framework of human rights. Above all, human rights require the elimination of any coercion between or within religious communities, including threats directed against dissidents, internal critics or converts. Under international human rights law, it falls upon the State to guarantee such strict non-coercion in this field, if need be by employing enforcement mechanisms, in line with rule of law principles. A litmus test of non-coercion is everyone's right to abandon a religious community and turn to another religion or to no religion, which is one of the few absolute guarantees of international human rights law. Apart from preventing violence occurring within and between religious communities, freedom of religion or belief also requires tackling all forms of *structural* religious coercion and discrimination. This implies repealing the criminalization of apostasy, proselytism or public critique of religion, even if deemed "blasphemous" by some. Far-reaching reforms may also be necessary in the area of family laws, which in quite a number of countries reflect traditional religious hegemonies as well as traditional gender roles, often with discriminatory implications in the intersection of both sex/gender and religion. School curriculums may also need a general overhaul, if they fail to reflect the religious and belief-related pluralism that has emerged in the country.

Reform policies enacted with the intention to eliminate direct, indirect and structural forms of religious coercion and discrimination have met with resistance by some religious communities or parts of them. Conservative criticism of human rights is often driven by fear for the future of traditional religious beliefs, values and identities in society. The perception may even be that the State uses the rhetoric of human rights to enforce a doctrinal anthropocentric worldview or a comprehensive humanistic value system, to the detriment of traditional religious beliefs, values and practices. However, this would be a profound misunderstanding. Human rights do not propagate a particular worldview or ideology. They do not follow Ludwig Feuerbach's belief that God is a mere product of human imagination and the projection of unfulfilled mundane yearnings,[39] a conjecture already a century earlier formulated by David Hume.[40] Nor do human rights establish a quasi-religious "cult of human reason". The idea is not to combat religions as "the opium of the people"[41] or replace them by some kind of post-religious doctrine. Indeed, turning human rights into an object of idolatry – a global civil religion or a humanist quasi-religion – would obfuscate their normative profile and ultimately undermine their authority.

Human rights are rights of equal freedom for all. Taking freedom seriously, however, requires respect for people's most different freely adopted orientations, including their freedom to stick to theocentric, cosmocentric and other non-anthropocentric religious worldviews. Freedom of religion or belief inter alia protects voluntary acts of surrendering oneself to God, i.e. positions that stand in the starkest possible contrast to an anthropocentric attitude. Of course, people are likewise free to hold anthropocentric views, if that strikes them more plausible. The important point is that they have broad freedom in this entire field. Moreover, just as human beings are free to adopt a humanistic ("post-religious") value system, they are free to shape their lives in accordance with traditional religious norms and values, as long as this is compatible with the equal freedom of others. For example, believers are free to understand and practice religious fast-

---

39 Cf. Feuerbach, Ludwig, *Vorlesungen über das Wesen der Religion*, Leipzig: Otto Wigand, 1851, 241.
40 Cf. Hume, David, *The Natural History of Religion, edited with an introduction by H.E. Root*, Palo Alto: Stanford University Press, 1956, 29: "There is a universal tendency among mankind to conceive all beings like themselves [...]."
41 Cf. Marx, Karl, *A Contribution to the Critique of Hegel's Philosophy of Right: Introduction*, trans. Allan McKinnon, vol. 3, *Collected Works*, New York: International Publishers, 1976.

ing rules as a strictly-binding divine command, provided they refrain from coercively imposing such rules on others.

The normative aspiration to shape pluralistic coexistence by enshrining respect for everyone's equal freedom implies that the specific authority, which human rights claim in order to fulfil this function, is from the outset a limited one. It is a *non-doctrinal authority,* which presupposes a spirit of *modesty,* i.e. a clear awareness of its inherent limitedness. For example, human rights do not – and cannot – compete with the Bible, the Qur'ān or any other holy book, nor do they contain any answers to the existential questions of human life.

Michael Ignatieff is right when insisting that human rights should not be termed a secular religion: "It is not a creed; it is not a metaphysics. To make it so is to turn it into a species of idolatry: humanism worshipping itself."[42] In spite of the historical significance that the UDHR can claim, it is not a sacred text. While providing binding normative standards for living together, human rights do not aim to replace the religious ethos in society or to remove community-based religious ceremonies, rites and liturgies. Turning the UN High Commissioner for Human Rights into a "high priest" of a worldwide civil religion would merely mock and undermine his position.

Authority and modesty are two sides of the same coin, because they both originate from the empowerment-function that human rights take on behalf of everyone's equal freedom. It is only with a clear awareness of their specific function – and thus of their inherent limitedness – that human rights can unfold the authority they need to be able to shape pluralist coexistence normatively. It is an authority best exercised in a "listening mode", i.e. in tandem with sensitivity to people's freely articulated wishes, needs, vulnerabilities and possibilities, not least in the field of religions and beliefs. Human rights would actually forfeit their specific authority when posing as an object of quasi-religious veneration, as Ignatieff warns. This danger is not merely hypothetical, since there are examples of a lack of modesty in human rights semantics. Freedom of religion or belief therefore has an important role to play, in that it keeps the entire system of human rights open for accommodating the broad range of free manifestations of people's profound convictions, thereby at the same time clarifying that human rights themselves are neither a crypto-religion nor a post-religious comprehen-

---

42 Ignatieff, Michael (ed.), *Human Rights as Politics and Idolatry,* Princeton: Princeton University Press, 2001, 53.

sive belief system.[43] The right to freedom of religion or belief can serve as a critical reminder in this regard.

Bibliography

Bielefeldt, Heiner, "'Western' versus 'Islamic' Human Rights Conceptions? A Critique of Cultural Essentialism in the Discussion on Human Rights," *Political Theory* 28 (2000), 90–121.

Bielefeldt, Heiner, *Auslaufmodell Menschenwürde? Warum sie in Frage steht und warum wir sie verteidigen müssen*, Freiburg: Herder, 2011.

Dawkins, Richard, *The God Delusion*, London: Bantam Press, 2006.

Durkheim, Émile, *Les formes élémentaires de la vie religieuse*, Paris: Félix Alcan, 1912.

Feuerbach, Ludwig, *Vorlesungen über das Wesen der Religion*, Leipzig: Otto Wigand, 1851.

Fikentscher, Wolfgang, "Die heutige Bedeutung des nicht-säkularen Ursprungs der Grundrechte," in: Ernst-Wolfgang Böckenförde/Robert Spaemann (eds.), *Menschenrechte und Menschenwürde. Historische Voraussetzungen – säkulare Gestalt – christliches Verständnis*, 43–73, Stuttgart: Klett-Cotta, 1987.

Hilpert, Konrad, *Menschenrechte und Theologie: Forschungsbeiträge zur ethischen Dimension der Menschenrechte*, Freiburg: Herder, 2001.

Hume, David, *The Natural History of Religion, edited with an introduction by H.E. Root*, Palo Alto: Stanford University Press, 1956.

Ignatieff, Michael (ed.), *Human Rights as Politics and Idolatry*, Princeton: Princeton University Press, 2001.

Islamic Council London (ed.), *The Universal Islamic Declaration of Human Rights* (1981), 21 Dhul Qaidah 1401/19 September 1981, http://www.alhewar.com/ISLAMDECL.html (accessed on 28.02.2022).

Joas, Hans, *The Sacredness of the Person. A New Genealogy of Human Rights*, Washington D.C.: Georgetown University Press, 2013.

---

43 This reflection draws on John Rawls, who in his *Political Liberalism* proposes a distinction between the legally binding concept of "political justice", on the one hand, and a multiplicity of "comprehensive doctrines", on the other. This differentiation is supposed to facilitate a broad endorsement of the guiding idea of political justice within a pluralistic society, which is characterized by a rich diversity of religious or non-religious worldviews, philosophies etc. His main point is that the guiding idea of political justice is *inherently limited* in its scope by having its focus on basic normative issues of fair coexistence and cooperation. Only on the understanding of such inherent limitedness can the idea of political justice claim a practical priority over the various existing worldviews ("comprehensive doctrines"). Whereas the idea of political justice claims a clear priority at the level of politics and law, the various comprehensive doctrines may in many ways exceed the realm of political justice. Rawls's purpose is the facilitation of an "overlapping consensus", which accommodates a broad variety of religions, philosophies and worldviews whose holders may nonetheless be able to endorse the main principles of political justice that normatively govern societal coexistence and cooperation.

Kant, Immanuel, "Critique of Practical Reason," in: Mary Gregor (ed.), *The Cambridge Edition of the Works of Immanuel Kant. Practical Philosophy*, 133–272, Cambridge: Cambridge University Press, 1996.

Kant, Immanuel, "Toward Perpetual Peace," in: Mary Gregor (ed.), *The Cambridge Edition of the Works of Immanuel Kant. Practical Philosophy*, 311–52, Cambridge: Cambridge University Press, 1996.

Kant, Immanuel, "What is Enlightenment?," in: Mary Gregor (ed.), *The Cambridge Edition of the Works of Immanuel Kant. Practical Philosophy*, 11–22, Cambridge: Cambridge University Press, 1996.

Little, David/Sachedina, Abdulaziz A./Kelsay, John, "Human Rights and World's Religions: Christianity, Islam and Religious Liberty," in: Nazila Ghanea (ed.), *Religion and Human Rights. Why Protect Freedom of Religion or Belief and Models for Protection of Freedom of Religion or Belief?*, 57–83, New York: Routledge, 2010.

Marx, Karl, *A Contribution to the Critique of Hegel's Philosophy of Right: Introduction*, trans. Allan McKinnon, vol. 3, *Collected Works*, New York: International Publishers, 1976.

Mayer, Ann E., *Islam and Human Rights: Tradition and Politics*, Boulder: Westview, ⁵2012.

Swidler, Arlene (ed.), *Human Rights in Religious Traditions*, New York: The Pilgrim Press, 1982.

The History Guide (ed.), *French Declaration of the Rights of Man and the Citizen*, August 1789, http://historyguide.org/intellect/declaration.html (accessed on 28.02.2022).

The Russian Orthodox Church. Department for External Church Relations (ed.), *The Russian Orthodox Church's Basic Teachings on Human Dignity, Freedom and Rights*, 2008, https://old.mospat.ru/en/documents/dignity-freedom-rights/ (accessed on 28.02.2022).

Troeltsch, Ernst: *Die Soziallehren der christlichen Kirchen und Gruppen*, Tübingen: J. C. B. Mohr, 1912.

United Nations Dag Hammarskjöld Library (ed.), *General Assembly Resolution 217 A*, December 10, 1948, http://www.un.org/en/sections/documents/general-assembly-reso lutions/ (accessed on 28.02.2022).

United Nations Human Rights Council (ed.), *Resolution 12/3*, October 1, 2009, www.ohchr. org/EN/HRBodies/HRC/RegularSessions/Session12/Pages/ResDecStat.aspx (accessed on 28.02.2022).

United Nations, *United Nations Charter*, article 1, para. 3, https://www.un.org/en/about-us/ un-charter/full-text (accessed on 28.02.2022).

University of Minnesota Human Rights Library (ed.), *Cairo Declaration of Human Rights in Islam*, Aug. 5, 1990, U.N. GAOR, World Conf. on Hum. Rts., 4th Sess., Agenda Item 5, U.N. Doc. A/CONF.157/PC/62/Add.18, 1993 [English translation], http://hrlibrary.umn. edu/instree/cairodeclaration.html (accessed on 28.02.2022).

Ushistory.org (ed.), *US Declaration of Independence of 1776*, www.ushistory.org/declaration/ document (accessed on 28.02.2022).

Waldron, Jeremy/Dan-Cohen, Meir (eds.), *Dignity, Rank, & Rights. With comments by Wai Chee Dimock, Don Herzog, & Michael Rosen*, Oxford: Oxford University Press, 2015.

Willems, Joachim, "Die Russisch-Orthodoxe Kirche und die Menschenrechte," in: Heiner Bielefeldt (ed.), *Jahrbuch Menschenrechte 2009. Schwerpunkt: Religionsfreiheit*, 152–65, Wien: Böhlau, 2008.

Suggestions for Further Reading

Bielefeldt, Heiner, *Philosophie der Menschenrechte,* Darmstadt: Wissenschaftliche Buchgesellschaft, 1998.

Bielefeldt, Heiner/Wiener, Michael, *Religious Freedom Under Scrutiny,* Philadelphia: University of Pennsylvania Press, 2020.

Hogan, Linda, *Keeping Faith with Human Rights,* Washington: Georgetown University Press, 2015.

Joas, Hans, *The Sacredness of the Person. A New Genealogy of Human Rights,* Washington: Georgetown University Press, 2013.

Little, David (ed.), *Essays on Religion and Human Rights: Ground to Stand On,* Cambridge: Cambridge University Press, 2015.

Morsink, Johannes, *Inherent Human Rights. Philosophical Roots of the Universal Declaration,* Philadelphia: University of Pennsylvania Press, 2009.

Salama, Ibrahim/Wiener, Michael, *Reconciling Religion and Human Rights. Faith in Multilateralism,* Elgar Human Rights Series, Cheltenham/Northampton: Edward Elgar Publishing Limited, 2022.

Waldron, Jeremy, *One Another's Equal. The Basis of Human Equality,* Cambridge/Mass.: Harvard University Press, 2017.

Michael J. Broyde and Shlomo C. Pill
The Concept of Human Rights in Judaism

In contemporary Western societies, human rights encompass a broad constellation of material moral needs and interests that are guaranteed to all people simply by virtue of the fact that they are people.[1] Religious and normative traditions, including Judaism and Jewish law recognize and protect many of these currently accepted human rights.[2] Indeed, religious legal traditions tend to be rather good at respecting and enforcing a broad range of *material* human rights and *material* human dignity. As explained below, Judaism recognizes the inherent equality and dignity of all people; respects natural liberty and autonomy; protects rights to life, bodily integrity, health, property, education, basic food, housing, and healthcare; and provides important legal rights closely resembling contemporary ideas of due process in the courts. One might even argue that religious traditions are more effective than modern, secular state systems at ensuring many basic material human needs because religious traditions are not mired by bureaucracy, political concerns, and commitments to various forms of free-market capitalism which leave significant segments of society vulnerable and without basic human needs like adequate food, housing, healthcare, and education.

Where religions often do a poor job at protecting human rights – and where modern states and non-state organizations tend to better succeed – is in the realm of recognizing and protecting less tangible, inchoate rights, especially the range of rights associated with freedom of religion, conscience, association, and the right to dissent from prevailing societal norms and values. One of the core human rights widely recognized by states and international conventions is the right to freedom of religion, and more particularly, the right to freely choose to not practice or believe in a particular faith, or any faith at all. The United States Constitution provides that "Congress shall make no law respecting an

---

1 For important recent scholarship providing useful overviews of the history, substance, and evolution of Western human rights discourses, see Stearns, Peter N., *Human Rights in World History*, New York: Routledge, 2012; Kao, Grace Y., *Grounding Human Rights in a Pluralist World*, Washington: Georgetown University Press, 2011.
2 For an overview of human rights valued by Judaism, see Konvitz, Milton R., *Judaism and Human Rights*, New York: Norton, 1972; Broyde, Michael J./Witte, John Jr. (eds.), *Human Rights in Judaism: Cultural, Religious, and Political Perspectives*, New York: Jason Aronson Publishers, 1998. On human rights in the Islamic and Christian traditions, see Witte, John Jr./Van der Vyver, Johan D., *Religious Human Rights in Global Perspective*, Grand Rapids: Eerdmans, 1996; Baderin, Mashood et al., *Islam and Human Rights: Advocacy for Social Change in Local Contexts*, New Delhi: Global Media Publications, 2006.

https://doi.org/10.1515/9783110561579-003

establishment of religion or prohibiting the free exercise thereof."³ The *Commonwealth Charter of Human Rights,* a non-binding aspirational statement of normative commitments adopted by over thirty Commonwealth countries, likewise affirms a commitment to religious freedom as an essential expression of human freedom. It states: "We emphasize the need to promote tolerance, respect, understanding, moderation and religious freedom which are essential to the development of free and democratic societies, and recall that respect for the dignity of all human beings is critical to promoting peace and prosperity."⁴ The United Nations' *Universal Declaration of Human Rights* similarly affirms that "[e]veryone has the right to freedom of thought, conscience and religion; this right includes freedom to change his religion or belief, and freedom, either alone or in community with others and in public or private, to manifest his religion or belief in teaching, practice, worship and observance."⁵

Religious freedom, as John Witte has put it, embraces "the principle of liberty of conscience by foreclosing government from coercively prescribing mandatory forms of religious belief, doctrine, and practice."⁶ This principle, however, is not often associated with normative faith systems.⁷ Yet, a large part of what makes religions what they are is their strong normative claims about correct practice and dogma to the exclusion of all others. Even when religious leaders do acknowledge the possibility that practitioners of other faiths may be believing and worshiping in a way that is essentially legitimate, such tolerance does not typically extend to members of their own religious communities that express dissent and autonomy in belief or practice by rejecting prevailing norms.⁸ Religions, especially nomos-centric faiths in which religious virtue is measured principally in terms of one's conformity to a wide-ranging and comprehensive set of behavioral norms, prescribe correct and unacceptable modes of conduct in both public and private life. The scriptures and teachings of such traditions, moreover, typically include a wide range of penalties and consequences – some imposed by

3 United States Senate (ed.), *Constitution of the United States,* amend. 1, https://www.senate.gov/civics/constitution_item/constitution.htm (accessed on 14.06.2022).
4 The Commonwealth (ed.), *Charter of the Commonwealth,* art. IV, https://thecommonwealth.org/charter (accessed online 14.06.2022).
5 United Nations (ed.), *Universal Declaration of Human Rights,* art. 18, https://www.un.org/en/about-us/universal-declaration-of-human-rights (accessed on 14.06.2022).
6 Gunn, Jeremy/Witte, John Jr., (eds.), *No Establishment of Religion: America's Original Contribution to Religious Liberty,* Oxford/New York: Oxford University Press, 2012.
7 Cf. the introduction in Witte/van der Vyver (eds.), *Religious Human Rights,* xvii–xxxv.
8 Cf. Novak, David, "Religious Human Rights in Judaism," in: Michael J. Broyde./John Jr. Witte (eds.), *Human Rights in Judaism: Cultural, Religious, and Political Perspectives,* 1–34, New York: Jason Aronson Publishers, 1998, 7–11.

temporal religious authorities and others by God – for religious infractions. Often, harsh punishments are prescribed for those who leave the faith expressing heretical or blasphemous ideas or who convert out by affirmatively adopting the tenets and practices of another religion.[9]

This article explores the practice of religious freedom within the rabbinic legal tradition.[10] It focuses on the extent to which rabbinic law – despite being a system of religious standards that makes strong prescriptive claims about exclusively correct practices and beliefs – has recognized the right of Jews to autonomously dissent from settled religious norms without attempting to coerce conformity and compliance with Jewish law. While rabbinic law

---

9 Cf., e.g., Elon, Menachem (ed.), *The Principles of Jewish Law*, Jerusalem: Keter Publishing House, 1975, 529; Affi, Ahmed/Affi, Hassan, *Contemporary Interpretation of Islamic Law*, Leicester: Troubador Publishing, 2014, 1–28; Helmholz, Richard H., *The Spirit of Classical Canon Law*, Athens: University of Georgia Press, 2010, 360–65.

10 Jewish law (called *halakhah* in Hebrew) is the term used to denote the entire subject matter of the Jewish legal system, including public, private, and ritual law. A brief historical review will familiarize the new reader of Jewish law with its history and development. The Pentateuch (the five books of Moses, the Torah) is the historical touchstone document of Jewish law, and according to Jewish legal theory was revealed to Moses at Mount Sinai. The Prophets and Writings, the other two parts of the Hebrew Bible, were written over the next 700 years, and the Jewish canon was closed around the year 300 B.C.E. From the close of the canon until 250 C.E. is referred to as the era of the *tanna'im*, the redactors of Jewish law, whose period closed with the editing of the Mishnah by Rabbi Judah the Patriarch. The next five centuries was the epoch in which the two *Talmud*s (Babylonian and Palestinian) were written and edited by scholars called *amoraim* ("those who recount" Jewish law) and *savora'im* ("those who ponder" Jewish law). The Babylonian Talmud is of greater legal significance than the Palestinian Talmud, and is a more complete work. The post-*talmudic* era is conventionally divided into three periods: the era of the *ge'onim*, scholars who lived in Babylonia until the mid-eleventh century; the era of the *ri'shonim* (the early authorities), who lived in North Africa, Spain, Franco-Germany, and Egypt until the end of the fourteenth century; and the *'aharonim* (the latter authorities), which encompass all scholars of Jewish law from the fifteenth century up. From the period of the mid-fourteenth century until the early seventeenth century, Jewish law underwent a period of codification, which led to the acceptance of the law code format of Rabbi Joseph Caro, called the *Shulḥan 'Arukh*, as the basis for modern Jewish law. Many significant scholars – themselves as important as Rabbi Caro in status and authority – wrote annotations to his code which made the work and its surrounding comments the modern touchstone of Jewish law. The most recent complete edition of the *Shulḥan 'Arukh*, Vilna: Rom, 1896, contains no less than 113 separate commentaries on the text of Rabbi Caro. In addition, hundreds of other volumes of commentary have been published as self-standing works, a process that continues to this very day. For a more literary history of Jewish law, see Elon, Menachem, *Jewish Law: History, Principles and Sources*, Philadelphia: Jewish Publication Society, 1993; and for a shorter review of the literary history of Jewish law, see Stone, Suzanne Last, "In Pursuit of the Counter-text: The Turn to the Jewish Legal Model in Contemporary American Legal Theory," *Harvard Law Review* 106 (1992), 813–94.

makes strong assertions about correct religious practice and belief, and un-abashedly affirms that Jews are obligated to observe such standards, it generally does not seek to coerce members of societies regulated by Jewish law to uphold their purely personal religious obligations. Instead, Jews living in Jewish communities governed by rabbinic law and rabbinic decisors are left free to be as religiously observant or non-observant as they wish. Social or formal legal sanctions were traditionally brought to bear only – though not always – if individual dissent from rabbinic laws threatened the well-being and cohesion of society or caused material harm to other individuals. This article uses several examples from various areas of rabbinic law to show that in practice rabbinic jurisprudence creates substantial space for religious dissent and religious freedom even within the confines of a rabbinically-regulated religious society.

This paper has five sections following this introduction. The next section reviews general human rights in Judaism without a sole focus on religious freedom. The next section dives into the legal sources of human rights in Judaism. The third and fourth sections explore the relationship between law and enforcement in the Jewish tradition, both civil and criminal. The fifth section synthesizes sections two, three, four and five into a grander theory of religious freedom in the Jewish tradition.

1 Human Rights in Judaism – General Overview

Many scholars have noted that Judaism does not speak in the language of rights – human rights or otherwise – and instead couches norms in the language of duties and obligations.[11] Nevertheless, the norms and values of Jewish law evince a strong commitment to many of the core protections typically enshrined in Western human rights discourses, and in some cases, the rabbinic tradition goes further in its robust respect for human life, health, property, and dignity.

The principle of inherent individual equality, which forms the necessary moral and logical starting point for any complex system of universal human rights, is enshrined in the Mishnah, the foundational second-century text of Jewish law that reflects the sum of rabbinic thinking over the previous several centuries.[12] The Mishnah ponders the reason God created only a single human being

---

11 Cf. Novak, "Religious Human Rights in Judaism," 5–6; Broyde, Michael J., "Introduction: Rights and Duties in the Jewish Tradition," in: Daniel Pollack (ed.), *Contrasts in American and Jewish Law*, New York: Yeshiva University Press, 2001, xxiii. See also Glendon, Mary Ann, *Rights Talk: The Impoverishment of Political Discourse*, Michigan: Michigan University Free Press, 1991.
12 See supra note 10.

from which the human race would descend; why not create an entire population of human beings from the very beginning? The Mishnah responds: "In order to better ensure peace among people; so that one person will to be able to say to another, 'my father is greater than your father'."[13] Instead, in the Jewish tradition, every human being ultimately traces his or her lineage to a single common ancestor; nothing makes any one person essentially different or better or more entitled to respect and rights than any other. This basic human equality is expressed in the biblical expression of the Golden Rule, "Love your neighbor as you love yourself," which the second century scholar, Rabbi Akivah affirmed is "a great and important principle of the Torah."[14] Similarly, in explaining why God required an annual census of the Jewish population, R. Yitzchak Arama (d. 1494) states: "They [individual members of the nation] were not like animals or inanimate objects; each one had an importance of his own like a king or priest [...] for they were all equal and individual in personal status."[15]

At the very beginning of the book of Genesis, the Torah affirms that there is something essentially special and significant about human beings, and that this specialness correlates to human beings having certain fundamental rights and duties towards each other.[16] When the Torah describes God's creation of human beings, it records God as saying, "And God created the human species in his image; in the image of God He created it; male and female He created them."[17] This theme – that human beings were created in the divine image – features prominently in rabbinic law and thought. While scholars have offered myriad explanations of what it might mean to say that people are created "in the image of God," at the very least this description is taken to imply an essential human dignity due and owed every person. Thus, while Rabbi Akivah argued that the Torah commands that people do unto others as they would have done unto themselves, another scholar, a contemporary of Rabbi Akivah named Ben Azzai took this idea even further. According to Ben Azzai, the critical crux of Jewish ethics is not "love your neighbor as you love yourself," since this leaves open the opportunity to treat others poorly as long as one does not demand better treatment for one's self. Instead, Ben Azzai argued, the essential principle of the Torah is encompassed in the phrase, "in the image of God He

---

13 Mishnah, Sanhedrin 4:5.
14 Jerusalem Talmud, Nedarim 9:4.
15 Arama, Isaac ben Moses, "Aḳeidat Yitsḥaḳ, Numbers 1:2, Gate 72:1," published online: *Sefaria*, https://www.sefaria.org/Akeidat_Yitzchak (accessed on 29.11.2021).
16 Cf. Novak, "Religious Human Rights in Judaism," 12.
17 Gen 1:27.

created it [humanity]."[18] Reciprocity is not sufficient; the Torah demands dignified and respectful treatment of human beings *qua* human beings in light of the basic fact that people reflect the divine. Thus, another Mishnaic sage, Rabbi Tanchumah maintained that mistreatment of people equates to mistreatment of God.[19]

As in Western human rights discourses, the foundational principle of human equality leads to numerous reciprocal rights and duties people have towards each other.[20] *Halakhah*, or Jewish law, contains numerous prescriptive and proscriptive rules that affirm many of the guarantees enshrined in contemporary human rights discourses, and in some instances goes even further in protecting important human concerns. The inviolability of human life is affirmed early on in the Torah, and is reinforced by a strict prohibition on murder.[21] Jewish law goes so far in recognizing other people's inviolable right to life that it recognizes no necessity defense to killing an innocent person; Jewish law prescribes that a Jew must passively allow him or herself to be killed rather than kill another without just cause.[22] Rights to bodily integrity are reinforced by a robust system of tort law compensation, and prohibitions against assault, kidnapping, and rape.

Related to these basic protections of individual life, dignity and bodily integrity, Jewish law includes a host of protections that help guarantee peoples' basic autonomy. This is evident in rabbinic understandings of law and governance in the Jewish tradition. Broadly speaking, important streams of Jewish thought maintain that restrictions on people's natural liberty and autonomy are binding only with the consent of the governed.[23] Thus, two important Talmudic sources maintain that majoritarian consent is a key element to the normativity of any rabbinic legislation. One source relates to the initial adoption of new legislation: "No legislation may be imposed on the public unless the majority thereof can conform to it."[24] The second rule relates to the continuing validity of enacted legislation: "Any law enacted by a legislative-court, but not accepted by a majority of the public, is no law at all."[25] The Talmud provides several examples of how

---

18 Cf. Jerusalem Talmud, Nedarim 9:4.

19 Cf. Sifre 4:12.

20 Cf. Pill, Shlomo C., "Jewish Law Antecedents to American Constitutionalism," *Mississippi Law Journal* 85 (2016), 665–69.

21 Cf. Exodus 20:12.

22 Cf. Babylonian Talmud, Sanhedrin 73a.

23 Cf. Pill, *Jewish Law Antecedents*, 657–65.

24 Babylonian Talmud, Avodah Zarah 36a.

25 Jerusalem Talmud, Avodah Zarah 2:8, 16a.

this principle operated in practice,[26] and Maimonides (1138–1204) confirmed this rule in his seminal twelfth century codification of Jewish law, *Mishneh Torah.*[27]

Indeed, rabbinic thought goes so far as to suggest that people's natural liberty and autonomy is so significant that Jews would not even be bound by Jewish law as laid out in the Torah had they not voluntarily consented to do so. The following passage illustrates how restrictions on natural liberty imposed by Torah law cannot be imposed absent willing consent.

> When God revealed Himself to give the Torah to the Jews, He first went to all the nations of the world [to offer them the Torah], but they did not want to accept it. [...] [Each nation asked about the content of the Torah's laws, and upon hearing them, declined to accept them] [...] Finally, God approached the Jews and offered them the Torah, and they opened their mouths and said, "whatever God will command us, we will do and we will listen" [Exodus 24:7].[28]

In other words, the Torah cannot be imposed on anyone; only those that accept it are bound by its rules. Another *Talmudic* passage intimates that had not the Jews willingly consented to be subject to the laws of the Torah, they would likely not be obligated to adhere to those obligations:

---

26 See, e. g., Babylonian Talmud, Bava Basra 60b (rejecting the proposed legislation that would ban the eating of meat and the drinking of wine as an expression of mourning over the destruction of the Temple in Jerusalem because "we may not pass a law that a majority of the people cannot adhere to"); Babylonian Talmud, Bava Kamma 79b (the Rabbis legislated against raising small domesticated animals, which wander about and damage cultivated fields, in the Land of Israel as a means of encouraging settlement. However, they did not outlaw the domestication of larger animals because to do so would impose upon the public a law that the majority was not willing to comply with).

27 Maimonides, "Mishneh Torah, The Laws of Ma'amarim 2:5–6," published online: Bar-Ilan University (ed.), *Online Responsa Project,* https://www.responsa.co.il/default.aspx (accessed on 08.03.2022). ("A *bet din* that sees fit to legislate must consider the matter and know beforehand whether or not the majority of the public can abide by the proposed law, for no law can be imposed on the public unless the majority can follow it. If the *bet din* enacted a law believing the majority of the public can conform to it, and afterwards the people resist the measure, and a majority of the public refuses to abide by it, the law is void and the *bet din* may not compel people to adhere to it.").

28 Sifre, Deuteronomy 33:2 [Hebrew]; see also Talmud Bavli, Avodah Zarah 2b; Ha-Adni, R. David ben Amram (d. 14th century), *Midrash ha-Gadol,* Deuteronomy 33:2, Jerusalem: Mossad HaRav Kook; Ha-Darshan, R. Shimon (d. 13th century), "Yalḵut Shim'oni, Deuteronomy 33:2 [Hebrew]," published online: *Sefaria,* https://www.sefaria.org/Yalkut_Shimoni (accessed on 19.06.2022).

Prior to the Sinaitic revelation, God suspended a mountain over them [the Jews], and said to them: "If you accept the Torah, good; but if not this shall be your grave." Rav Acha bar Yaakov responded, "If so, this episode provides a strong basis for rejecting our obligation to the Torah!" Rava explained, "That is true, but they [the Jews] subsequently consented to the Torah's laws without coercion."[29]

Property rights also feature prominently in Jewish law and thought – not only rights to own and dispose of private property,[30] but also numerous duties associated with private property ownership that protect the material needs and interests of the indigent. The Torah prescribes expansive obligations towards the poor, requiring Jews to "not harden your hearts and shut your hand against your indigent neighbor. Rather, you shall surely open your hands and lend him whatever he is lacking."[31] Rabbinic law expands on this idea by obligating Jewish communities to establish communal charity and welfare funds to provide food, housing, clothing, healthcare, and other necessities for the poor, all the while emphasizing that the mechanisms for distributing charity must be designed to minimize affronts to recipients' dignity.[32] Providing for people's material needs is regarded as so critical, that Jewish law even prescribes that people seeking food or clothing must be provided these basic necessities without prior investigations into the truth of their claimed needs.[33] The *halakhah* further prescribes special duties of care to widows, orphans, immigrants and non-citizens, and other vulnerable members of society;[34] contains expansive provisions protecting the rights of workers to receive their wages in a timely manner;[35] and includes protections for debtors.[36] Rabbinic law also instituted expansive rights to education, imposing on Jewish societies the duty to ensure that their members receive adequate religious and vocational educations in order to become self-sustaining and contributing members of the community.

This broad respect for human beings as made in the image of God leads the *halakhah* to embrace numerous other rights and protections. Jewish law, for instance, prescribes a broad range of procedural safeguards in court processes to help ensure that defendants accused of crimes and litigants in civil cases are af-

---

29 Babylonian Talmud, Shabbos 86A.
30 See, e.g., Babylonian Talmud, Bava Basra 100a.
31 Deut 15:7–8.
32 Cf. Sefer ha-Ḥinukh, no. 66; *Shulḥan ʿArukh*, Yoreh Deʿah 247:1–259:6.
33 Cf. *Shulḥan ʿArukh*, Yoreh Deʿah 251:10.
34 Cf. Exod 22:20–23.
35 See generally Maimonides, "Mishneh Torah, The Laws of Hiring Workers," https://www.responsa.co.il/default.aspx (accessed on 08.03.2022).
36 Cf. Deut 24:10–13.

forded broad access to due process.[37] Judicial proceedings cannot take place in the absence of the defendant or his or her representative; courts must be presided over by competent, impartial judges; testimony is only accepted from witnesses who have no interest in the outcome of a case, and who otherwise are not suspected of perjury; all parties in court are afforded the opportunity to present evidence and respond to and impeach the claims made against them; and the courts must help litigants unable to organize their own claims and defenses to do so. Jewish law further maintains a strong presumption of innocence in criminal cases. Criminal convictions require a majority vote of at least two judges; and convicted defendants are given the opportunity to reopen their cases upon the discovery of new claims or evidence until sentencing is carried out.[38]

This brief survey suggests that Judaism and Jewish law embrace many material human rights typically associated with contemporary liberal rights discourses. However, the Jewish approach to less tangible human rights – especially rights to freedom of religious practice and conscience, and rights of free expression, association, and dissent – is more complicated. The following sections trace the development of Jewish law, thought and practice on issues related to the right to religious freedom and self-expression from biblical roots through rabbinic interpretation and application. The upshot of this millennia-long story of Jewish legal practice, is that while Torah and rabbinic writings suggest strict limits on the rights of Jews to reject, violate, and dissent from normative Jewish law and practice, actual practice proved these restrictions malleable. On the ground, when rabbinic authorities used judicial and political power to enforce *halakhah*, they rarely sought to apply an obligatory standard to compel Jews to comply with Jewish religious law. Instead, the rabbis regularly used force to punish conduct that caused or threatened material harm to other people or communities, whether such behavior technically violated any Torah norms. Likewise, rabbinic authorities scarcely used force to punish private violations of ritual *halakhah*, unless such misconduct affected the material interests of other people or the community. Put differently, rabbinic applications of Jewish law carved out a substantial scope for individual religious dissent as violations of ritual law were not punished *per se*, but were corrected by coercive force only when they also impacted the more mundane, material needs and interests of other people or the Jewish community.

---

37 See generally Quint, Emanuel, *A Restatement of Rabbinic Civil Law,* vol. 1, *Laws of Judges and Laws of Evidence,* Jerusalem: Gefen Books, 1990.
38 Cf. ibid.

2 Religious Coercion in the Torah and Talmud

The Torah – the first five books of the Hebrew Bible – comprises the foundational written text of Jewish law. According to rabbinic tradition, the Torah is the
written record of God's speech to Moses over the course of the Jews' forty-year
sojourn in the wilderness en route from Egypt to Canaan. This text includes
the background origin story of creation; the Jews descent into slavery and ultimate exodus from Egypt; narratives of events that took place during their travels
to Canaan; and laws – many, many rules and principles that form the basis for
normative Jewish religious practice.

Some of the Torah's laws are from a scriptural text and ritualistic in nature.
Among its many laws, the Torah prescribes the observance of the Sabbath by ab-
staining from work;[39] prohibits idolatry;[40] regulates the offering of animal sacrifices to God;[41] and establishes holidays.[42] Aside from these traditionally "religious" norms, the Torah includes numerous civic regulations that closely
resemble the kinds of standards one might expect to find in any ordered society.
The Torah prohibits murder, theft, and kidnapping;[43] prescribes standards of liability for tort damages by and against persons and property;[44] regulates inheritance and loans;[45] and describes government institutions and formulates standards of judicial procedure.[46] The Torah prescribes various judicially-enforced
punishments for the violation of both kinds of norms. Thus, alongside prescribed
death penalties for murder and kidnaping,[47] and financial liability for theft and
torts,[48] blasphemy, performing work on the Sabbath, and idolatry are capital offenses.[49] Likewise, the ritual prohibitions against shaving with a straight razor,
eating sanctified food while in a state of ritual impurity, and eating non-kosher
food are all punishable by court-administered lashes.[50]

---

39 Cf. Exod 20:8 – 10.
40 Cf. Exod 20:2 – 5.
41 Cf. Lev 1:1 – 4:35.
42 Cf. Lev 23:1 – 44.
43 Cf. Exod 20:12, 21:16; Lev 19:11.
44 Cf. Exod 21:22 – 36.
45 Cf. Num 27:8 – 11; Deut 24:10 – 13.
46 Cf. Deut 16:18 – 20, 17:8 – 20.
47 Cf. Exod 21:12 (murder); Exod 21:16 (kidnaping).
48 Cf. Exod 21:22 – 36; Lev 5:23.
49 Cf. Lev 24:16, 20:2; Exod 31:15.
50 Cf. Lev 11:3 – 8, 19:27; 22:4.

The bifurcation of Jewish legal precepts into "ritual" and "civic" norms has a long tradition in rabbinic thought.[51] Rabbinic thought distinguishes between public and private offenses, between legal violations that only impact one's self and those actions that also affect other individuals or the public at large. The rabbis termed the first kind of norms, laws that pertaining to the relationship "between Man and God," while the second type are laws relating to affairs "between Man and his fellow."[52] According to Maimonides, laws governing the relationship between Man and God include "every commandment, whether it be a prescription or a prohibition, whose purpose is to bring about the achievement of a certain moral quality or of an opinion or the rightness of actions, which only concerns the individual himself and his becoming more perfect."[53] These laws include things like the obligation to pray; the range of obligations and prohibitions related to the Jewish Sabbath, such as reciting the *ḳiddush* blessing over a cup of wine, eating three festive meals, and refraining from the thirty-nine kinds of prohibited work; observance of Jewish holidays, including eating *matsah* on Passover, and taking the Four Species during *Succot*; and the laws of kosher food. Laws that pertain to peoples' relationships with each other, by contrast, are those that prohibit various kinds of injury and violence; order and regulate business transactions, such as loans, sales, leases; establish rules of inheritance; establish conditions of valid contracts; regulate land use and relations between neighbors; and provide remedies and punishments for violations of these rules.[54]

As explained below, rabbinic law often treated interpersonal offenses as more severe than ritual violations, and often finds greater legal flexibility in those areas of the law that pertain to Jews' religious obligations to God than in areas of the law that govern relations and proper conduct between human beings. The Mishnah, for instance, teaches that *Yom Kippur*, the Day of Atonement on which people's sins are forgiven through prayer and fasting, can only atone for a person's offenses against God. With respect to "sins between a person and his fellow," however, "Yom Kippur does not atone, unless one has appeased

---

51 Cf. Sperber, Daniel, *On the Relationship of Mitzvot between Man and His Neighbor and Man and His Maker*, Jerusalem: Urim Publications, 2014, 13.
52 Cf. Maimonides, "The Guide for the Perplexed III:35," https://www.responsa.co.il/default.aspx (accessed on 08.03.2022).
53 Ibid.
54 Cf. Maimonides, "The Guide for the Perplexed III:35," https://www.responsa.co.il/default.aspx (accessed on 08.03.2022).

his fellow [who he wronged]."[55] Additionally, the secondary rules of decision that guide rabbinic adjudication create substantial leeway for decisors to modify normative standards governing ritual matters pertaining to man's relationship with God in response to serious economic, health, emotional, political, and communal needs.[56] God is understood to be accommodating and willing to compromise on His own interest, so to speak. This is not the case with respect to Jewish laws governing interpersonal affairs, however. In such matters, rabbinic decision makers are warned against taking liberties with the rights and obligations of human beings. Any legal leniency offered to one party entails a corresponding legally unjustified burden upon the other party, which cannot be imposed without his or her consent.[57]

While the text of the Torah provides the broad outlines of a legal system, rabbinic thinking has always maintained that Jewish law does not begin or end with scripture. The Torah itself indicates that the rabbis – the personification of "the judge that will be in those days"[58] – have wide latitude to enrich the landscape of Jewish law through the interpretation and application of biblical texts, and through the legislation of additional – "rabbinic" rather than "biblical" – laws.[59] The rabbis of the Mishnaic and Talmudic eras, from approximately 150 B.C.E until around 500 C.E., exercised substantial discretion in interpreting and applying biblical rules, and in legislating additional legal obligations and prohibitions.

---

55 Mishnah, Yoma 8:9. See also Maimonides, "Mishneh Torah, The Laws of Repentance 2:11–12," https://www.responsa.co.il/default.aspx (accessed on 08.03.2022). ("(11) Repentance and Yom Kippur only atone for transgressions between man and God, such as one who eats a forbidden food, or has a forbidden sexual relationship. But transgressions between man and his fellow, such as hurting his fellow, or cursing his fellow, or stealing from him, those are not forgiven until he gives his fellow what he owes him, and [his fellow] is appeased. (12) Even if he returned the money he owed, he must appease his fellow and ask him to forgive him. Even if he only perturbed his fellow verbally, he must make amends and meet with him until he forgives him.")
56 See, e.g., Feinstein, R. Moshe, "'Iggrot Mosheh: 'Oraḥ Ḥayim 5:29,"; Ha-Kohen, R. Shabbtai, "Ḳitsur be-Hanhagat 'Issur ve-Hetter § 3,"; Epstein, R. Yechiel Michel, "'Arukh ha-Shulḥan: Yoreh De'ah 242:66," published online: *Sefaria*, https://www.sefaria.org/texts (accessed on 15.06. 2022).
57 Cf. Bi'ur ha-Grah to *Shulḥan 'Arukh*, 'Oraḥ Ḥayim 331:3.
58 Deut 17:9. Cf. Berger, Michael, *Rabbinic Authority*, New York et al.: Oxford University Press, 1998, 31–40.
59 Cf. Maimonides, "Mishneh Torah, The Laws of Ma'amrim 1:1–2:3," https://www.responsa.co.il/default.aspx (accessed on 08.03.2022).

In some cases, the Talmudic rabbis legislated new religious duties and restrictions designed to protect against inadvertent violations of biblical rules.[60] For instance, the Torah prohibits the consumption of mixtures of milk and meat.[61] While this stricture was understood to include only mammal meat – cows, deer, sheep, etc. – the rabbis legislated a broader prohibition against the consumption of mixtures of milk and poultry as well on the theory that meat and poultry are so similar that unless they enacted a blanket prohibition on the consumption of all animal flesh with milk, people would accidentally violate the biblical stricture.[62]

In other instances, the rabbis used various interpretive techniques to soften the sometimes-harsh sting of biblical rules. Thus, while the Torah prescribes the death penalty for an array of different ritual and civil offenses, the rabbis rigorously defined the elements of particular offenses, and imposed numerous procedural and evidentiary hurdles that made the obligatory imposition of Torah-mandated capital punishment all but impossible.[63] Thus, Rabbi Akivah, an important second century rabbi declared that had he been head of the *Sanhedrin*, the rabbinic High Court in Jerusalem, he would have used his judicial discretion to impose numerous procedural and evidentiary hurdles so as to ensure that no defendant would be found guilty of murder.[64] In a similar vein, the Talmud describes how late in the Second Temple period, the head of the *Sanhedrin*, the rabbinic High Court that had primary jurisdiction over capital cases, elected to remove the Court from its proper seat in the temple courtyard to instead assemble in one of the city's nearby shops. The Talmud explains that that was a conscious decision made in order to enable the Court to avoid mandatory jurisdiction over capital cases under Torah law, which could only be exercised when the Court was sitting in the temple courtyard.[65]

While the rabbis chose to limit the practical and legal applicability and enforceability of many of the Torah's civil and religious norms, this did not mean that they left society without enforceable standards of behavior. At the same time that they limited the mandatory applicability of Torah laws, the rabbis expanded their authority to exercise discretion in defining and punishing what they regarded as societal harms in the manner they saw fit. The Talmud thus prescribed that

---

60 Cf. Elon, *Jewish Law*, 490.
61 Cf. Exod 23:19.
62 Cf. Babylonian Talmud, Chullin 113a.
63 See generally, Mishnah, Sanhedrin ch. 1–9.
64 Cf. Babylonian Talmud, Makkot 7a.
65 Cf. Babylonian Talmud, Avodah Zarah 8b.

"we may [...] punish not in accordance with the law,"[66] by which the rabbis meant, they had the authority to use their own discretion to take such measures as they deemed necessary to ensure good social order.[67] This power permitted the rabbis to punish offenses not actually proscribed by the Torah, and to do so in ways and in accordance with procedures not sanctioned by formal Jewish law, so long as the rabbis regarded such measures as necessary for the preservation of law and order.[68]

The Talmudic rabbis also contemplated the coercive enforcement of purely ritual norms, at least in theory. Although the Talmud imposes high evidentiary burdens of proof and prescribes burdensome procedures that must be followed before a defendant can be convicted of a capital offense or be subjected to forms of corporal or financial punishment, it recognizes that properly constituted and authorized rabbinical courts, or *batte din*, may punish infractions of religious law, whether such offenses have harmed others or pertain only to personal ritual obligations.[69] For instance, the Talmud prescribes the use of lashes in order to compel recalcitrant Jews to fulfill the ritual obligations to take up the Four Species and to sit in a *sukkah* hut during the holiday of Succot.[70] In fact, the Talmud states explicitly that "just as a person can be punished for violating a negative prohibition, he can be compelled to fulfill a positive duty," and it makes no difference whether that obligation is a financial duty that impacts others or a purely ritual commandment.[71]

Examining rabbinic texts of the Talmudic period, create the inference that what was advocated in theory was never implemented in practice. Talmudic sources contain numerous accounts of judicial law enforcement by the rabbis. In none of these instances, however, do we find the rabbis followed the procedures, processes, and evidentiary standards they acknowledged to be critical components of the Torah's comprehensive approach to Jewish law.[72] Nor do we find cases in which the rabbis used formally sanctioned Torah law processes to coerce people to comply with ritual obligations, or to punish people for violations of their private religious duties. Instead, the Talmud is replete with instances of rabbis using their extra-legal authority and judicial power to flexibly

---

66 Cf. Babylonian Talmud, Sanhedrin 46a.
67 Cf. *Shulḥan ʿArukh*, Ḥoshen Mishpaṭ 2.
68 Cf. Elon, *Jewish Law*, 533–36.
69 Cf. Ben Asher, Jacob, *ʾArbʿah Turim*, Ḥoshen Mishpaṭ, 425.
70 Cf. Ketubot 86a–b.
71 Cf. Ketubot 86a.
72 Cf. Saiman, Chaim N., *Halakha: The Rabbinic Idea of Law*, Princeton: Princeton University Press, 2019, ch. 2–3.

enforce standards of behavior they deemed necessary for the proper civic functioning of Jewish society.[73]

3 The Question of Authority

Rabbinic authority to define and shape the practical expression of Jewish law in this discretionary way was not and is not unrestrained. A significant limitation on rabbinic discretion over the interpretation and application of the law is determining which scholars and jurists qualify to fill the office of "Rabbi" given the interpretive and legislative authority this role possesses. From biblical through early Talmudic times, the institution of *semikhah*, an ordination, was the chief method by which rabbis were given formal discretionary rabbinic authority to interpret, apply, and thus shape Jewish law.[74] In rabbinic tradition, the institution of *semikhah* began when Moses laid his hands on the head of Joshua to signal a formal grant of judicial authority to the person that would eventually succeed him as the leader of the Children of Israel. Subsequently, *semikhah* was given by teachers – who had themselves been ordained by their own teachers in an unbroken chain stretching back to Moses and Joshua – to their students.[75] Scholars who possessed *semikhah* were authorized to exercise the wide range of discretionary rabbinic powers discussed above, while non-ordained scholars lacked this right.[76]

---

73 See for example Tractate Sanhedrin 46a and 72a. For discussions of the court's exigency jurisdiction, see Herring, Basil F., *Jewish Ethics and Halakhah for Our Time: Sources and Commentary*, New York: Ktav Publishing House, 1984, 158–59; Quint, Emanuel B./Hecht, Neil S., *Jewish Jurisprudence: Its Sources and Modern Applications*, New York: Harwood Academic Publishers 1980, 139–213; Kirschenbaum, Aaron, "The Role of Punishment in Jewish Criminal Law: A Chapter in Rabbinic Penological Thought," *Jewish Law Annual* 123,9 (1991), 132–35.

74 Cf. 'Arb'ah Ṭurim, Ḥoshen Mishpaṭ 1; Elon, *The Principles of Jewish Law*, 563. This idea was well said by the great Jewish Law authority of the last century, Rabbi Abraham Isaiah Karlitz (known as Ḥazon 'Ish d. 1953) who notes in Pe'er ha-Dor 3:139, n. 30 that the main purpose of the punishments found in Jewish Law is to underscore in people's minds and sensibilities the gravity of these offenses, rather than to mete out the court directed punishments, which was rarely – if ever – implemented and has not been applied in nearly two millennium. He notes that "It is widely stated that a Court that executes more than once every 70 years is called bloodthirsty. How amazing is it Jewish law used cross-examination restrictions and implementation to restrict execution – rather it is to teach an ethical lesson." (Our thanks to Rabbi Yona Reiss for sharing this source with us.)

75 See Hecht, Neil S. et. al. (eds.), *An Introduction to the History and Sources of Jewish Law*, Oxford: Oxford University Press, 1996, 124–27.

76 Cf. Babyloian Talmud, Bava Kamma 84a–b; Elon, *The Principles of Jewish Law*, 563.

At some point before the completion of the Talmud around 500 B.C., the institution of *semikhah* lapsed. This was likely a result of Roman persecutions of the Jews living in Judea following the Jews' failed *Bar Kochba Revolt* in the early second century. Numerous ordained rabbis were executed during this time, teaching Torah was proscribed by imperial rule on pain of death, and the remaining Jews were exiled from Judea. Since *semikhah* could only be conferred by a scholar who had been ordained himself, and in the biblical Land of Israel, the combination of exile, the killing of scholars, and the prohibition of teaching Torah led to the last ordained rabbis dying out without being able to continue the chain of *semikhah* by ordaining their students.[77] From this point onward, rabbis lacked any formal authority to enforce biblical law.[78]

However, the loss of formal *semikhah* did not mean that rabbis could no longer enforce the law. In rabbinic constructions, the last generation of ordained rabbis enacted legislation authorizing their non-ordained scholarly successors to exercise judicial powers over cases deemed necessary to ensure the proper functioning of society. The Talmudic formulation of this authorization states that it gave non-ordained rabbis the legal power to hear and decide litigious matters that occur commonly and involve financial loss.[79] In practice, this grant of judicial authority is understood to be more broad, and has been held to include the power to administer divorces and conversions – both of which must be overseen by a properly constituted court – as well as the license to take extra-legal measures necessary to preserve social order within Jewish communities.[80]

Critically, rabbinic practice and understandings of Jewish law may be characterized by the exercise of discretion. The formally ordained Talmudic rabbis made conscious choices about (1) whether to characterize specific norms as "ritualistic" or "interpersonal"; (2) about which areas of biblical Jewish law they would use judicial powers to enforce; and (3) about using interpretive and procedural devices to avoid enforcing the letter of the law when they thought that doing so would be socially detrimental. These rabbis made choices about how and when to exercise their power to set and enforce extra-legal standards of behavior. Moreover, the last generation of formally ordained rabbis made a choice to authorize later non-ordained scholars to adjudicate cases under Jewish law, and made choices about which kinds of cases those non-ordained judges would be empowered to hear. Additionally, the non-ordained rabbis of the post-Talmudic era decided which extra-legal measures they would take to en-

---

77 See generally Ibn Haviv, R Levi, *Ḳunṭres ha-Semikhah*, Yerushalayim: n.p., 2005.
78 Cf. *'Arb'ah Turim*, Ḥoshen Mishpaṭ 1.
79 Cf. Babylonian Talmud, Bava Kamma 84a–b.
80 Cf. *Bet Yossef*, Ḥoshen Mishpaṭ 1:4 (s.v. u-masḳinan).

force norms and standards they deemed necessary for the well-being and proper functioning of Jewish societies.

In all of these many choices made by Jewish law authorities about how to enforce Jewish legal norms in practice, we find that time and again the rabbis chose to enforce Jewish law almost exclusively in cases concerning civil law, or "matters between man and his fellow." The observance of ritual law was rarely coerced, and when it was, it was because the physical well-being of the Jewish community was threatened, or the community needed to distance itself from violators of religious norms as an expression of the community's own associational rights.

4 Principles of Rabbinic Law Enforcement

The following sections illustrate that a broad survey of rabbinic legal writings and practice over the centuries suggests the existence of a three-tiered framework for the discretionary enforcement of Jewish law.[81] First, throughout Jewish legal history, rabbinic authorities have responded to actions that caused tangible harm to others or threatened the physical well-being of Jewish communities by exercising both legal and extra-legal judicial authority to punish and deter such behavior. Critically, these sanctions could result in civil liability, criminal fines, imprisonment, and various kinds of corporal punishment, depending on the time, place, and scope of the rabbis' law enforcement power under local non-Jewish law.[82]

Second, when conduct fell short of posing tangible threats to other people or to the community, but undercut the religious foundations and commitments that constituted the community as a *Jewish* community, rabbinic authorities typically responded by utilizing social sanctions that asserted the community's right to not associate with individuals that did not share its mission and values. Such

---

81 This material is not novel and is a synthesis of secondary material found in many different articles. For a review of six excellent articles, cf. Herring, Basil F., *Jewish Ethics and Halakhah for Our Time: Sources and Commentary*, New York: Ktav Publishing House, 1984; Quint, *Jewish Jurisprudence*, 139–213; Kirschenbaum, *The Role of Punishment in Jewish Criminal Law*, 132–35; Bleich, J. David, "Jewish Law and the State's Authority to Punish Crime," *Cardozo Law Review* 12, 3–4 (1991), 829; Enker, Arnold N., "Aspects of Interaction Between the Torah Law, the King's Law, and the Noahide Law in Jewish Criminal Law," *Cardozo Law Review* 12, 3–4 (1991), 1137; Levine, Samuel, "Capital Punishment in Jewish Law and its Application to the American Legal System: A Conceptual Overview," *Saint Mary's Law Journal* 29, 4 (1997), 1037.
82 Cf. Pill, Shlomo C., "Freedom to Sin: A Jewish Jurisprudence of Religious Free-Exercise," *Regent University Law Review* 34, 1 (2021), 1–67.

measures included social ostracization, the denial of various rights and privileges associated with membership in the Jewish community, exclusion from participation in communal functions, economic boycotts, and others. Importantly, when dealing with such behavior, rabbinic law enforcement did not aim to compel compliance with Jewish law norms. Such religious offenders were left largely free to violate Jewish law; they were simply prevented from maintaining the paradoxical position of being members in good standing of the Jewish community while simultaneously flagrantly rejecting that same community's basic values and commitments[83]

Third, and perhaps most surprisingly, rabbinic authorities have traditionally taken a rather non-interventionist approach to enforcing strictly religious or ritualistic Jewish law norms and values. While public and flagrant violations of certain religious standards could undermine Jewish communal cohesion, and were addressed with social sanctions, private ritual offenses that did not tangibly harm others or impact the community as a whole rarely formally punished. Even when they had the police power to do so, rabbinic authorities seldom tried to compel individual Jews to comply with what they regarded as appropriate religious standards of behavior in ritual matters. Nor were rabbinic judges zealous in applying social sanctions to exclude from the community individuals whose religious offenses remained private and personal rather than publicly flagrant. As shepherds of their flocks, rabbis had a duty to make judgments and determinations about appropriate public and private religious behavior, and routinely identified and criticized misconduct when it occurred if they deemed it appropriate and useful to do so. However, the use of coercive measures designed to compel religious compliance or exclude ritually lax Jews from the Jewish community were the exception rather than the rule in the rabbinic enforcement of Jewish law.[84]

Put differently, rabbinic choices about which Jewish legal norms and values should be enforced and in what way exists on a spectrum. On one extreme, the harshest coercive penalties were reserved for offenses – whether offenses against formal Jewish law, or otherwise – that caused tangible material harm to other people or the community. At the other extreme were private ritual violations, which were condemned by the rabbis, but not generally punished in ways designed to stamp out religious dissent or compel compliance with the community's ritual standards. Between these two poles lay a range of offensive conduct

---

83 Pill, "Freedom to Sin," 34.
84 Pill, "Freedom to Sin," 34–35.

that could be and was addressed with a variety of other sanctions designed to preserve the character and constitution of Jewish religious communities.

Before turning to specific examples of how rabbinic law enforcement worked in practice, it is important to appreciate the broad standards for when rabbinic law enforcement would be applied and when it would not. In sum, in deciding how and when to use various means to enforce Jewish law, rabbinic authorities appear to have made a conscious decision to generally refrain from compelling compliance with Jewish religious norms. The exception to this was when religious dissent was public, flagrant, and undermined the religious constitution of the community, in which case the violator was excluded from communal privileges as an expression of the community's associational rights, as well as in cases where ritual violations caused material harms to the community, in which case it was civic standards of good behavior that were imposed. In effect, then, rabbinic enforcement of Jewish law typically carved out significant room for the free exercise of religion. Rabbinic authorities did not use legal or extralegal means to force religious dissenters into compliance. So long as a person's ritual (mis)behavior did not harm others, that person remained largely free – at least in a legal sense – to do as he or she wished. Private religious misconduct could lead to strained relations with one's more traditionally observant friends and neighbors, and public flouting of the community's common religious standards could lead to exclusion from the community. However, such informal social sanctions and secondary consequences of the community's decision to not associate with those who reject its values did not fundamentally alter the basic position that sinners were free to sin, and that the rabbis would not typically force normative religious observance, even when they had the power to do so.

5 Internal and External Concerns Regarding Religious Freedom

5.1 Rabbinic Law Enforcement as Protecting Jewish Civil Society

Coercive rabbinic law enforcement was most prominent when it faced what legal systems typically classify as criminal behavior. Beginning in the biblical era, continuing through Talmudic times, and throughout the medieval and early modern periods when Jewish communities in both Christian and Muslim lands often enjoyed a measure of political autonomy and delegations of police powers by local rulers, rabbinic authorities were very active in regulating behavior that they viewed as impacting the material wellbeing of other people or the Jewish community, often zealously enforcing these standards using a variety of coercive means designed to compel compliance. Murderers were often killed or maimed; assailants were whipped, killed, or had limbs amputated, depending on the severity and frequency of their misbehavior; thieves, who are only subject of civil liability under formal Torah law, were fined, whipped, imprisoned, and sometimes killed; wife-beaters were whipped or maimed; and those found to be in contempt of court faced a range of civil and corporal penalties designed to compel compliance and warn off future refusals to comply with judicial directives.[85] In all these cases, rabbinic judges and law enforcement officials demurred from enforcing formal Torah law using proper judicial and evidentiary procedures; they developed flexible and pragmatic methods for insuring that behavior that harmed others was punished, discouraged, and remedied with little regard for the enforcement of religious standards as such.

One of the most common and severely punished criminal offenses in medieval Jewish communities was *mesirah*, or the act of informing on fellow Jews to non-Jewish authorities.[86] The *moser*, or "informer", was generally recognized as posing a grave threat to both individual Jews and to the Jewish community.[87] A disgruntled Jew's informing on other Jews or the community to non-Jewish authorities for real or contrived offenses could lead to the accused being imprisoned, tortured, or killed, and to the community facing fines, progroms and massacres, expulsions, and other consequences. Rabbinic authorities thus often classified the *moser* as a *rodef*, Jewish legal term that literally means "pursuer" and is used to refer to someone actively trying to kill, rape, or otherwise seriously harm others.[88] Talmudic law prescribes that the *rodef* must be killed by anyone in a position to do so to rescue his intended victims from harm,[89] and this reasoning was applied to informers in Jewish communities throughout the middle ages and early modern periods.[90] Informers were regularly tried, convicted, and executed by communal and rabbinic authorities empowered to do so.[91] Even when local communities lacked a grant of such police powers from local

---

85 See generally Schreiber, Aaron M., *Jewish Law Decision Making: A Study Through Time*, Philadelphia: Temple University Press, 1979, 375–422.
86 Cf. Broyde, Michael J., "Informing on Others to a Just Government: A Jewish Law View," *The Journal of Halacha and Contemporary Society* 41 (2002), 5–49.
87 Cf. Babylonian Talmud, Bava Kama 116b, 117a–b; Babylonian Talmud, Gittin 7a.
88 Cf. Resp. Ro'sh 17:1.
89 Cf. Babylonian Talmud, Sanhedrin 73a.
90 Cf. *Shulḥan 'Arukh* 388:1–16.
91 Cf. Schreiber, *Jewish Law*, 379–84.

rulers, informers were made to "disappear" to protect their potential individual and communal victims. In at least one notable case in Spain 700 years ago, a particularly dangerous informer was killed in the middle of the local synagogue during prayers on the Jewish high holy day of Yom Kippur.[92] Of course, such actions – as well as the less extreme forms of dealing with informers – did not meet the procedural and evidentiary tests of formal Torah law, and the rabbinic judges or communal authorities that ordered such measures to deal with informers did not possess the *semikhah*-ordination required to try capital cases. Nevertheless, rabbinic authorities chose to take measures to protect the community and its members from harmful behavior by others under their jurisdiction.[93]

This all suggests a very important point: The rabbis' imposition and enforcement of criminal laws was not premised on any desire or interest to uphold Jewish religious law. In meting out penalties for theft, assault, murder, rape, and other offenses, the rabbis were not really interested in upholding the law of the Torah or actualizing some religious ideal of God's rule in society. In many cases, rabbinic decisors made clear that such law enforcement activities were not premised on any prerogative to uphold the religious standards of Jewish law.[94] What the rabbis were interested in – and this is important to highlight – was the effective administration of civil justice and law and order in the Jewish communities and societies in which they functioned. Put differently, rabbinic judges cared little for enforcing Jewish religious norms and values on society. They were primarily – if not exclusively – interested in using the judicial, police, and law enforcement powers they were allowed to exercise under local state laws and under Jewish law, to prescribe and enforce standards of behavior that insured that society functioned well, productively, safely, and predictably for people. At times, of course, religious and civic norms overlapped; the rabbis did not refuse to prosecute and punish murderers merely because murder also happened to be a religious prohibition proscribed by the Torah. But when the rabbis executed or imprisoned murderers, they did not do so under formal Torah law. They did so because murders posed a threat to the life and wellbeing of other members of the community and to the foundations of good civil society as a whole.

---

92 Cf. Resp. Zickron Yehudah, no. 75; Resp. 'Edut Bihosef 1:34.
93 See, e. g., Resp. Ro'sh 17:1.
94 Cf. Prishah to Ḥoshen Mishpaṭ 425:5.

5.2 Rabbinic Law Enforcement in Civil and Sexual Matters: A Question of Consent

In the realm of civil law – torts, contract obligations, property rights, and the like – rabbis drew distinctions between what they regarded as interpersonal and ritual duties related to money and property. Like in the criminal law context, rabbinic judges often went well beyond the bounds of formal Jewish law in order to impose compensatory and punitive liability on parties that harmed others through theft, torts, nonpayment of contracts; employment injustices; fiduciary malfeasance; and similar offenses.[95] At the same time, rabbinic authorities declined to punish and enforce a range of Torah law violations pertaining to financial matters because they regarded such misconduct as essentially religious and ritualistic rather than interpersonal in nature. In the absence of a real harm to another party, the rabbis declined to enforce what they viewed as religious norms regulating economic life.

Civil law offenses against other people are also religiously prohibited in the Jewish tradition. One not only has to compensate others for tortuously harming them; it is a sin to do so.[96] Likewise, Jewish law prescribes upholding one's contractual promises as a ritual duty,[97] and prohibits certain kinds of financial transactions on a religious level, even if all parties to the deal agree to the terms.[98] Nevertheless, it is important to appreciate that in rabbinic law, it is not the fact that a particular civil wrong is prohibited by the Torah that triggers legal enforcement of the parties' relative rights and duties. Instead, even when a religious sin has been committed, it is the existence of a nonconsensual wrong to another party that induces rabbinic courts to act. There are numerous religious offenses that involve civil wrongs to others that rabbinic authorities have regarded as nonjusticiable because, despite the existence of a legal violation, there is no genuine victim to whom the defendant owes a compensatory duty.

---

95 Cf. Schreiber, *Jewish Law*, 401–05.

96 Cf. Babylonian Talmud, Bava Kamma 51a (referring to the act of creating a dangerous obstacle in the public domain as a sin). See also Babylonian Talmud, Kiddushin 42b; Maimonides, "Mishneh Torah, the Laws of Property Torts 5:1," https://www.responsa.co.il/default.aspx (accessed on 08.03.2022). ("It is forbidden to directly damage or cause damage to another's property."); Resp. Ḥatam Sofer, Yoreh Deʻah no. 241.

97 Cf. Babylonian Talmud, Ketubot 86a.

98 Cf. Babylonian Talmud, Makkot 3b (price gauging).

5.2.1 Ribbit (Usury) as an Example

A prime example of this phenomenon is rabbinic treatment of the Jewish law prohibition on *ribbit*, or usury. The Torah prohibits borrowing and lending money on interest.[99] All parties involved in these kinds of forbidden usurious transactions – creditors, debtors, co-signers, lawyers, and witnesses – are all regarded as committing very serious sins.[100] Indeed, Jewish law views interest payments as ill-gotten gains; despite the fact that borrowers are usually more than willing to make interest payments in order to secure funds, many rabbinic authorities liken money paid as interest to stolen property.[101] Thus, Jewish law prescribes that creditors that have violated the *ribbit* prohibition by taking interest on loans are obligated to return these funds to the debtors that paid them.[102]

There is a debate among the Talmudic rabbis about whether and under what conditions rabbinical courts should compel creditors to return interest payments to borrowers. In large part, this issue hinges on whether the prohibition on *ribbit* is classified as a ritual or civil law matter, in other words on whether this restriction pertains to Man's relationship with God or Man's relationship with other human beings. R. Yochanan rules that rabbinic courts cannot compel lenders to return interest payments to borrowers, seemingly because he views the prohibition on usury as a ritual matter between Man and God. On this view, creditors must contend with God over their usurious lending practices, and returning the funds to the debtor would do little to obviate the underlying sin. Alternatively, R. Yochanan may think that because *ribbit* is a ritual sin against God, the creditor should voluntarily return the interest out of regard for God, and not due to judicial compulsion. R. Elazar, by contrast, prescribes that the repayment of *ribbit* is subject to judicial coercion because the Torah's regulation of interest payments is fundamentally a civil matter between human beings. Since the prohibition is designed to regulate the relationships and exchanges of money between creditors and debtors, rabbinic courts are empowered to extract ill-gotten interest payments from lenders and return the funds to their rightful owners.[103]

Post-Talmudic authorities adopted the view of R. Elazar, and have ruled that courts should compel creditors to repay interest received from borrowers.[104]

---

99 Cf. Lev 25:36–37.
100 Cf. Babylonian Talmud, Bava Metziah 75b.
101 Cf. *'Arb'ah Ṭurim*, Yoreh De'ah 160.
102 Cf. *Shulḥan 'Arukh*, Yoreh De'ah 161:5.
103 Cf. Babylonian Talmud, Bava Metzia 61b–62a.
104 Cf. *Shulḥan 'Arukh*, Yoreh De'ah 161:5.

At first glance this may appear to undermine the central claim laid out in this paper that rabbinic legal practice has largely declined to actively enforce ritual law or compel members of the Jewish community to comply with accepted standards of religious behavior in matters pertaining exclusively to the relationship between Man and God. Indeed, forcibly extracting interest voluntarily paid by a borrower to a lender pursuant to a loan agreement willingly executed by both parties suggests that even in the absence of the lender causing any harm to the debtor, he can be compelled to uphold his religious obligation to return his wrongfully gotten *ribbit*. However, rabbinic authorities have applied an important qualification to the rule that courts force lenders to return interest payments received from their debtors. Specifically, court action to compel a creditor's divestment from *ribbit* funds is only appropriate in cases where the borrower brings an action to recover those funds.[105] When a borrower fails to bring suit against the lender over the illegal *ribbit*, he is deemed to have waived his right to those funds and forgiven the lender's improper collection of interest on the loan. In such cases, while the creditor may have a strictly religious duty to return the funds, rabbinic courts have not generally ordered or forced him to do so.[106] Indeed, some authorities go so far as to suggest that once the debtor has forgiven the interest payments, the lender does not have any obligation to divest from the *ribbit*. Such cases are no different than a victim waiving his or her right to collect compensation from a tortfeasor or thief, both of whom would have no legal or religious obligation to pay for their wrongful actions due to the victim's having forgiven their liability.[107]

In other words, while in principle rabbinic law provides for compelling a creditor to comply with his religious duty to repay collected interest, it does so only if the debtor who made the interest payments regards himself as having been wronged by the lender's conduct and seeks restitution. Absent claims to recover for this interpersonal harm, rabbinic authorities have been unwilling to compel lenders to repay *ribbit*, despite the acknowledged fact that collecting and retaining interest payments is a very serious sin.

Bound up with pragmatic rabbinic permissiveness with respect to enforcement of the Torah prohibition against interest lending is an important shift in rabbinic thinking about *ribbit* that moved this stricture from the sphere of interpersonal to ritual law. The Torah's own presentation of this prohibition suggests

---

105 Cf. Magen 'Avraham, Yoreh De'ah 161:14.
106 Cf. Pithe Teshuvah to *Shulḥan 'Arukh*, Ḥoshen Mishpaṭ 161:5.
107 Cf. ibid. See generally, Reisman, Yisroel, *The Laws of Ribbis: The Laws of Interest and their Application to Everyday Life and Business*, Brooklyn, N.Y.: Mesorah, 1995, 344–54.

that the prohibition on lending on interest is a civil concern – a law concerning Man's relationship with other human beings. Thus, in one of the several places in which the Torah records the prohibition on taking interest, it rationalizes the restriction as a means of ensuring that "your brother may be able to live with you."[108]

An economic framework in which Jews cannot lend money to other Jews on interest only works in a relatively insular, largely Jewish society, like the one envisioned by the Hebrew Bible. Once Jews and non-Jews began to both inhabit the same social, economic, and political space, however, this stricture became not only untenable but also self-defeating. While the Torah prohibits Jews from lending to other Jews on interest, it permits them to collect interest on loans made to non-Jews; likewise, Jewish borrowers are allowed to borrow on interest from non-Jewish, but not from Jewish lenders. Consequently, in a society comprised of both Jewish and non-Jewish residents, Jewish lenders would avoid lending to fellow Jews, and instead opt for more profitable interest-bearing loans to gentiles. Similarly, non-Jewish creditors would take advantage of the militated credit market available to Jews to charge Jews higher interest rates than they would charge their non-Jewish borrowers.[109] In this context, rather than helping "your brother live with you," the *ribbit* prohibition resulted in Jews having only limited access to above-market rate credit. As the Talmudic rabbis put it, it "closed the door to borrowers".[110]

Rabbinic authorities responded to this contingency by gradually coming to a reconceptualization of the Torah's prohibition on interest-bearing loans that classified this law as a matter between Man and God, rather than one pertaining to the relationship between Man and Man. Once viewed as a ritual matter, the prohibition on *ribbit* began to be treated as a formal rather than functional rule, and this opened the door to the development of various financial structures that could be used to circumvent the restriction.[111] Some such arrangements were deemed impermissible, such as one whereby a Jew would extend an interest-bearing loan to a Jew by laundering the loaned funds through an interest-bearing loan to a non-Jew who would then supply those funds to the Jewish debtor in

---

108 Lev 25:36.
109 Cf. Epstein, R. Baruch Halevi, "Torah Temimah, Lev. 25:36," published online: *Sefaria*, https://www.sefaria.org/Torah_Temimah_on_Torah%2C_Leviticus.1.1?lang=bi (accessed on 15.06.2022).
110 See, e.g., Babylonian Talmud, Bava Metzia 68a.
111 Cf. Broyde, Michael J., *Sharia Tribunals, Rabbinical Courts, and Christian Panels: Religious Arbitration in America and the West*, Oxford: Oxford University Press, 2017, 60 – 62 (pointing out the formalism of *heter 'iskah* usages).

another interest-bearing loan as a small profit.[112] Other financing models became rabbinically acceptable, however, such as the 'iskah arrangement whereby interest-bearing loans are structured as capital investments in a joint business venture between borrower and lender with a guaranteed fixed rate of return.[113] Indeed, over time, the reliance on a *pro forma* 'iskah arrangement became standard among Jews, even as such financing arrangements functioned as ordinary loans in everything but name.[114]

The permissiveness with which rabbinic authorities have treated interest leading between Jews was thus largely facilitated by the conceptual characterization of *ribbit* as a ritual rather than civil law matter.[115] As a civil prohibition on predatory lending, there was little room for accommodation or leniency; restrictions on interest-bearing loans had to be enforced to protect the vulnerable human parties that such practices harmed. As a ritual sin, however, the rabbis could tolerate all manner of legal fictions that formally transformed loans into capital investments, though the function and outcome of such arrangements remained the same. Moreover, once *ribbit* lending as a broad legal category was adjudged to be a ritual sin against God, rabbinic enforcement of this rule could be limited to cases that raised the obvious specter to interpersonal harm, such as those in which a debtor sued to recover interest he had already paid on a Biblically prohibited *ribbit* loan.

Another example of the rabbis' non-enforcement of religious violations that do not cause sufficiently cognizable harm to others is the Torah's obligating Jews to come voluntarily to court and testify about any matter which they havewhich they have pertinent information.[116] Often, the failure of such a witness to come forward in violation of this religious duty can result in a litigant losing a case he or she should have won, and consequently, in the litigant suffering a financial loss. While the rabbis could have treated witnesses' failure to appear in court as a tort and subject such individuals to civil liability to compensate litigants for losses suffered as a result of their refusal to testify, they refused to do so.

---

112 Cf. *Shulḥan 'Arukh*, Ḥoshen Mishpaṭ 168:2.
113 See generally Grunstein, Leonard, "Interest, Ribit, and Riba: Must These Disparate Concepts be Integrated, or is a More Nuanced Approach Appropriate for the Global Finance Community?," *Banking Law Journal* 130 (2013), 439–80.
114 Cf. ibid.
115 This is evidenced by the way the laws of *ribbit* are organized within Jewish legal codes. Rather than including *ribbit* laws under the general heading of "Ḥoshen Mishpaṭ" – the section of Jewish law codes that includes laws of property, contract, torts, civil procedure, and the like – the laws of *ribbit* are included under the ritual-law focused "Yoreh De'ah" heading alongside laws pertaining to kosher food, ritual impurity, and similarly ritualistic subjects.
116 Cf. *Shulḥan 'Arukh*, Ḥoshen Mishpaṭ 28:1.

This harm was classified as *grama'*, or a loss produced by causation too attenuated to result in legally enforceable civil liability.[117] The fact that a religious law was violated was insufficient to trigger any liability or coercive enforcement measures since the harm caused was regarded as too attenuated, speculative, and indefinite to warrant law enforcement resources designated to protecting others from harm.

The rabbis made similar judgments in deciding that certain kinds of tort injuries with speculative chains of causation could not be a basis for civil liability.[118] In many such cases, the Talmudic rabbis noted that the defendant "not liable in human law, but liable by the law of heaven".[119] In other words, while acknowledging that the tortious conduct was a violation of the defendant's religious obligations to God, the rabbis declined to use their judicial powers to remedy such offenses – likely because the interpersonal harm element was too uncertain to warrant enforcement.

Likewise, in cases of a defendant's withdrawal from some kinds of oral contracts, the rabbis recognized that while a ritual offense may have been committed, legally-enforceable liability should not necessarily follow. Under formal Jewish law, oral agreements not concretized by a *kinyan*, an act that signifies a meeting of the minds and each party's commitment to adhere to the terms of the contract, are not binding.[120] Parties can withdraw or refuse to uphold their obligations under such agreements, and face no legal liability for doing so.[121] Even so, however, the Talmudic rabbis maintained that withdrawing from such an agreement without good cause was a serious wrong, and affirmed this view by declaring a curse on those who engaged in such conduct: "May He who exacted payment from the Generation of the Flood and from the Generation of the Tower of Babel also exact payment from those who do not keep their word."[122] Reneging on an agreement is thus regarded as a serious religious wrong. Nevertheless, rabbinic practice has not used civil liability to punish parties for reneging on agreements or to compel them to uphold their religious obligation because rights of non-breaching parties to contractual performance do

---

117 Cf. ibid.
118 Cf. Babylonian Talmud, Bava Kama 55b–56a.
119 Ibid.
120 Cf. *Shulḥan 'Arukh*, Ḥoshen Mishpaṭ 198:1. See generally Herzog, Isaac, *The Main Institutions of Jewish Law*, vol. 2, *The Law of Obligations*, London: Soncino Press, ²1967, 1–47.
121 Cf. *Shulḥan 'Arukh*, Ḥoshen Mishpaṭ 198:5.
122 Mishnah, Bava Metziah 4:1.

not vest without a *ḳinyan*, and so, the breaching party is not regarded as having caused any legally cognizable harm.[123]

Rabbinic treatment of various kinds of civil offenses under Jewish law suggests that the mere fact that a religious law was violated was neither sufficient nor necessary to trigger rabbinic law enforcement measures designed to compel compliance, punish misconduct, or remedy wrongs. Misconduct that caused or threatened material harm to others or to society was punished, whether such behavior offended the technical duties and restrictions of formal Jewish law. At the same time, actions that violated Jewish ritual laws were not punished, and compliance with strictly religious norms were not enforced unless religious misconduct also caused material harm to others. The hallmark of the use of force to compel compliance with Jewish norms was the existence of sufficiently concrete injuries or threats to individuals or the community such that any failure to enforce the law would result in material injuries and damage to the fabric of Jewish and general society.

5.2.2 Between Sexual Sin and Sexual Violence

Like many religious traditions, Judaism prescribes an expansive and strict sexual ethic. Jewish law regulates marriage, divorce, and family life, and the who, what, where, when, and how of sexual relationships generally.[124] Indeed, sexual offenses are regarded as particularly serious in that they – along with murder and idolatry – are considered one of the three kinds of religious violations for which Jews are obligated to martyr themselves rather than commit.[125] In practice, however, rabbinic authorities rarely punished Jews for committing private sexual offenses in which all parties were willing participants.[126] Rabbinic enforcement of the Torah's sexual mores was largely limited to cases in which one party was likely to have been sexually victimized by another, or where sexual conduct between consenting parties also had the secondary effect of harming innocent third parties or the community. In the absence of such harm, however, religious misconduct of the sexual variety was typically not seriously punished.

The distinction between rabbinic enforcement and non-enforcement of Jewish law, and between ritualistic and interpersonal offenses in the sexual realm is

---

123 Cf. *Shulḥan 'Arukh*, Ḥoshen Mishpaṭ 204:1, 4.
124 See generally, Maimonides, "Mishneh Torah, The Laws of Prohibited Sexual Relationships," https://www.responsa.co.il/default.aspx (accessed on 08.03.2022).
125 Cf. Babylonian Talmud, Sanhedrin 74a.
126 Cf. Sefer Me'irot 'Enayim, Ḥoshen Mishpaṭ 425:12.

well illustrated by a Jewish law opinion authored by Rabbi Moshe Feinstein, a preeminent twentieth century rabbinic authority.[127] In this responsum, Rabbi Feinstein deals with a question posed about the *halakhic* consequences of an adulterous relationship between a married Jewish woman and a non-Jewish man where all parties – the wife, her consort, and her husband – consented to the extramarital affair. The question arises in significant part because black-letter Jewish law prescribes that aside from adultery being a grave sexual sin in Judaism, after engaging in an extramarital affair, an adulterous wife must separate from her husband and the couple must divorce.[128] In Rabbi Feinstein's case, the questioner wondered whether the same rule applies even when both spouses consent to the affair.

In a long opinion, Rabbi Feinstein considered the question from a number of different angles. One of the possibilities that he considers is that the Torah's prescription for divorce in cases of adultery may only apply to cases where an adulterous relationship also entails some measure of *infidelity*.[129] Perhaps, he suggests, divorce is mandated only when a Jewish wife *betrays* her husband and her marital bond by engaging in an extramarital affair without her husband's approval. In the case at hand, however, both husband and wife endorsed the adulterous relationship. There was no betrayal of the marital bond; merely a rather unconventional arrangement between the husband and wife about the terms of their marital relationship. In such a case, Rabbi Feinstein supposes, perhaps dissolution of the marriage is not required.[130] Importantly, this view seems to be grounded in a recognition that sexual sins often comprise two parts. On the one hand, illicit sex is a ritual sin against God; on the other hand, prohibited sexual relationships can also entail an interpersonal sin against other people, whether the victim of a nonconsensual sexual advance, or a betrayed spouse. Rabbi Feinstein never supposes that adultery is *permitted* by Jewish law merely because the spouses agree to the affair; extramarital sexual relationships are strictly prohibited by Jewish law. This prohibition, however, is a ritual one. On an interpersonal level, however, spousal permission transforms adultery into an open-marriage relationship; the ritual sin remains, but the interpersonal wrong is negated through consent.

Rabbi Feinstein's recognition of the dual ritual and interpersonal nature of adultery closely tracks an important distinction implied and also explicitly delineated in many of the major codifications, restatements, and commentaries

---

127 Cf. Resp. 'Iggrot Mosheh, 'Even ha-'Ezer 4:44.
128 Cf. Babylonian Talmud, Ketubot 9a; Babylonian Talmud, Sotah 18b.
129 Cf. Resp. 'Iggrot Mosheh, 'Even ha-'Ezer 4:44(5).
130 Cf. ibid.

on Jewish law. The *halakhah* imposes a duty to rescue others from harm, and goes so far as to direct Jews to if necessary kill an assailant in order to save the life of the victim.[131] The same rule applies to saving a potential victim from being raped; bystanders may – and have a duty to – intervene to rescue the victim, and to if necessary kill the rapist in order to do so.[132] In stating this rule, the seminal sixteenth century Jewish law code, *Shulḥan 'Arukh*, frames the issue in terms of ritual sin, but emphasizes that the authorization to take action to prevent a sexual union prohibited by Jewish law exists only when this sin also entails harm to a victim.[133] The *Shulḥan 'Arukh* rules that "one who is chasing after another male or after any woman with whom he is prohibited from having a sexual relationship *to rape them* – aside from an animal – we save the victim, even at the cost of the life of the pursuer."[134] In other words, Jewish law authorizes the use of force to prevent sexual sin only in cases where the sin also involves a human victim, such as cases of rape. Where both sexual partners are willing participants in the commission of the sin, however, Jewish law does not authorize the use of force to prevent the sin and compel the parties involved to abide by ritual Torah norms.[135]

Rabbinic authorities permitted the imposition of punishments for sexual sins when such sins also harmed others or undermined the foundations of civil society. In addition to cases of non-consensual sex discussed above, judicial power was deployed to punish ritual sexual misconduct that resulted in potential dangers to the community at large. In one famous 13th century Spanish case, a Jewish widow engaged in a sexual relationship with a Muslim and became pregnant.[136] She gave birth to twins, one of whom died in childbirth while the local Muslim community took custody of the surviving child. Apparently, the entire affair resulted in significant disruption for the community, and produced tensions between the Jews and the local Muslim population. The local ruler, one Don Juan, directed the local rabbinical court to judge and punish the woman for the affair, and the court did so, ultimately settling on disfiguring her nose "in order to ruin her beauty that she beatified herself for her lover."[137]

While the judgement in that case is indeed harsh, it is important to point out the circumstances under which the rabbinic court came to judge the case at all.

---

131 Cf. Babylonian Talmud, Sanhedrin 73a.
132 Cf. ibid.
133 Cf. *Shulḥan 'Arukh*, Ḥoshen Mishpaṭ 425:3.
134 *Shulḥan 'Arukh*, Ḥoshen Mishpaṭ 425:3.
135 Cf. Sefer Me'irot 'Enayim, Ḥoshen Mishpaṭ 425:12.
136 Cf. Responsa Ro'sh 18:13.
137 Ibid.

Records of the matter suggest that, first of all, local rabbinic authorities took little legal cognizance of the affair between the Jewish widow and her Muslim paramour – and certainly took no steps to punish the woman for this serious religious infraction – until after the matter was brought before the local ruler who directed the rabbinic court to deal with the matter.[138] Significantly, at that place and time, the common penalty for adultery meted out by non-Jewish courts was to have the guilty woman burned to death.[139] Thus, once ordered to deal with the affair by the local ruler, the rabbinic court was put in a position of not only having to penalize the inter-religious relationship, but of doing so in a way that non-Jewish authorities would consider sufficiently credible.[140] Of course, this all took place under the looming backdrop of the Jewish community's own precarious status and relationship with the non-Jewish authorities under whose rule they lived. Failure to deal with the matter, and deal with it harshly, could endanger the community's security and stability by incurring the wrath of the local Muslim community seeking custody of the child, and the displeasure of the local ruler who wanted the affair and the resulting inter-communal tensions addressed.

The material concerns and pressures – as distinct from religious sensibilities – that gave rise to the harsh corporal punishment for this sexual affair between the Jewish divorce and Muslim man exemplify the standard black-letter rule in Jewish law. The *'Arb'ah Turim*, an important 14th century restatement of rabbinic law, prescribed a similar approach to dealing with cases of sexual relationships between Jews and non-Jews.[141] While such relationships are strictly prohibited by rabbinic law, violators should not be punished unless they are apprehended while committing an actual sexual act "in public," but not in private.[142] The critical trigger for corporal punishment is not the commission of the religious sin of sexual intercourse between Jew and a non-Jew. Instead, judicial punishment is appropriate only when there is another, more mundane and material, social and civil wrong at play. Public sex acts that flout the norms of the community may be sanctioned because they are *public sex acts*, and are socially unacceptable. The Talmud takes a similar stance in recording that one rabbinic authority flogged a married couple for engaging in sexual intercourse in public.[143] In that

---

138 Cf. ibid.
139 Cf. 'Assaf, Simḥah, *ha-'Onshin 'Aḥarei Ḥatimat ha-Talmud, ha-Po'el ha-Tsa'ir*, Jerusalem: Yonovits, 1922, 69.
140 Cf. ibid. For other examples of this concern, see Resp. Rivash 233 and Resp. Ro'sh 17:1.
141 Cf. *'Arb'ah Turim*, Ḥoshen Mishpaṭ 425.
142 *'Arb'ah Turim*, Ḥoshen Mishpaṭ 425.
143 Cf. Babylonian Talmud, Sanhedrin 56a.

case, there was no technical religious sin at all; married couples are, of course, permitted to engage in sexual conduct, and nothing in Jewish religious law specifically proscribes public engagement in otherwise ritually acceptable sexual behavior. In that case, as in the case described by the *'Arb'ah Turim*, and the medieval Spanish affair between the Jewish widow and her Muslim lover, the essential issue was not whether a ritual sin had been committed, but whether specific behavior is socially unacceptable, and therefore deserving of legal sanction designed to compel compliance with social norms.

5.3 Rabbinic Law Enforcement Contextualized: When Sins Harm Others

The foregoing discussion suggests a very important principle of rabbinic legal practice. Namely, even in times and places when rabbinic authorities had the judicial and political power to use force to enforce Jewish law upon members of the Jewish community, they largely declined to do so to compel compliance with the ritual norms and values of the Torah. In fact, rabbinic authorities have noted explicitly that even grave violations of ritual aspects of Jewish law do not, in and of themselves, license the imposition of corporal punishment. In the eyes of rabbinic law, penalties for violations of Jewish law are only appropriate when, as the important scholar Rashi put it, the Torah violation entails "shame, disgrace, and harm to a victim".[144] Ritual offenses that do not impact other people, however, are between man and God, and not to be sanctioned by human authorities.

The *'Arb'ah Turim* restatement of Jewish law expresses this rule as follows: "One who running [...] [to attempt] to violate any of the commandments of the Torah – even to desecrate the Sabbath or commit idolatry [both serious capital offenses under Torah law] – is not killed, except in court with a warning and with witnesses."[145] There is an important subtext here that needs to be spelled out: As noted above, the rabbis of the Talmudic period imposed numerous procedural and evidentiary hurdles on the judicial process, which rendered the legally-authorized enforcement of Torah norms rare if not impossible. The *'Arb'ah Turim* referenced these procedural protections by noting that violators of ritual Jewish law can be killed or otherwise punished only with "witnesses" and "warnings". Moreover, only courts staffed by the kinds of formally ordained

---

144 Rashi *to* Sanhedrin 73a (s.v. 'aval ha-rodef 'aḥar behemah).
145 *'Arb'ah Turim*, Ḥoshen Mishpaṭ 425.

judged mentioned earlier were empowered to implement Jewish law using the kinds of procedures being referenced here by the *'Arb'ah Ṭurim*. The author of the *'Arb'ah Ṭurim* is thus stating that ritual violators may be judged and punished only by judges who possess biblical *semikhah* following the stringent and cumbersome rule of procedure and evidence described by the Talmud. Put differently, the text is asserting that in contemporary practice (and really in any rabbinic practice following the Talmudic period), Jews who violate ritual Jewish law are not subject to corporal punishments for their infractions.[146]

The major exception to this rule, of course, is that ritual offenses that also harm other people or the community can be – and routinely were – punished. Murder, theft, tortious conduct, and rape are all religious sins proscribed by the Torah, and, as discussed above, all were routinely sanctioned by rabbinic authorities. The same was true for countless other ritual sins the violation of which negatively impacted others.

5.3.1 Blasphemy

Consider the quintessentially ritualistic offense of blasphemy. The Torah prescribes the death penalty for "cursing the Name [of God]". In response to an actual incident the Torah records as having taken place among the Jews wandering through the wilderness during the 40 year wanderings in the desert where certain individuals blasphemed and cursed God in public.[147] A similar case of public blasphemy was presented to Rabbi Asher ben Yechiel, the chief rabbinic figure of 13th century northern Spain, in which an individual who had been recently released after having been imprisoned by the local non-Jewish authorities cursed God over his troubles.[148] The matter was brought before a local rabbinic court that decided to execute the offender for his crime, but before doing so, the court decided to ask R. Asher ben Yechiel, the preeminent rabbinic authority in the region, his opinion on the matter. R. Asher began his opinion by expressing surprise at the fact that the court wished to execute someone for blasphemy: "About all other lands that I know about, there is no place in which [the Jewish community] judges capital crimes, except here in Spain. And I wondered at this;

---

146 Cf. Rema to *Shulḥan 'Arukh*, Ḥoshen Mishpaṭ 425:1.
147 Cf. Lev 24:10 – 16. The definition and punishment for this offense can be found in the Babylonian Talmud, Keritut 7a–b and Succah 53a.
148 Cf. Responsa Ro'sh 17:8.

how can they try capital crimes without a Sanhedrin? [...] And I have never agreed with them on carrying out executions."[149]

After noting his surprise and opposition to rabbinic courts executing convicts, R. Asher nevertheless reluctantly endorses the court's decision to carry out its sentence on the blasphemer.[150] Significantly his justifications for doing so have nothing to do with the grave nature of the defendant's sin. Instead, R. Asher notes that practical, material concerns can justify the use of force to enforce Jewish law in general, and in the case presented in particular. First, R. Asher noted that rabbinic courts in Spain operate pursuant to a royal command directing Jews to police their own communities.[151] He further argued that, in general, the use of force to uphold societal norms can be justified as a measure designed to better protect Jewish lives since, if rabbinic courts did not try and punish criminal offenses in a way that the non-Jewish authorities considered adequate, those cases would be handled by the royal courts and "more blood would be spilled during trials controlled by non-Jews non-Jews."[152] These concerns all coalesce in the case of the Jewish blasphemer. R. Asher noted that in this case the defendant's blasphemy was not merely a private sin; "he desecrated the name of God *in public*, and it was already heard by the non-Jews as well, who take very seriously anyone who speaks against their religion."[153] The matter was thus not merely a sin, but a public scandal. Moreover, since this instance of blasphemy was already known to the non-Jewish authorities, the rabbinic court was put in a position where it had to deal seriously with the offense – just as a local non-Jewish court would have dealt with one of their own coreligionists who committed blasphemy – in order to maintain the confidence of the non-Jewish authorities and the continued license to govern the Jewish community internally. R. Asher made clear that punishing the blasphemer was not justified on religious grounds *per se*; it was not the fact that the defendant sinned, but the fact that his sinning had wider material implications for the community that necessitated a strict corporal response that justified the execution.

---

149 Ibid.
150 Cf. ibid.
151 Cf. ibid.
152 Ibid.
153 Ibid.

5.3.2 Education

The Jewish law approach to educating children offers another useful example of how ritual law becomes enforced law when religious sins impact others. The Torah prescribes a religious duty to educate children in Jewish law and tradition.[154] "It is a positive commandment [of the Torah] for a person to teach his son Torah."[155] The rabbis have understood this duty to include religious teachings, but also moral training, vocational or professional education, and life skills like swimming.[156] Jewish law and practice is heavily structured around this fundamental educational imperative. The traditional Passover *Seder* is structured to provide educational opportunities for children; group Torah study, and Torah teaching in family and communal settings is a central feature of Jewish living; and virtually all contemporary observant Jewish communities maintain various programming opportunities geared towards children's religious education. While the duty to educate is thus an important religious obligation, it also has broader material concerns. Put simply, a Jewish child will find itself unable to function as a Jewish adult in the Jewish community unless it has received an adequate Jewish education.[157] More broadly, children who are left uneducated in secular matters will find themselves ill equipped to secure gainful employment, run their own households, and generally do things people need to do to live successful lives. In light of these realities, rabbinic law was not content with leaving educational duties to the realm of ritual law; instead, Jewish law authorities have prescribed the enforcement of this obligation. As R. Moshe Isserles wrote: "We compel a person to hire teachers for his children; and if he is not present in the city, but has assets [...] we seize his assets [in his absence] and hire teachers for his son."[158]

The fact that it is the harm to the child that triggers rabbinic enforcement of the duty to educate rather than the religious obligation itself is made clear by contrasting the obligation to educate one's children with the obligation to edu-

---

154 Cf. Deut 6:7.
155 *Shulḥan ʿArukh*, Yoreh Deʿah 245:1.
156 Cf. Babylonian Talmud, Kiddushin 29b (obligation to teach one's child to swim); *id.* ("Rabbi Yehuda said: 'One who does not teach one's child a trade teaches them to be a thief.'"); Pseudonymous Case, 9 Piske Din Rabbaniyim [Israeli Rabbinic Court] 251, 259 (1974). ("Even if neither parent will educate the children in the study of Jewish law [...] still a parent owes his children – and children should receive from their parents – a close and robust relationship through which a child can develop into an adult with adult characteristics and an adult demeanor.")
157 Cf. "*Ḥinukh*," Encyclopedia Talmudit, 16:161–162 (1978).
158 Rema *to Shulḥan ʿArukh*, Yoreh Deʿah 245:4.

cate one's self. In Jewish law, education goes beyond teaching children; adults are religiously obligated to set aside regular times to study Jewish texts and traditions as well.[159] The duty to engage in Torah study can be framed as an extension of the duty to educate children: "If one's father did not teach him Torah, a person is obligated to teach himself."[160] Like the education of children, adult education is a very central component of religious life, so much so that many devout Jews devote years to full-time Torah study. Despite the importance of adult learning, in contrast with its approach to educating children, rabbinic law never mandates the active enforcement of the obligations of adults to self-educate. The reason for this distinction seems straightforward: While one's failure to fulfill the ritual duty to educate his or her children will actually harm those children, an adult's willful decision to not improve his or her Torah knowledge does not harm any victims, and so there is no basis in rabbinic legal practice for compelling anyone to comply with this ritual norm.

5.4 Between Religious Coersion and Religious Community: The Case of Ḥerem and Rights of (Dis)Association

All this does not mean that Jewish ritual law was not important to the rabbis. On the contrary, the endless minutiae of ritual *halakhah* – from proper modes of Sabbath observance, kosher food and drink standards, prayer practices, the proper celebration of Jewish holidays, and even the rules of long defunct practices such as animal sacrifices in the Temple in Jerusalem and the laws of ritual purity and impurity – were endlessly debated, interpreted, and taught by rabbinic authorities in every place and time that Jews found themselves in. Community rabbis delivered sermons encouraging proper ritual practice and chastising their flocks for sin. More importantly, the private ritual practice of Jewish law was a chief way in which Jewish communities in the premodern era constituted and defined themselves. Jewish communities were *Jewish* primarily in the sense that they were communities constructed around and for individual and collective observance of rabbinic Jewish law.

Rabbinic authorities regularly sanctioned violators of ritual Jewish law using a variety of methods designed to shun offenders and to distance them from the

---

159 Cf. Maimonides, "Mishneh Torah, The Laws of Torah Study, ch. 1," https://www.responsa. co.il/default.aspx (accessed on 08.03.2022).
160 *Shulḥan ʿArukh*, Yoreh Deʿah 245:1.

structured community.[161] Such sanctions, generally subsumed under the general heading of *ḥerem* (literally "excommunication"), included a wide range of different measures that ranged in type and severity. A minor form of *ḥerem*, called *niddui*, involved informal social ostracism; Jews were prohibited from sitting within six feet of the offender, the subject of a *niddui* would not be counted towards the ten-man quorum required for public prayers, and could not wash his clothes, cut his hair, or shave.[162] More serious *ḥerem* practices included additional economic restrictions on members of the community speaking and doing business with the excommunicated individual.[163] Additional such measures included public humiliation; the denial of ritual privileges, such as being called upon to read from the Torah in the synagogue or leading prayers; the denial of communal privileges, like the right to vote or hold public office. In extreme cases, grievous offenders could face banishment from the Jewish community.[164] Importantly, while serious corporal punishments and financial penalties were typically imposed only for wrongs that harmothers, *ḥerem* sanctions were at times deployed against individuals who violated Jewish ritual laws and norms.[165]

It is important to understand that the use of *ḥerem* for ritual offenses was subject to limitations that distinguished this practice from the coercive enforcement of ritual norms. Most importantly, *ḥerem* was used as a penalty for breaches of "communal discipline" rather than ordinary private religious indiscretions.[166] "Adultery, polytheism, Sabbath violations, and other central tenets of the faith [...] were never subject to shunning by the Jewish tradition unless the person engaged in this conduct in a public manner."[167] Such public ritual misconduct was not merely an offense against God; private offenses against God

---

161 For an overview of these methods, see "Ḥerem," in: *Encyclopedia Talmudit*, vol. 16, Jerusalem: Yad HaRav Herzog, 1976, 326.

162 Cf. Babylonian Talmud, Mo'ed Katan 17a; Maimonides, "Mishneh Torah, The Laws of Torah, Study 7:4," https://www.responsa.co.il/default.aspx (accessed on 08.03.2022).

163 Cf. Maimonides, "Mishneh Torah, The Laws of Torah, Study 7:4," https://www.responsa.co.il/default.aspx (accessed on 08.03.2022).

164 See generally Schreiber, *Jewish Law*, 417–21.

165 Cf. *Shulḥan 'Arukh*, Yoreh De'ah 334:1, 43. See also Kook, R. Isaac, *Resp. Da'at Kohen*, Yoreh De'ah 193 (discussing sanctions against a community that failed to excommunicate a prominent member for eating and drinking on Yom Kippur); Resp. Rambam no. 157 (Freiman ed.) (*ḥerem* for a *kohen* (priest) that married a divorcee, which is ritually prohibited); Rema *to Shulḥan 'Arukh*, Ḥoshen Mishpaṭ 325:1; 'Assaf, *ha-'Onshin 'Aḥarei Ḥatimat ha-Talmud* , 114.

166 See Broyde, Michael J., "Forming Religious Communities and Respecting Dissenters' Rights: A Jewish Tradition for a Modern Society," in: Michael J. Broyde./John Witte Jr. (eds.), *Human Rights in Judaism: Cultural, Religious, and Political Perspectives*, New York: Jason Aronson Publishers, 1998, 52.

167 Broyde, "Forming Religious Communities," 55.

were for God to deal with, and did not warrant serious social or legal sanctions. Instead, such public ritual misconduct was an affront to the community, an attempt to openly flout, reject, and undermine the religious structure and foundations of the Jewish community and the religious norms and values through which the community constituted itself. In response to such behavior, Jewish communities and rabbinic authorities used the *ḥerem* and related forms of social sanction as a means of exercising their rights of association. Jews who refused to "buy in" to the constitutive foundations of the Jewish community and expressed such dissent in a public manner were not forced to observe Jewish law, but they could not reject the Jewish community and be members in good standing in the community at the same time. Instead of using legal means to compel sinners to behave appropriately, rabbinic authorities recognized sinners' basic rights to dissent from Jewish norms while also disassociating from such sinners whose behavior *de facto* placed them outside the religiously constituted Jewish communal structure.

Jewish communities have always been made up of members who maintained varying levels of ritual observance. Private laxity in matters of Jewish ritual was a recognized fact of life that did not warrant punitive measures designed to compel compliance with religious law. Jews were largely free to practice as piously or as irreverently as they wished, as there was no inquisitor peering into their homes looking to catch them in a ritual sin. However, when religious misconduct moved from private to the public space and indicated a rejection of the religious foundations of the Jewish community or threatened the religion-based cohesiveness of Jewish communal life, rabbinic law prescribed the use of *ḥerem* as an exercise of the community's right to disassociate from subversive members.[168]

6 Human Rights and Religious Freedom in Modern Jewish Discourse

In one sense, the Jewish tradition managed to achieve an ideal model for Human Rights: on the one hand, the rabbinic legal corpus provided enough positive law to guide Jews to form charitable, kind and caring communities in which judicial and political institutions ensured respect for the material needs and entitlements of community members. Yet, at the same time, the implementation of Jewish law offered freedom in practice to allow people the liberty of conscious needed to be intellectually free from ideas they wished to reject. Many legal systems failed to

---

168 See Broyde, "Forming Religious Communities," 55–56.

achieve both of these values: one could have all the freedom one wanted in an uncaring society, or none of the freedom, but the closeness and support of a deeply enmeshed society. The Jewish legal tradition sought to have both values expressed.

Indeed, a review of the modern Jewish legal tradition sees the complexity of the model in play. Like any balanced tradition where two competing values need to be expressed, where exactly the suitable middle should reside is subject to some controversy and evolution. There have been times when a slightly more nationalistic and restricted view of Judaism wherein the human right of religious dissent was more tolerated, and times when less charity and community were expressed. Israeli values – for example – excellently embody this problem. Israel is – and always has been – a Jewish and democratic state: attempts to undermine its democratic nature by pointing to its Judaism have never succeeded, just as attempts to undermine its Jewish nature by pointing to the democratic tradition have never been rewarded. But, that does not mean that the pendulum does not swing. Over the last 50 years there have been repeated shifts in the exact location of middle. That discourse has focused on at least four questions.

First, is the question of governmental recognition of pluralistic Jewish faiths in the diaspora. Who a Jew is outside of Israel has been a troubling issue within Israel since its creation.[169] Second, there is the question of public prayer at the Western Wall and the related question of Jewish prayer at the Temple Mount. Since 1967, only Orthodox Jewish prayer is authorized at the Western Wall and only Islamic prayer is authorized on the Temple Mount. Both are now being questioned in the name of religious freedom.[170] Third is the question of the diversity of processes used to convert to (and the validity of converting from) Judaism. The move to Israel of about a million Russian individuals, many of uncertain Jewish ancestry has created a substantial question about how to convert to Judaism and what exactly is the relationship between being Jewish and being Israel.[171] Fourth, the Jewish community in the diaspora has been forced to confront

169 Cf. Kaplan, Yehiel S., "Immigration Policy of Israel: The Unique Perspective of a Jewish State," *Touro Law Review* 31 (2015), 1089.
170 Cf. Kershner, Isabel, "Israel Approves Prayer Space at Western Wall for Non-Orothdox Jews," published online: *The New York Times*, 2016, https://www.nytimes.com/2016/02/01/world/middleeast/israel-western-wall-prayer.html (accessed on 24.02.2022); Sharon, Jeffrey, "Discreet Jewish prayer continues on Temple Mount despite minister's comments," published online: *The Jerusalem Post*, 2021, https://www.jpost.com/israel-news/discreet-jewish-prayer-continues-on-temple-mount-despite-ministers-comments-682617 (accessed on 24.02.2022).
171 Cf. Kravel-Tovi, Michal, *When the State Winks: The Performance of Jewish Conversion in Israel,* New York: Columbia University Press, 2017.

again the problems of significant anti-Semitism.[172] The universalistic tendencies of the Jewish tradition are most popular and accomplished in a society in which the Jew functions consistent with his or her faith without fear of trial or attack. The communitarian competent naturally seems much more valuable to society when it is embattled. This is not unique to the Jewish tradition.

We suspect that how open the human right of religious freedom in the Jewish tradition will be in the future depends very much on these four issues, with a particular emphasis on the final factor – the rise of anti-Semitism. Jew hatred reinforces and justifies Jews' emphasizing more particularistic streams of the Jewish tradition, and a sustained rise of antisemitism will likely result in the human rights tradition of the Jewish texts being naturally less present in Jewish discourses.[173] That would be a shame and a return to the historically more common antisemitic model of the last centuries, but seems to be a political possibility, sadly enough.

7 Conclusion

The foregoing overview of classical rabbinic approaches to the coercive enforcement of Jewish law norms suggests something very important about Jewish law approaches to human rights. Judaism, like many other faith traditions does a fairly good job at recognizing and prescribing the protection of various material human rights such as rights to life, property, education, housing, clothing, fair employment conditions, freedom of contract, and equal treatment under law. At the same time, rabbinic practice maintained a fairly robust respect for private religious conscience and dissent from Jewish ritual norms. Unlike some other religious-legal traditions that sought to compel compliance with their own ritual norms, and punished religious dissent with force, in practice Judaism largely avoided doing so. Ritual misconduct was sanctioned, but typically only when and because it had the effect of harming other people or the community. Rather

---

[172] See, e.g., American Jewish Committee (ed.), *The State of Antisemitism in America 2021*, https://www.ajc.org/AntisemitismReport2021 (accessed on 01.03.2022).

[173] The ideas of these last few chapters are derived from a few works we have written, including; "Religious Alternative Dispute Resolution in Israel and Other Nations with State-Sponsored Religious Courts: Crafting a More Efficient and Better Relationship Between Rabbinical Courts and Arbitration Law in Israel," *Touro Law Review* 36, 4 (2021), 901–42; and "Privatizing the Temple Mount *Haram es-Sharif*) and the Western Wall (*Kotel*)," *Journal of Law, Religion and State* 10 (2020), 23–47, https://www.broydeblog.net/uploads/8/0/4/0/80408218/jlrs_adv_broydezeligman.pdf (accessed on 01.03.2022); as well as the many other works cited in this article.

than seeking to directly force Jews into religious compliance, rabbinic practice focused on using ordinary tools of membership and association to cultivate Jewish communities of like-minded Jews who were at least publically respectful of the norms and values of rabbinic law. In doing so, rabbinic authorities largely succeeded in carving out what can be viewed as a sphere for private freedom of religion and conscience within a normative Jewish framework.

Bibliography

Affi, Ahmed/Affi, Hassan, *Contemporary Interpretation of Islamic Law*, Leicester: Troubador Publishing, 2014.

American Jewish Committee (ed.), *The State of Antisemitism in America 2021*, https://www.ajc.org/AntisemitismReport2021 (accessed on 01.03.2022).

Arama, Isaac ben Moses, "Aḵeidat Yitsḥaḵ, Numbers 1:2, Gate 72:1," published online: *Sefaria*, https://www.sefaria.org/Akeidat_Yitzchak (accessed on 29.11.2021).

'Assaf, Simḥah, *ha-'Onshin 'Aḥarei Ḥatimat ha-Talmud, ha-Po'el ha-Tsa'ir*, Jerusalem: Yonovits, 1922.

Baderin, Mashood et al., *Islam and Human Rights: Advocacy for Social Change in Local Contexts*, New Delhi: Global Media Publications, 2006.

Berger, Michael, *Rabbinic Authority*, New York et al.: Oxford University Press, 1998.

Bleich, J. David, "Jewish Law and the State's Authority to Punish Crime," *Cardozo Law Review* 12, 3 – 4 (1991), 829 – 57.

Broyde, Michael J./Witte Jr., John (eds.), *Human Rights in Judaism: Cultural, Religious, and Political Perspectives*, New York: Jason Aronson Publishers, 1998.

Broyde, Michael J., "Forming Religious Communities and Respecting Dissenters' Rights: A Jewish Tradition for a Modern Society," in: Michael J. Broyde./John Witte Jr. (eds.), *Human Rights in Judaism: Cultural, Religious, and Political Perspectives*, 35 – 76, New York: Jason Aronson Publishers, 1998.

Broyde, Michael J./Zeligman, David, "Privatizing the Temple Mount (Haram es-Sharif) and the Western Wall (Kotel)", *Journal of Law, Religion and State* 9 (2020), 23 – 47.

Broyde, Michael J., "Introduction: Rights and Duties in the Jewish Tradition," in: Daniel Pollack (ed.), *Contrasts in American and Jewish Law*, xxiii–xxix, New York: Yeshiva University Press, 2001.

Broyde, Michael J., "Informing on Others to a Just Government: A Jewish Law View," *The Journal of Halacha and Contemporary Society* 41 (2002), 5 – 49.

Broyde, Michael J., *Sharia Tribunals, Rabbinical Courts, and Christian Panels: Religious Arbitration in America and the West*, Oxford: Oxford University Press, 2017.

Elon, Menachem (ed.), *The Principles of Jewish Law*, Jerusalem: Keter Publishing House, 1975.

Elon, Menachem, *Jewish Law: History, Principles and Sources*, Philadelphia: Jewish Publication Society, 1994.

Enker, Arnold N., "Aspects of Interaction Between the Torah Law, the King's Law, and the Noahide Law in Jewish Criminal Law," *Cardozo Law Review* 12, 3 – 4 (1991), 1137 – 56.

Glendon, Mary Ann, *Rights Talk : The Impoverishment of Political Discourse*, Michigan: Michigan University Free Press, 1991.

Grunstein, Leonard, "Interest, Ribit, and Riba: Must These Disparate Concepts be Integrated, or is a More Nuanced Approach Appropriate for the Global Finance Community?," *Banking Law Journal* 130 (2013), 439–80.
Gunn, Jeremy/Witte, John Jr., (eds.), *No Establishment of Religion: America's Original Contribution to Religious Liberty*, Oxford/New York: Oxford University Press, 2012.
Hecht, Neil S. *et. al.* (eds.), *An Introduction to the History and Sources of Jewish Law*, Oxford: Oxford University Press, 1996.
Helmholz, Richard H., *The Spirit of Classical Canon Law*, Athens: University of Georgia Press, 2010.
Herring, Basil F., *Jewish Ethics and Halakhah for Our Time: Sources and Commentary*, New York: Ktav Publishing House, 1984.
Herzog, Isaac, *The Main Institutions of Jewish Law*, vol. 2, *The Law of Obligations*, London: Soncino Press, ²1967.
Levine, Samuel, "Capital Punishment in Jewish Law and its Application to the American Legal System: A Conceptual Overview," *Saint Mary's Law Journal* 29, 4 (1997), 1037–52.
Kirschenbaum, Aaron, *The Role of Punishment in Jewish Criminal Law: A Chapter in Rabbinic Penological*, New York: New York University Press, 1991.
Kao, Grace Y., *Grounding Human Rights in a Pluralist World*, Washington: Georgetown University Press, 2011.
Kaplan, Yehiel S., "Immigration Policy of Israel: The Unique Perspective of a Jewish State," *Touro Law Review* 31, 4 (2015), 1089–1135.
Kershner, Isabel, "Israel Approves Prayer Space at Western Wall for Non-Orthodox Jews," published online: *The New York Times*, 02.01.2016, https://www.nytimes.com/2016/02/01/world/middleeast/israel-western-wall-prayer.html (accessed on 24.02.2022).
Konvitz, Milton R., *Judaism and Human Rights*, New York: Norton, 1972.
Kook, Abraham Isaac, "Da'at Kohen," published online: Bar-Ilan University (ed.), *Online Responsa Project*, https://www.responsa.co.il/default.aspx (accessed on 08.03.2022).
Kravel-Tovi, Michal, *When the State Winks: The Performance of Jewish Conversion in Israel*, New York Chichester/West Sussex: Columbia University Press, 2017.
Maimonides, "Mishneh Torah," published online: Bar-Ilan University (ed.), *Online Responsa Project*, https://www.responsa.co.il/default.aspx (accessed on 08.03.2022).
Novak, David, "Religious Human Rights in Judaism," in: Michael J. Broyde./John Jr. Witte (eds.), *Human Rights in Judaism: Cultural, Religious, and Political Perspectives*, 1–34, New York: Jason Aronson Publishers, 1998.
Pill, Shlomo C., "Freedom to Sin: A Jewish Jurisprudence of Religious Free-Exercise," *Regent University Law Review* 34, 1 (2021), 1–67.
Pill, Shlomo C., "Jewish Law Antecedents to American Constitutionalism," *Mississippi Law Journal* 85 (2016), 643–96.
Quint, Emanuel B./Hecht, Neil S., *Jewish Jurisprudence: Its Sources and Modern Applications*, New York: Harwood Academic Publishers, 1980.
Quint, Emanuel, *A Restatement of Rabbinic Civil Law*, vol. 1, *Laws of Judges and Laws of Evidence*, Jerusalem: Gefen Books, 1990.
Reisman, Yisroel, *The Laws of Ribbis: The Laws of Interest and their Application to Everyday Life and Business*, Brooklyn, N.Y.: Mesorah, 1995.
Saiman, Chaim N., *Halakha: The Rabbinic Idea of Law*, Princeton: Princeton University Press, 2019.

Schreiber, Aaron M., *Jewish Law Decision Making: A Study Through Time*, Philadelphia: Temple University Press, 1979.

Sharon, Jeffrey, "Discreet Jewish Prayer Continues on Temple Mount Despite Minister's Comments," published online: *The Jerusalem Post*, October 20, 2021, https://www.jpost.com/israel-news/discreet-jewish-prayer-continues-on-temple-mount-despite-ministers-comments-682617 (accessed on 02.24.2022).

Sperber, Daniel, *On the Relationship of Mitzvot between Man and His Neighbor and Man and His Maker*, Jerusalem: Urim Publications, 2014.

Stearns, Peter N., *Human Rights in World History*, New York: Routledge, 2012.

Stone, Suzanne Last, "In Pursuit of the Counter-text: The Turn to the Jewish Legal Model in Contemporary American Legal Theory," *Harvard Law Review* 106 (1992), 813–94.

Witte, John Jr./Van der Vyver, Johan D., *Religious Human Rights in Global Perspective*, Grand Rapids: Eerdmans, 1996.

Suggestions for Further Reading

Brafman, Yonatan/Batnitzky, Leora, *Jewish Legal Theories: Writings on State, Religion, and Morality*, Waltham: Brandeis University Press, 2018.

Broyde, Michael J./Witte Jr., John (eds.), *Human Rights in Judaism: Cultural, Religious, and Political Perspectives*, New York: Jason Aronson Publishers, 1998.

Broyde, Michael J., *Sharia Tribunals, Rabbinical Courts, and Christian Panels: Religious Arbitration in America and the West*, Oxford: Oxford University Press, 2017.

Fadl, Khaled Abou El, *The Great Theft: Wrestling Islam from the Extremists*, New York: HarperOne, 2007.

Glendon, Mary Ann, *Rights Talk: The Impoverishment of Political Discourse*, Michigan: Michigan University Free Press, 1991.

Kaye, Alexander, *The Invention of Jewish Theocracy: The Struggle for Legal Authority in Modern Israel*, New York: Oxford University Press, 2020.

Milton R., *Judaism and Human Rights*, New York: Norton, 1972.

Pill, Shlomo C., "Rabbinic Reflections of the Religious and Civil Value of the Separation of Church and State," *Studies in Judaism, Humanities, and the Social Sciences* 23, 1 (2018), 23–36.

Pill, Shlomo, "Religionsfreiheit, Jüdisch," in: *Das Lexikon für Kirchen- und Staatskirchenrecht*, vol. 4, Paderborn et al.: Ferdinand Schöningh, 2020, 650–652.

Witte, John Jr./van der Vyver, Johan D., *Religious Human Rights in Global Perspective*, Grand Rapids: Eerdmans, 1996.

Clare Amos

The Concept of Human Rights in Christianity

Introduction

"No one interested in where human rights came from can afford to ignore Christianity."[1] There is a sort of double paradox about the relationship between Christianity and the development of human rights.[2] If one goes back in history even a
century or so Christianity cannot necessarily be seen as a natural bedfellow of
what would now be called "human rights" – indeed there are only too many instances from the Constantinian era until recent times when the opposite could be
illustrated.[3] The distinctive vision of voluntary suffering and vulnerability – following in the pattern first followed by Jesus Christ himself – which lies at the
heart of the Christian faith, seems to place a fundamental question-mark as to
whether it is appropriate for those who call themselves Christian to be eager
to claim "rights" for themselves. And yet it is undoubtedly true that the formal
development of international human rights structures and ideology in the middle of the 20th century owed much to the work of Christian thinkers, theologians
and political activists, both Protestant and Roman Catholic, whose work and vision was undergirded by their religious motivation and commitment. However
paradoxically the standards that these thinkers sought to implement as normative for all humanity were not by and large[4] viewed by them as distinctively
"Christian". Rather they were intended to be rooted "in a shared moral basis
taken to be universally common to all people, a basis [...] described as "secular"
or perhaps "pluralistic" in present day parlance."[5] A corollary is that there has

---

1 Moyn, Samuel, *Christian Human Rights*, Philadelphia: University of Pennsylvania Press, 2015,
169.
2 I am grateful to Skylar Salim, intern in the WCC Interreligious Department for some months in
2016 – 17 who assisted me with some initial research for this chapter.
3 There is a notable (and probably accurate) remark by Paul Zagorin which would horrify many
contemporary Christians, that "Of all the great world religions past and present, Christianity has
been by far the most intolerant", Zagorin, Paul, *How the Idea of Religious Toleration Came to the
West*, Princeton: Princeton University Press, 2003, 1.
4 Though this may be more true for the Protestant rather than the Roman Catholic figures involved in the discussions that led to the UDHR.
5 Little, David, "Foreword," in: John Nurser (ed.), *For all Peoples and all Nations. The Ecumenical Church and Human Rights*, Geneva: WCC Publications, 2005, xi.

https://doi.org/10.1515/9783110561579-004

been comparatively little reflection done on theological resources stemming from a distinctively Christian framework. The history of human rights from a Christian perspective has been the object of far more reflection than the theology. A further corollary is perhaps that now that the apple has been eaten, Pandora's box has been opened and the genie has been let out of the bottle, the implications of modern understandings of human rights have taken the western world at least considerably further down a number of roads than some Christians would necessarily have wished to travel.

This chapter seeks to "tell the story" of key moments of Christian involvement in human rights, including Christian involvement in the formal development of human rights structures in the mid-20th century onwards. It will inevitably be selective and partial. Interwoven with this, it will also seek to explore some aspects of the Christian theological underpinning of human rights – noting that the story and the theology in fact resonate with and challenge each other. Finally, some suggestions will be offered for drawing on central motifs of Christian theology as a tool for Christian theological engagement with human rights.

1 The Christian Faith, Human Dignity and Human Rights

Perhaps the single most important contribution that Christianity has made to the development of human rights is to link human rights and human dignity. This linkage is now such a common assumption, made of course even in the preamble to the Universal Declaration on Human Rights ("Whereas recognition of the inherent dignity and of the equal and inalienable rights of all members of the human family [...]") that it can be difficult to realize that originally the two concepts of "human rights" and "human dignity" were not necessarily viewed as virtually co-terminous. For example, the *Declaration of the Rights of Man and of the Citizen* promulgated in 1789 as part of the French Revolution had nothing explicit to say about human dignity, and indeed the progress of the revolution might suggest that not all that much attention was paid to the concept. The US Declaration of Independence in 1776, with its stirring call that "all Men are created equal, that they are endowed by their Creator with certain unalienable Rights, that among these are Life, Liberty, and the pursuit of happiness" does not use the actual word "dignity" either, although that concept does not seem to be very far away.[6]

---

6 The famous reflection of Alexander Hamilton in 1775 comes closer still. "The sacred rights of

Conversely, the traditional Natural Law teaching of the Roman Catholic Church, based heavily on the writings of Thomas Aquinas, was very slow to translate the discussion of "dignity" into actual practical rights for men and women. The focus on "dignity" in the writings of Immanuel Kant probably sowed some seeds: but they did not quickly result in a vision that gave such dignity physical or political expression.

It has been cogently argued that it was global political developments in the 1930s and 1940s that enabled, indeed compelled, such a correlation between human dignity and human rights, with the former resulting in the latter, and the latter rooted in the former. And it was Christians, both Roman Catholics and Protestants, who *par excellence* made this correlation. It was the advent of totalitarian regimes, both of the right and the left in the 1930s, the horrors of the Second World War in the first half of the 1940s, and the western Christian preoccupation with the Communist advance in the second half of that decade which forced that correlation. Intriguingly, the monstrous reality of the Holocaust (Shoah), which is – from the perspective of later generations – an example of the denial of human dignity and human rights, does not seem to have had initially as much influence on the political and theoretical discussions about dignity and rights as one might have expected. However, the fact that many of the post-Second World War trials of Nazis employed the concept of "crimes against humanity" suggests that there was some unspoken understanding.[7]

It is likely that it was Pope Pius XII, in a Christmas Day message in 1942, at the height of the Second World War and indeed at a time when its outcome must still have felt in the balance, who was the first major Christian leader explicitly to make the linkage between human dignity and human rights in a very public way.[8] The focus of the Pope's address was on peace. The first of the five points that the Pope offered in his message read as follows:

---

mankind are not to be rummaged for, among old parchments, or musty records. They are written, as with a sun beam in the whole volume of human nature, by the hand of the divinity itself; and can never be erased or obscured by mortal power." Cf. Hamilton, Alexander, *The Farmer Refuted: or, a More Impartial and Comprehensive View of the Dispute between Great-Britain and the Colonies, February 25*, New York: James Rivington, 1775.

7 See, for example, *Charter of the International Military Tribunal* (Nuremberg Tribunal), Article 6 (c).

8 His predecessor Pope Pius XI, in a message two months before his death in 1938 had noted the connection between dignity and rights, although in a way that feels somewhat exclusive and partisan, "Christian teaching alone gives full meaning to the demands of human rights and liberty because it alone gives worth and dignity to human personality", The New York Times Archives (ed.), *Pope Bids Church to Guard Man's Rights*, October 13, 1938, https://www.nytimes.

Dignity of the Human Person. He who would have the Star of Peace shine out and stand over society should cooperate, for his part, in giving back to the human person the dignity given to it by God from the very beginning [...] He should uphold respect for and the practical realization of [...] fundamental personal rights [...] The cure of this situation becomes feasible when we awaken again the consciousness of a juridical order resting on the supreme dominion of God, and safeguarded from all human whims; a consciousness of an order which stretches forth its arm, in protection or punishment, over the unforgettable rights of man and protects them against the attacks of every human power.[9]

In this statement human rights are linked to human dignity, and dignity in turn is connected to "a juridical order resting on the supreme dominion of God" – which is, of course, being implicitly contrasted with the dominions of the day.

A couple of years earlier in 1940 George Bell, the Anglican bishop of Chichester, highly influential in the ecumenical movement, and later to become the first Moderator of the World Council of Churches Central Committee, had written, "Of course you can dress up the ideas of 1789 and adapt them to the conditions of 1940. But the present situation is the result of secularism. To add a further dose of secularism to what the patient has already absorbed is to add poison to poison [...] no amount of secular Declarations, no number of claims for human rights, without spiritual sanctions, will save us from destruction."[10]

What both Pius XII and George Bell seem to be hinting at is something that will become explicit in the late 1940s among Christian proponents of human rights, namely the embedding of human rights in human dignity and in turn understanding human dignity as ultimately derived from the biblical account of creation set out in Genesis 1:26–28. In relation to humanity, the central and distinctive motif of this creation narrative is that human beings are created "in the image and likeness of God", which offers them a certain innate dignity, and further are given a special role in administering God's creation (the expression "steward" or "vice-regent" is often used). The corollary is that to mistreat human beings and to demean their dignity through ignoring their rights constitutes a refusal of the rule and dominion of God and of God's goal in creation.

This biblical text, and especially its affirmation that human beings are created "in the image of God" has in the last 75 years become the primary Christian theological cornerstone for reflection on human rights. Although the belief that

com/1938/10/13/archives/pope-bids-church-guard-mans-rights-tells-prelates-here-to-lead-in.html (accessed on 28.06.2022).
9 Pius XII, *The Internal Order of States and People* (Christmas Message for 1942). Cf. David Hollenbach, *Claims in Conflict: Retrieving and Renewing the Catholic Human Rights Tradition*, New York: Paulist Press, 1979, 60.
10 Bell, George, *Christianity and World Order*, Harmondsworth: Penguin, 1940, 104.

human beings reflect the image of God has been understood and interpreted in a variety of ways, and alternatively seen in terms of either gift or law, its centrality to the issue is unarguable.

Explicit reference to this text does not appear in the *Universal Declaration on Human Rights* promulgated in 1948, but it seems likely that it was in the minds of many of those who were responsible for the composition of the statement. Its widespread use since that time in international "rights" discussions by Christians is illustrated by the quotations below, deliberately chosen to give a sense of the range both of date and of ecclesiastical tradition:

- The worth of the person, his liberty, his rights arise from the order of naturally sacred things which bear upon them the imprint of the Father of Being and which have in him the goal of their movement. A person possesses absolute dignity because he is in direct relationship with the Absolute, in which alone he can find his complete fulfilment. *(Jacques Maritain, Christianity and Democracy: The Rights of Man and Natural Law, 1943)*
- The dignity of man is the dignity of the image of God. *(Pius XII Christmas Broadcast of 1944)*
- Out of nothing, He (God) made all things and filled them with the fullness of His own wisdom and goodness. Hence, these are the words the holy psalmist used in praise of God: 'O Lord, our Lord: how admirable is thy name in the whole earth.' And elsewhere he says: 'How great are thy works, O Lord! Thou hast made all things in wisdom.' Moreover, God created man 'in his own image and likeness,' endowed him with intelligence and freedom, and made him lord of creation. *(Pacem in Terris, Encyclical of Pope John XXIII on Establishing Universal Peace in Truth, Justice, Charity and Liberty, April 11, 1963)*
- Since man was created in the image of God, it follows that all men, regardless of colour, race, nationality, culture, or sex have equal and inherent worth. *(Frederick Nolde, 1968)*
- Our concern for human rights is based on our conviction that God wills a society in which all can exercise full human rights. All human beings are created in the image of God, equal and infinitely precious in God's sight and ours. Jesus Christ has bound us to one another by his life, death and resurrection, so that what concerns one concerns us all. *(World Council of Churches, Fifth Assembly, Nairobi, 1975)*
- All theological statements on human rights derive from the Christian anthropology of the human person made in the image of God. *(World Alliance of Reformed Churches, approx. 1975)*
- According to the teaching of the Book of Genesis, man is made in the image of God (Cf. Gn 1:26–27). This signifies that every human being is endowed

with intelligence, will and power which exist in this full perfection, free of contingency; only in God. These gifts of God constitute the essential basis of the rights and dignity enjoyed by man as such, independent of his particular personal talents, background, education or social status. *(The Church and Human Rights, Pontifical Council for Justice and Peace, 1975, 2nd edition 2011)*

- The doctrine of human rights is man's attempt at exercising his responsibility as God's steward on earth in that it seeks to challenge all the injustices that distort the image of God in man. It is an attempt to establish a social condition where there are harmonious relations among all the people of the world and where people are able to realise their full potential as God created them. *(Archbishop Winston Ndungane, former Anglican archbishop of Capetown, 1979)*
- A common [Christian] understanding does exist in the basic doctrine that all theological statements on human rights derive from the Christian anthropology of the human person created in the image of God. *(1980 Consultation of WCC, LWF, WARC, Pontifical Council for Justice and Peace)*
- The basis for all that the Church believes about the moral dimensions of economic life is its vision of the transcendent worth – the sacredness – of human beings. The dignity of the human person, realized in community with others, is the criterion against which all aspects of economic life must be measured. All human beings, therefore, are ends to be served by the institutions that make up the economy, not means to be exploited for more narrowly defined goals. Human personhood must be respected with a reverence that is religious. When we deal with each other, we should do so with the sense of awe that arises in the presence of something holy and sacred. For that is what human beings are: we are created in the image of God (Gn 1:27). *(Economic Justice for All: Pastoral Teaching on Catholic Social Teaching and the U.S. Economy, United States Catholic Bishops, 1986, #28)*
- This does not mean that the Bible does not provide an adequate basis for theological reflection on human rights [...] The dignity of human beings, the chief reason for human rights, arises from the idea of persons being created in the image of God. *(Russel Botman, Reformed World, 1998).*
- The human rights theory is based on human dignity as its fundamental notion. This is the reason why the need arises to set forth the Church's view of human dignity: According to the Biblical revelation, God not only created human nature but also endowed it with qualities in His image and after His likeness (cf. Gen 1:26). It is the only ground which makes it possible to assert that human nature has an inherent dignity. St. Gregory the Theolo-

gian, speaking about human dignity as related to the act of divine creation, wrote: "God has endowed all human beings so generously so that by distributing His gifts equally He may also show the equal dignity of our nature and the abundance of His grace" (Oration 14, On the Love for the Poor). *(The Russian Orthodox Church's Basic Teaching on Human Dignity, Freedom and Rights, adopted by the Bishops' Council of the Russian Orthodox Church in 2008.)*

– God has created all human beings in the image of God, and the inherent equal dignity of all human beings is the basis for the radical message of equality found in Christianity. The foundations of the church's efforts for universal human rights are therefore faith in God, the Creator, faith in Jesus Christ, who shows God's care for all sides of human life and the Church's calling and mission, also inspires the Church's human rights involvement, encouraging a confrontation with oppression, inequality and injustice. *(The Church of Norway General Synod, 2014)*

The central position that this text from Genesis has played and continues to play in Christian human rights discourse can call us to address three questions. The first is the primary question, already noted, of the relationship between human rights and religion – and specifically the Christian religion. That is a question very widely raised by both religious and secular authors in both popular and academic writing.[11] The second question which is much less discussed is whether the *imago dei* language of Genesis 1:26–28 is the only or the primary theological resource that Christianity has to draw on in discussion of human rights? Given that Genesis 1:26–28 comes from that part of Christian scripture which is shared with another faith (Judaism) are there not, or should there not, be resources particular to Christianity and its New Testament, such as reflection on the nature and work of Christ, which could be drawn on for discussion of the relationship between human rights and the Christian tradition? The third question is less obviously related to Genesis 1:26–28, though I believe it is certainly implied there: what is the relationship between human rights and human responsibilities, between claims and duties? This in turn cannot be disentangled from the relationship between the individual and communal dimensions of "rights".

---

11 It is intriguing that a short op ed piece written for the Credo column of the secular UK newspaper *The Times* on 28 April 2018, https://www.thetimes.co.uk/past-six-days/2018-04-28/register/religion-and-human-rights-are-a-double-lock-on-dignity-vxdr0326r (accessed on 26.02.2022) begins by observing, "Although human rights have erroneously been described as a secular religion, from the medieval era onwards religion and human rights have reinforced each other."

Responses to the second and third questions will surface in the course of this chapter, but to return to the first question: to what extent, if indeed at all, is modern international reflection on human rights inspired by the Christian tradition and by Christian theology? There are starkly contrasting views offered by different scholars. For example, the American political philosopher Louis Henkin has succinctly set out the view that religions and human rights are distrustful of each other. He believes that religions have often been suspicious of human rights because:

> [They] are much older than the human rights idea and have seen no need for that idea. Religions laid claim to conceptions of the good, of the good society, long ago, without any idea of rights […] they do not welcome the ideological independence of human rights […] religions have not had confidence in an ideology that does not claim divine origin and inspiration and has no essential place for the Deity.[12]

The suspicion, Henkin believes is however mutual. Those who have developed an ideological underpinning for human rights are suspicious about religion because: "[It] does not see human rights as integral to a cosmic order. It does not derive from any sacred text. Its sources are human, deriving from contemporary human life in human society."[13] Henkin adds, "Though some Christian theologians have argued that Western human rights theory is grounded in religious faith, human rights morality is in fact autonomous."[14] This can be contrasted with the succinct comment by the classic German theologian Emil Brunner, "Human rights live wholly from their ground in faith. Either they are *ius divinum* or – a phantom."[15]

These diverging views cannot be totally divorced from history or from context. Brunner's remark comes from 1947 – those years immediately after the Second World War which were the heyday of the birth of modern civil rights. The issue at the time for Christian theologians was that one needed to ground people's rights in something wider or broader than their putative "rights" as citizens or inhabitants of a state – because the state had – certainly in Nazi Germany – so patently failed to honor or even acknowledge any such rights. The Nazi regime had of course even questioned whether many of its victims had the right to be considered properly human at all. So it was important to ground human "rights"

---

12 Henkin, Louis, "Religion, Religions and Human Rights," *The Journal of Religious Ethics* 26 (1998), 229–39, 232.
13 Ibid., 231.
14 Ibid., 229.
15 Brunner, Emil, "Das Menschenbild und die Menschenrechte," *Universitas* 2, 3 (1947)/2, 4 (1947), 385–91, quoted in Moyn, *Christian Human Rights*, 125.

in something wider, broader, and deeper than the nation or even a person's immediate physical or specific situation – to link them to a something "transcendental" that did not depend on immediate contingent realities. The suggestion made by Hans Joas that the development of human rights is linked to what he describes as the "sacralization of the person" is perhaps a helpful response to the dichotomy and polarity of the two viewpoints expressed above. Joas suggests that the belief in universal human rights and human dignity arose as the result of a "process in which every single human being has increasingly, and with ever-increasing motivational and sensitizing effects, been viewed as sacred, and this understanding has been institutionalised in law."[16] Joas's language may not precisely be locating the underpinning of human rights in religious awareness, but it is certainly not far off doing so. And although the idiom is different the quotation from Jacques Maritain offered above expresses even more powerfully a similarly "sacralizing" view of human nature. In a lecture given at the World Council of Churches in 2012, Rowan Williams, then Archbishop of Canterbury, drew attention to the vital importance of human rights holding on to their roots in the sacred:

> We need a vocabulary of the sacred [...]. It is this that religious doctrine offers to the institutions and dialects of 'human rights', and it is a vital contribution. It is essential that, in an age that is often simultaneously sentimental, utilitarian and impatient, we do not allow the language of rights to wander too far from its roots in an acknowledgement of the sacred.[17]

This seems to take us back to the language of the "image of God" in Genesis 1:26 – 28. How does this biblical passage link with a phrase such as the "sacralization of the person"? Does not the idiom of human beings created in the divine image and likeness offer a fertile soil for developing a framework in which human beings can be given the respect due to the sacred? It is intriguing that in 1947 George Bell uses language that implies this: "The rights of men derive directly from their condition as children of God and not of the State [...] [given] the sacredness of the human personality."[18]

---

16 Joas, Hans, *The Sacredness of the Person: A New Genealogy of Human Rights*, Washington DC: Georgetown University Press, 2013, 5.
17 Williams, Rowan, "Lecture by Archbishop of Canterbury on Human Rights and Religious Faith," published online: World Council of Churches (ed.), https://www.oikoumene.org/re sources/documents/lecture-by-archbishop-of-canterbury-on-human-rights-and-religious-faith (accessed on 18.01.2022).
18 Bell, George, "The Church in Relation to International Affairs (address at Chatham House)," *International Affairs* 25, 4 (1949), 405 – 14.

2 Genesis 1 and the Image of God

If we return to Genesis 1:26 – 28 we can note that the presentation of the creation of humanity in Genesis 1:26 – 28 differs considerably from comparative accounts in Mesopotamian literature where ordinary[19] non-royal human beings are primarily created as slaves to relieve the gods of the burden of work. In such accounts, human beings have only duties. They do not have rights. Yet it would also be true to say, that the full liberating implications, which can be drawn from the text of Genesis, have not necessarily been realized throughout the history of Christian scriptural interpretation of the passage.

It may well be that during the last century, Christian interpretation of Genesis 1:26 – 28 had been influenced by wider reflection on human rights as well as influencing such reflection in return. The Gospel affirmation that "the Spirit [...] will guide you into all the truth" (John 16:13, NRSV) offers an affirmation that a readiness to realize more fully the implications of what is implied within scripture is a legitimate aspect of theological methodology within the Christian tradition. It is also an affirmation in itself of the dignity that God has bestowed on the human creation through the use of reason. One clear example of such development in biblical interpretation in relation to Genesis 1:26 – 28 has been that the significance of the fact that both "male and female" are created in God's image and likeness is now much more readily noted, certainly in relation to the dignity and rights of women. It is remarkable how 18th century "human rights" statements were in fact quite literally declarations about the rights of men. The rights of women were hardly discussed at all. The reality is that until very recently the specific rights of women were viewed as rather marginal.

In much of the discussion which links human rights to Genesis' language of *imago dei* the focus is, as we have already seen, inevitably on the "rights" and "dignity" of humanity. Yet in the context of Genesis this language is also a summons to human responsibility. The writer of Genesis clearly envisages human beings as tasked with acting as God's stewards or vice-regents in relation to the rest of creation. And if they are to "reflect" God in the way that the language of image implies, that surely means that they need to be able to demonstrate something of

---

19 However, in a number of ancient Middle Eastern texts in which the concept of sacral or divine kingship appears kings are seen as in some way reflecting the "image of God". The implication of this is that the Hebrew Bible democratises the language "image of God" by relating it to all human beings. The corollary is that all human beings should be treated as "royal" – with royal prerogatives and rights – which has interesting implications for reflection on human rights.

the character of God, which, from the Christian perspective means they have the duty of expressing justice, compassion, faithfulness and even love. All this is part of what it means to be in the image of God.

Genesis 1:26 – 28 is of course part of the common scripture that is shared by Christians and Jews. It is clearly an important text also within the Jewish tradition where it is seen in quasi-legal terms. For example, there is an intriguing traditional discussion between second century rabbis which seeks to pinpoint the essence of the Torah and which "cuts down" the commandments, to focus on what is most important. Beginning from the traditional Jewish statement that Moses received 613 commandments from God, it goes on: David reduced them to eleven (Ps. 15), Micah to three (Mic 6:8), Isaiah to two (Isa 56:1), and Amos to one (Amos 5:4). The poem then observes that Rabbi Akiva said that the most important principle in the Law was "Love your neighbour as yourself: I am the LORD." (Lev 19:18), but, according to the poem, Rabbi Ben Azzai taught a greater principle: "When God created the human being, he created the human in the likeness of God" (Gen 1:27).[20]

So, the theological understanding of human beings as *imago dei* is thus being viewed as a commandment, essentially a legal principle, a responsibility as well as a "right". This is then reinforced in Genesis 9:6 when the prohibition against murder is specifically tied to humanity's status as created in the image of God. Such a development of course facilitates a connection with the legal framework of human rights legislation. Of course the link that is made at this juncture between human creation in the image of God and the injunction against bloodshed also acts as an important reminder that the most fundamental human right of life – from which all others must surely flow – is the right to life itself.

In the Christian tradition fundamental reflection on Genesis 1:26 – 28 was undertaken by Thomas Aquinas in the 13th century, based on the earlier work of Augustine of Hippo and Anselm. Aquinas' work on natural law undergirds and influences his reflection on this topic. According to Aquinas *(Summa theologiae 1:93* and *De veritate 10:1)* the human being is the "image of God" in three ways. Firstly, according to the natural order because of his or her ability to know and love *qua* human being. Secondly, according to the order of grace – because of ability to know and love God. Then thirdly according to the order of glory a human being is the *imago Dei* when he or she knows and loves God in heaven. The journey of the Christian life is, for Aquinas. a growing into perfection as God perfects the resemblance of the *imago Dei* in each one of us that begins in our human nature as rational creatures and ends in our glory as saints

---

20 Talmud Yerushalmi, Nedarim 9:4

who have become partakers of the divine nature (cf. 2Pet 1:4) and as such, have become like God. The essential principle which Aquinas seems to be adopting is that there is a connection between the rationality (ability for thought) of the human person and their possession of the image of God. There was of course no immediate direct connection between such reflection and the development of human rights, and indeed Aquinas' views on heresy and how heretics needed to be treated are the antithesis of modern understandings about freedom of religion as a human right. Nonetheless, it is true that once Christianity had consciously decided to advocate for human rights, Aquinas' work has made a significant contribution to its theological underpinning, especially within the Roman Catholic tradition. There is a delicious remark made by Julie Clague, that "Christianity should consider the language of human rights as a direct descendant of natural law origins – though admittedly Thomas [Aquinas] is a more distant relation than some in the family tree that traces the genealogy of rights. And, as in all families, there are a number of skeletons in the closet."

These two theological reflections on Genesis 1:26–28 – from the Jewish tradition and by Aquinas – predate the modern era. They are usefully complemented by the perspectives of two Reformed theologians, John Calvin and Karl Barth, Calvin from the Reformation period and Barth from modern times. Both write extensively on the subject: the comments below focus on ideas that their interpretation of this biblical passage have contributed to the understanding of human rights.

In the case of John Calvin the language of "mirror" (one of Calvin's favorite metaphors) is important. Human beings in some way reflect God, just as a mirror reflects images. Calvin rejected the view, popular among some figures from the patristic age, that there is a difference between the "image" and "likeness". The use of both expressions in Genesis 1:26–28 is rather an example of poetic parallelism, which is common in Hebrew literature. For Calvin the image of God rests in the human soul: "For although God's glory shines forth in the outer man, yet there is no doubt that the proper seat of his image is in the soul."[21] Yet although the soul is the central focus of the image, Calvin still believes that no part of an individual human being is left untouched by the "image of God". However, a key insight offered by Calvin – and influential in later Reformed and evangelical theology – is the fact that the "Fall" had a drastic impact on this "image" and "likeness". Before the Fall Adam and Eve were intelligent and obedient, and the image of God was clearly seen in them. After the Fall, the image was frightfully marred. Although human reason and will contin-

---

21 Calvin, John, *Institutes of Religion*, 1.15.3.

ued, though tainted, the mirror was shattered.[22] The image of God may not have been not completely obliterated in human beings but it was deeply marred. It is like something that has been badly burned – like ash is both related to the wood it was before it was burnt, but is also completely unrecognizable, with no semblance of what it was before. What might the marring of the image of God in humanity imply for theological reflection on human rights?

The key contribution of Karl Barth to the concept of the image of God (certainly in any discussion about human rights) is his stress on its link to relationship. For Barth it is not anything intrinsic in human beings themselves that can be named as "image of God". "It [the image] does not consist in anything that man is or does. It consists as man himself consists as the creature of God."[23] Drawing an analogy with the way that the creation of humanity is introduced by the divine plural "Let us", which he believed led us in the direction of the Trinity, Barth gives attention to the pluralities in these verses, including of course the plurality of gender, "male and female". Barth stresses that what is essential in the "image of God" is the nature of human relationship and communion, reflecting the communion and love within the divine Trinity. This relationship which allows human beings to be described as in the "image of God" is multifaceted and refers to communion both between different human beings and between human beings and God. "For it is not God in us but rather we are in relation to God through *imago dei*."[24] This relational understanding provides an important resource for reflecting upon the communal dimensions of human rights. Although Barth himself did not emphasize the link between the relational sense of *imago dei* and the biblical understanding of "covenant", it is surely implied, since divine-human covenants are one of the, perhaps the primary, way in which the relationship between God and human beings is affirmed. Perhaps is not surprising therefore that some have seen in the Decalogue, the code at the heart of the Sinai covenant, a sort of biblical prototype of human rights.[25]

With this theological background in mind let us turn to some key moments in the modern development of human rights. The role that Christian institutions, in particular the Vatican and the World Council of Churches played in such developments, is notable.

---

22 Ibid., 1.15.4.
23 Barth, Karl, Church Dogmatics III/1, London: T&T Clark Ltd, 1958, 184.
24 Ibid.
25 See for example, Harrelson, Walter, *The Ten Commandments and Human Rights*, Philadelphia: Fortress Press, 1980.

3 Human Rights and the Christian Ecumenical Movement

I turn first to the World Council of Churches. It is widely acknowledged that the World Council of Churches and its ecumenical precursors played a fundamental role in the development of the international framework on human rights. It has been said that the World Council of Churches, "has done more for human rights among the peoples of the world than any other single international body."[26] Conversely, at different points in its own history, how the World Council of Churches has chosen to respond to, and reflect upon, human rights is a touchstone and test for its own integrity.

It is no accident that the first Assembly of the World Council of Churches, in Amsterdam in 1948 and the ratification of the *Universal Declaration on Human Rights* (UDHR) at the UN General Assembly in December of the same year, took place in such chronological proximity. For both developments happened in part at least, due to the events that had dominated the world stage for the previous decade, namely the Second World War and its aftermath. The horrors of Nazism, and its readiness to persecute individuals on the grounds of race, ethnicity, religion and sexuality, provided the stark backcloth against which both the World Council of Churches came into being and the United Nations itself was established. The wider dangers of nationalism, and the atrocities committed in its name, had also become apparent, in Asia as well as in Europe. It is telling that the first explicit rights spelled out in the UDHR are "the right to life, liberty and security of person" (Article 3), rights which had been brutally ignored in the period that led up to these events. During the years of the Second World War both President Franklin D Roosevelt in the United States and Prime Minister Winston Churchill in the United Kingdom in talking about global freedom began to speak in the language of rights. Roosevelt concluded his famous *Four Freedoms* speech with the words, "Freedom means the supremacy of human rights everywhere. Our support goes to those who struggle to gain those rights or keep them. Our strength is our unity of purpose."[27] The following year Churchill looked for-

---

26 Stackhouse, Max L., "Public Theology, Human Rights and Mission," in: Arthur S. Dyke (ed.), *Human Rights and the Global Mission of the Church*, Boston Theological Institute Annual 1, 11–21, Cambridge, MA: Boston Theological Institute, 1985, 16.
27 Roosevelt, Franklin D., *The Four Freedoms, Address to Congress January 6*, 1941 (Records of the United States Senate; SEN 77 A-H1; Record Group 46; National Archives).

ward to the time "when this world's struggle ends with the enthronement of human rights."[28]

Roosevelt's speech energized a number of churchpeople, especially in the United States and Britain, and particularly from what would be described as liberal Protestant church circles, to engage with a vision for developing a United Nations that was more than a grouping of nations and powers, and which could help establish fundamental rights for human beings which would transcend the authority of a state. Characteristic of such thinking was the assumption that the fundamental human right – on which all others could and should be based – was freedom of belief and religion. For example, the British Joint Committee on Religious Liberty produced a substantial essay in 1947 which argued that "religious freedom is the fundamental human freedom in which alone the true dignity of human personality can be fostered and its highest capacities flower."[29] Especially prominent in these discussions was the Lutheran theologian Otto Frederick Nolde, who in 1944 became the Executive Secretary of the Joint Committee for Religious Liberty established by the Federal Council of Churches of the USA and the US Foreign Missions Conference. At the founding conference of the UN in San Francisco in 1945, Nolde and other members of the church delegation that were present, pleaded passionately "that the UN must not just be seen as a state instrument. Rather, it must also give expression to the aspirations of the people of the world. The lack of this, they argued, was one of the main reasons why the League of Nations had failed. Therefore, they urged for a preamble stating this vision and the inclusion of an article that would guarantee people direct access to the UN's deliberations."[30] This resulted in seven references to human rights being included within the UN Charter signed in 1945. Over the next three years the full horror of the Nazi holocaust became more widely known, and this significantly helped to prompt the signing of the UDHR in 1948. Nolde's considerable influence on the complete eventual text is well known and it is widely believed that he was responsible for the actual wording of Article 18, *The Right to Freedom of Thought and Religion:* "Everyone has the right to freedom of thought, conscience and religion; this right includes freedom to change his religion or belief, and freedom, either alone or in community with others and in public or private, to manifest his religion or belief in teaching, practice, worship and observance."

---

28 Churchill, Winston S., *Letter to the Archbishop of Canterbury,* 29 October 1942.
29 Quoted in Nurser, *For all People and all Nations.*
30 Weiderud, Peter, "Otto Frederick Nolde: A Human Rights Pioneer," in: Peter N. Prove/Luke Smetters (eds.), *Faith and Human Rights: Voices from the Lutheran Communion,* Geneva: The Lutheran World Federation, 2006, 16.

By this time Nolde had also become Director of the CCIA, the Churches' Commission on International Affairs, in effect the arm of the WCC and the ecumenical movement established to engage with the international United Nations institutions, so it is hardly surprising that the statement on human rights issued by the WCC's 1948 Assembly anticipated the priorities of the UDHR:

> We are profoundly concerned by evidence from many parts of the world of flagrant violations of human rights. Both individuals and groups are subjected to persecution and discrimination on grounds of race, color, religion, culture or political conviction. Against such actions, whether of governments, officials, or the general public, the churches must take a firm and vigorous stand, through local action, in cooperation with churches in other lands, and through international institutions of legal order. They must work for an ever wider and deeper understanding of what are the essential human rights if men are to be free to do the will of God.[31]

As many commentators, from within the World Council of Churches as well as outside it, have noted, the focus of the human rights interest at the Amsterdam Assembly, which was largely dominated by the churches from North America and Western Europe, was primarily on what might be called "freedom" rights – imposing a negative obligation on states not to interfere with the rights of an individual to pursue his or her happiness. The report from Amsterdam suggested that churches "should press for freedom of speech and expression, of association and assembly, the rights of the family, of freedom from arbitrary arrest, as well as all those other rights which the true freedom of man requires."[32] The Assembly also offered a *Declaration on Religious Liberty* which reads as though it is an expansion of what would appear in the UDHR later in the same year. This was again understood as primarily relating to the right of an individual. There were four cornerstones of religious liberty which were listed as follows:

1. Every person has the right to determine his own faith and creed.
2. Every person has the right to express his religious beliefs in worship, teaching and practice, and to proclaim the implications of his beliefs for relationships in a social or political community.
3. Every person has the right to associate with others and to organize with them for religious purposes.
4. Every religious organization, formed or maintained by action in accordance with the rights of individual persons, has the right to determine its policies and practices for the accomplishment of its chosen purposes.[33]

---

31 WCC First Assembly (ed.), *Report of the Church and the Disorder of Society*, Amsterdam, 1948.
32 Ibid.
33 WCC First Assembly (ed.), *A Declaration on Religious Liberty*, Amsterdam, 1948.

It is important to notice that these rights are intended to be rights of individual human beings: they are *not* rights given to religions, or churches. This is a subject that we will touch upon again later.

The focus on religious liberty needs to be understood partly in the context of the period – when the rise of communist regimes in Eastern Europe seemed – certainly to Western Christians – to threaten religious freedom in the region. Rightly or wrongly those in the World Council of Churches who pressed for such freedom believed that by doing so they were supporting their Christian brothers and sisters who were living in difficult circumstances in the East. The problem, of course, was however that such support could, in the days of the Cold War, all too easily shade into an uncritical backing for western governmental aims.

Nolde was to remain the Director of CCIA until his retirement in 1969, and certainly for the earlier part of this period the human rights priorities of the ecumenical movement were to remain those of the liberal western, predominantly American, Protestant churches. The right of an individual's freedom of religion and belief was somehow considered paramount, and the importance of other human rights were linked at least in part to enabling this fundamental right to flourish. Nolde had himself however come to reject the view that had been urged by a number of Christians in the 1940s that a reference to God should be written in to the UDHR. Nor did he allow himself to be seduced by the aspiration that appears to have been subconsciously present in some Protestant churches at the time that affirming the right to religious freedom might offer scope for Christian, and specifically Protestant, missionary activity. Nolde – and through him the CCIA – took the view that Christian faith and theology required him to support the human right of all people to be free to choose their own expression of religion and belief. In other words, it was actually more "Christian" to encourage genuine and complete freedom of religion for all, rather than seek to privilege Christianity in any way! Nonetheless, although he encouraged the secular framing of the UDHR he noted, "In interpreting the Declaration, the Christian has an obligation to contend that such rights as man claims in society derive from the Christian view of man's nature and destiny, by virtue of his creation, redemption and calling."[34] So even though the language used in the UDHR was appropriately secular it was also appropriate, even required, that a Christian should view it through the spectacles of the biblical tradition, I suspect

---

34 Nolde, O. Frederick, "The United Nations Acts for Human Rights," release by the American Committee for the World Council of Churches in the Michigan Christian Advocate, 30 December 1948 (CCIA Archives, "UN International Bill of Human Rights," 1947–48, 428.3.24, World Council of Churches, Geneva, Switzerland).

in particular, Genesis 1:26–28, which does seem to have been the main Christian theological underpinning of World Council of Churches work for human rights during this period!

Although in reflecting on the World Council of Churches we are theoretically focusing on the ecumenical movement, in reality most of the engagement with human rights within this movement, practically, and even more so theologically, is owed to two ecclesiastical traditions, the Lutheran and Reformed/Presbyterian. This is due in part to their comparative strength in the United States during the foundational period of the 1940s, and their considerable dominance of the ecumenical movement in the years since. Each of the two traditions also has specific theological thrusts, which make commitment to human rights especially congenial.

For the Lutheran tradition – and Nolde himself was a Lutheran – the profound theological focus on freedom fits very comfortably with the language of freedom in which human rights are so often expressed. Similarly, the Lutheran foundational doctrine of "justification by faith" emphasizes the rights – and perhaps also responsibilities – of individual human beings.[35] It has been observed that, facilitated perhaps by the Lutheran doctrine of "the two kingdoms", "the Lutherans did not just baptize the UDHR but see in its rights the secular analogies to the essential terms of the Gospel by which all persons should be able to live."[36] The theological idiom of the "two kingdoms" has enabled the Lutheran tradition to draw an analogy between the righteousness and justice of God as it is established by God and applies in the kingdom of God, and the importance of justice offered by secular law. They are not however the same, and an essential task of Christians rooted in the gospels is to "constructively and critically challenge all human rights proposals from the perspective of faith and love, and enable Christians to engage in the struggle for human rights with a level of hope and courage that surpasses what the law alone can generate within us."[37] This "analogical" approach was the one taken by the Lutheran World Federation at its Fifth Assembly in Evian in 1970.

---

35 It is important to remember that biblical terms such as "justification" in their Hebrew (*tsadaq*) and Greek (*dikaio*) origins, are cognate with words such as "right", "righteousness".
36 Nelson, Robert J., "Human Rights in Creation and Redemption," in: Arlene Swidler (ed.), *Human Rights in Religious Traditions*, New York: The Pilgrim Press, 1982, 11.
37 Villa-Vicencio, Charles, *A Theology of Reconstruction: Nation-building and human rights*, Cambridge: CUP, 1992, 141. The author draws here on the study, *Theological Perspectives on Human Rights*, produced by the Lutheran World Federation in 1977. The text is marginally adapted from the original for the sake of syntax.

For the Reformed tradition, the link between the more liberal forms of Calvinism and the rise of democratic forms of government was a driver for human rights. The excellent studies of Calvin's *Geneva* offered by John Witte[38] illustrate the way in which from the beginning of the Calvinist tradition Calvin's own legal background complemented his theological acumen and produced an environment in which the language of "rights" (even if not understood fully in the modern sense) was affirmed and influential. The importance of the concept of "covenant" within Reformed Theology is also a helpful and probably not a completely accidental link with the modern international framework for human rights.

Of course, deeply embedded within the memory and DNA of these two Protestant traditions is the passion for freedom of religion, over against popes or kings, which was so much the part of the quest of the Reformation era, perhaps especially in the Puritan tradition of the English-speaking world.[39] Along with this though sometimes more in vision than in actuality, went a spirit of egalitarianism – of the equality of all human beings and a distrust of hierarchies. The pre-eminent place given to freedom of religion and belief when measured alongside other human rights – certainly in the 1950s – must be in part due to the historic importance such freedom had played in the story of the very foundation of these churches. Moreover rooting of human rights in the language of *imago dei* – itself a religious concept which spoke of the relationship between God and human beings – perhaps encouraged a special privileging of religious rights, which, as already suggested above, were viewed both as enabling the visible "flowering" of human dignity and the lynch-pin on which other rights depended. The Lutheran and Calvinist understanding of the church – which sees it fundamentally as a voluntary association of individual religious believers – itself encourages a sense of the primacy of the individual over the community when it comes to reflecting on the rights and wrongs of rights.

The 1960s and 1970s saw some significant shifts in the understanding of human rights, and, within the Christian ecumenical tradition, the exploration of some new theological paradigms. The World Council of Churches was also active – and in some ways actually prompted these developments.

---

38 Witte, John Jr., *The Reformation of Rights*, Cambridge: CUP, 2005.
39 A passionate article by the Baptist scholar Glen Stassen in fact makes a plea for the recognition of the Baptist Richard Overton as the "author and originator of the first comprehensive doctrine of human rights" in 1646. Overton's focus was clearly on religious liberty. Stassen, Glen, "Solid Ground IV: Incarnational Discipleship and Recovery of a Historically Realistic Jesus," *Baptistic Theologies* 4, 2 (2012), 40–54.

By the 1960s the sense of post-war optimism and hope for a new humanity had rather dissipated in countries such as the USA. In the socialist states of Eastern Europe there was strong critique of laissez-faire western economic systems which seemed to prioritize the needs of individuals over communities. In other parts of the world the urgent pressure to throw off the shackles of colonialism was paramount and had also created an awareness of the very selective nature of "western" human rights. The realization of the prevalence of racism, and the abysmal lack of human rights that were experienced by those who were on racism's receiving end also began to change the terms of the discussion.[40]

At the United Nations this shift was represented by the ratification of two detailed covenants which appeared in 1966, and which were intended to give concrete and legal expression to the sentiments expressed in the UDHR. The first of these was the *International Covenant on Civil and Political Rights*; the second was the *International Covenant on Economic, Social and Cultural Rights*. Although they both appeared in the same year, and in fact both began with the same article opposing colonialism, – "All peoples have the right of self-determination" – the first of these covenants feels like a direct heir of 1948, representing the classic "first generation" of human rights, and the second is a marker of the shift in human rights thinking that was taking place in the 1960s. It can be considered representative of "second generation" understanding of rights, in which the focus is now no longer on the protection of individuals from the state, but rather enabling and encouraging individuals to contribute to and to benefit from their participation in the wider community and in the state. The "rights" involved are themselves of a different nature to those on which the early period of international human rights focused: now concerns were issues like the right to work, to equal pay, to strike, to form trade unions, to education, to medical services, to an adequate standard of living.

These developments strongly impacted on the life of the World Council of Churches, which also underwent a substantial shift in its thinking on human rights, including the question of the relative importance of individual versus community rights. In particular, from the early 1960s, the determined struggle against racism, especially in Africa, was a significant factor in ecumenical life and thinking. An ecumenical consultation held by the World Council of Churches at St Pölten, Austria in 1974 in which the voices of East European Christians were prominent was a marker of this change. Freedom of religion still played a role in the discussions, but those who met at St Pölten were quite clear that it

---

40 See particularly, Traer, *Robert, Faith in Human Rights: Support in Religious Traditions for a Global Struggle*, Washington, D.C.: Georgetown University Press 1991, chapter 12, 187–201.

was not to be seen as an end in itself – but rather the means by which other rights could be promoted. So for example the final consultation statement includes the following:

> [31] The WCC has frequently declared that religious liberty is a basic human right. This right is required so that the full responsibility of Christian faith may be undertaken. This right is not a privilege or an exclusive freedom of the church. Human solidarity demands that we should be aware of the inter-relatedness of all rights, including the rights of those of other faiths or no faiths [...]. The rights to religious liberty exist in order to serve the religious community according to the commands of the gospel.[41]

The shift was sharply set out in a paper presented at the consultation by a church delegation from East Germany, entitled, *The Meaning of Human Rights and the Problems they pose.*[42] An initial short extract from this paper gives a flavor of its argumentation: "The building of a socialist society can be regarded as an inclusive effort to create social conditions in which human rights can become a reality [...] The right to a different opinion is often regarded in traditional bourgeois circles as the most important of human rights [...] under socialism, [...] human rights are rights to participate in shaping society."

The St Pölten consultation constructed a list of what it called six fundamental human rights, which were then ratified at the WCC Assembly in Nairobi the following year. These were:
1. the right to basic guarantees of life,
2. the rights to self-determination and to cultural identity, and the rights of minorities,
3. the right to participate in decision-making within the community,
4. the right to dissent,
5. the right to personal dignity,
6. the right to religious freedom.

It is notable that "religious freedom" comes at the bottom of the list. No longer does it hold the pre-eminent place that it initially enjoyed in the 1940s.

This shift in the content of human rights was also mirrored in the theological underpinning that was constructed. Drawing again on *The Meaning of Human*

---

41 Cf. Commission of the Churches on International Affairs (ed.), *Human Rights and Christian Responsibility, Report of the Consultation, St. Pölten, Austria, 21–26 October 1974,* Geneva: Oikoumene, 1975, 1–3.
42 A version of the paper prepared for the St Pölten conference by the UN Working Group of the GDR Regional Committee of the Christian Peace Conference can be accessed as "The Meaning of Human Rights and the Problems They Pose," *Ecumenical Review* 27, 2 (April 1975), 139–46.

Rights and the Problems they pose we can see a sharp challenge being offered to what had been, until then, the received theological wisdom on the topic. In a section of the document titled "The theological aspect" the discussion critiques the focus on creation which had hitherto been prevalent:

> The argument appealing to the creation as the basis of human rights has been employed since the Enlightenment and is still the one most commonly used even today. "Since man was created in the image of God, it follows that all men regardless of colour, race, nationality, culture or sex have equal and inherent worth." But the weakness and difficulties of this argument are easily overlooked. Strictly speaking the Genesis passages lead to the (old controversial) question whether and to what extent the dignity and noble status attributed to the first man (image of God) also apply to the generations which follow. Were they not withdrawn or at least qualified by the Fall? [...] But the decisive point is that, in the Old and New Testaments, the right to give life and to take it away, to grant freedom and to restrict it, to confer dignity on man and to dishonour him, is vested in God himself, as Creator and Lord. The outstanding examples here are Job and Jesus himself, God's man (Job 1:21 and Mark 8:31–33). According to the biblical tradition, inviolability of life, dignity and property are not a constitutive element of the human being. This is the point at which the severe criticism levelled at human rights by the dialectical theologians also begins. "Holy Scripture understands man as God sees him and it approaches his rights and duties from the same angle." "It betrays no knowledge of any human rights to which man could appeal as a basis for any claims." "The very rights listed in the Universal Declaration would be used by any human being who was assured of them only to achieve his or her humanity without obligations or considerations for other human beings." "We cannot really confess Jesus Christ and him crucified unless we take quite seriously the truth that God sees man only as represented in Jesus Christ, represented indeed as man *had* to be in him, namely as the lawbreaker and the condemned.[43]

It is interesting how the traditional Reformed/Calvinist unease about the language of *imago dei* gets married here to socialist concerns. From the perspective of the writers of this document there was a systemic "fallenness" and sinfulness reflected in the world order of the day. The writers of the document then continue by pointing to two other theological avenues, both of which are connected with the person and work of Christ.

The first of these suggests that human rights should indeed be located in human dignity, but in human dignity restored through the action of God in Jesus Christ:

> The statements in the Bible about the sinfulness of all human beings and the redemption achieved for them all (Rom 3:21–24) provide another possibility. In Christ man's dignity is

---

43 Ibid., 143–44.

restored. The access to God thereby opened up is the basis of true human dignity and true human right.[44]

However, the document then uses a second theological avenue to refer to the specific example of the life of Jesus in more detail:

> He had dealings with people from a great variety of sections and classes of society, disregarding and flouting all the social conventions of his time. By this practical demonstration of his acceptance of them as fellow human beings, He helped others to get their due, 'without respect of persons'. Standing up for the rights of others is one specific practical way of expressing love for the neighbour [...]. It must be pointed out, however, that in saying that, it is easy to overlook the way in which Jesus took sides, demonstrated his compassion for the outsider and the outcast, the sinner, the tax-collector, the prostitute and the leper.[45]

Then alongside acknowledging this bias to the poor on the part of Jesus, the document then raises the question as to whether it is "Christian" to insist on one's rights at all:

> The message of Jesus includes the summons: 'Anyone who wishes to be a follower of mine must leave self behind; he must take up his cross and come with me. Whoever cares for his own safety is lost; but if a man will let himself be lost for my sake and for the Gospel, that man is safe' (Mark 8.34 ff) [...] The notion that humanity and co-humanity must be secured in such a way that renunciation, sacrifice and suffering are excluded is foreign to the Bible. Far more characteristic of and central to the whole Bible is the affirmation that the way of the just often requires him to surrender his own preferences, claims and securities (see Mark 10.21; Matt 5.38 – 48).[46]

The challenges that the discussions at St Pölten posed are perhaps reflected in the very general nature of the affirmation of human rights made in the final report:

> It is our conviction that the emphasis of the Gospel is upon the value of all human beings in the sight of God, on the atoning and redeeming work of Christ that has given to man his true dignity, on love as the motive for action, and on love for one's neighbor as the practical expression of an active faith in Christ.[47]

What is perhaps most significant here is the Christological underpinning of human rights, which had not previously been a substantial element in the theo-

---

44 Ibid., 144.
45 Ibid., 144 – 45.
46 Ibid., 145.
47 World Council of Churches, *Human Rights and Christian Responsibility*.

logical discussion. Conversely it is also telling that the use of the language of *imago dei* is absent from this statement. "Dignity" is not given to human beings merely through their creation, but only through redemption in Christ.

It is interesting to notice however, how at this conference at St Pölten the insights of the Lutheran/Reformed traditions found themselves married to concerns of Christians from the Soviet bloc of Eastern Europe to produce a theological underpinning of human rights which is markedly more Christological in its focus than traditional theology had hitherto been, and which in several ways even appears ambivalent about such rights. Certainly, there is a strong whiff around of the suggestion that previous understandings of human rights were culturally conditioned and linked to the capitalist underpinning of the western world. The *Universal Declaration of Human Rights* had named property-ownership as a fundamental human right (Article 17). For some of those present at St Pölten, the question was probably present as to whether it was legitimate for human beings to own property at all – certainly not if such ownership disadvantaged others. One significant aspect of this development is that it helped to emphasize the importance of communitarian rights alongside, or even over against, individual rights: as the editorial of the issue of *The Ecumenical Review* which published the papers from St Pölten noted: "The issue of the freedom of the individual versus the interests of the state is closely related to the question of the importance of economic and social rights as against other rights."[48] The editorial also made clear that human rights could not be viewed apart from human duties or responsibilities, and quoted Article 29 of the UDHR to reinforce this argument.[49]

During the following decade, the Lutheran and Reformed Communions continued their own confessional reflections on human rights, influenced to a degree by the insights of the St Pölten meeting. In 1977 a declaration of the Lutheran World Federation offered not exactly a list of rights, but rather drew attention to three basic elements, all of which they believed needed to be present in all human rights – though perhaps not in the same proportion in all of them. These elements were freedom, equality and participation, all of which it was suggested had their roots in the biblical tradition.[50] Around the same time the World Alliance of Reformed Churches, guided by the theologian Jürgen Moltmann, developed a *Theological Basis of Human Rights*, with a slightly different triad of principles, "liberation by Jesus Christ, creation in the image of God, and hope

---

48 Uncredited editorial, in *Ecumenical Review* 27, 2 (1975), 93–96.
49 See further on Article 29 below, p. 106.
50 Cf. Todt, Heinz-Eduard, "Theological Reflections on the Foundations of Human Rights," *Lutheran World* 24, 1 (1977), 45–58.

in the coming Reign of God". The document however also developed an understanding of *imago dei*, which seems to adhere closely to Karl Barth's relational understanding of the concept. "The image of God is the human being who co-responds to God." This co-responding needs to be demonstrated by humans co-responding to God, in their relationship to other human beings, to the non-human creation, and in the succession of generations.[51]

The St Pölten consultation, its changed direction of human rights and the new theological trajectories it proposed made its mark on the ecumenical world. It has influenced the World Council of Churches, and in particular the work of the CCIA, to this day. Current World Council of Churches work draws on both the "first generation" and "second generation" models of human rights – and indeed now focuses on "third generation"[52] rights as well. One very practical and widely known example of support for "second generation" rights is the World Council's Ecumenical Accompaniment Programme in Palestine and Israel. However in recent years, perhaps prompted by current concerns about the vulnerable situation of Christian communities, both in the Middle East, and in countries such as Pakistan, the World Council of Churches has also been giving renewed attention to the issue of religious freedom. One of the most widely received documents published by the World Council of Churches in recent years, in 2011, *Christian Witness in a Multi-Religious World: Recommendations for Conduct* includes a strong affirmation of the importance of freedom of religion and belief as a – perhaps the – core human right:

> Freedom of religion and belief. Religious freedom including the right to publicly profess, practice, propagate and change one's religion flows from the very dignity of the human person which is grounded in the creation of all human beings in the image and likeness of God (cf. Genesis 1:26). Thus, all human beings have equal rights and responsibilities. Where any religion is instrumentalized for political ends, or where religious persecution occurs, Christians are called to engage in a prophetic witness denouncing such action.[53]

---

51 See in particular Moltmann, Jürgen, *On Human Dignity: Political Theology and Ethics*, trans. and intro. M. Douglas Meeks, Philadelphia: Fortress Press, 2007, 11.

52 This includes a particular interest in environmental and ecological concerns.

53 World Council of Churches/Vatican City: Pontifical Council for Interreligious Dialogue/Deerfield, IL: World Evangelical Alliance (eds.), *Christian Witness in a Multi-Religious World: Recommendations for Conduct*, Geneva, 2011, https://www.oikoumene.org/en/resources/documents/wcc-programmes/interreligious-dialogue-and-cooperation/christian-identity-in-pluralistic-societies/christian-witness-in-a-multi-religious-world (accessed on 26.02.2022). The document was published jointly by the World Council of Churches, the Pontifical Council for Interreligious Dialogue and the World Evangelical Alliance.

What has perhaps not happened however for the last 30 years – at least under the direct auspices of the World Council of Churches – has been ongoing systematic theological reflection on human rights, or at least not such reflection in official documents and statements.[54]

4 Human Rights and the Roman Catholic Church

The story of the World Council of Churches' involvement with human rights is complemented by that offered by the Roman Catholic Church, both centrally at the Vatican, as for example at the Second Vatican Council, and in the global life of the Church. During the last 150 years this Church has experienced a complete sea-change from the 1864 promulgation of *The Syllabus of Errors* by Pope Pius IX, in which error was declared to have no rights! In some measure the hostility on the part of the Roman Catholic Church towards human rights through much of the nineteenth century was due to the stress on "rights" during the French Revolution of 1789.[55] Unlike the *Declaration of Independence* (USA) and the *American Constitution and Bill of Rights*, which had been promulgated a few years earlier, and whose advocates were largely rooted in the Christian Protestant tradition, the rhetoric of the French Revolution was profoundly anti-religious, and this certainly affected attitudes towards human rights, at least in (Catholic) Europe for the next century. However during the last half century there have been considerable efforts made to explore how elements of human rights seem to surface in earlier Roman Catholic history: this has led, for example, to the figure of Bartholome de las Casas being viewed as a precursor of human rights in relation to his work on behalf of the indigenous people of the Americas. Las Casas also acts as an important corrective to the view that, in Christian circles, human rights is preeminently an anglophone preoccupation.[56]

---

54 For example, in 2008, the 60th anniversary year of the UDHR the WCC issued a "Statement on Universal Declaration on Human Rights" which referred to various practical examples of human rights work. However, it is notable that the only "theological" aspect of the Statement is a reference back to the Nairobi 1975 WCC statement, quoted earlier in this document, https://www.oikoumene.org/en/resources/documents/executive-committee/2008-09/statement-on-universal-declaration-of-human-rights (accessed 21.06.2022). However as this book was at its final stage before publication a new publication on Human Rights with significant World Council of Churches input did appear: Prove, Peter et al., *Strengthening Christian Perspectives on Human Dignity and Human Rights*, Geneva: WCC Publications & Globethics.net, 2022.
55 In particular the *Declaration des droits de l'homme et du citoyen*, 1789.
56 Ruston, Roger, *Human Rights and the Image of God*, London: SCM Press, 2004, 119–55.

We referred above to the importance of the link made by Pope Pius XII in 1942 between human dignity and rights. In fact, the language of dignity in relation to human beings has a long and glorious pedigree in the Catholic Church – as an ancient collect for Christmas, which comes ultimately from a prayer book dating back to the seventh century, opens with an affirmation of human dignity as the gift of God:

> O God who did wonderfully create,
> And yet more wonderfully restore,
> The dignity of human nature,
> Grant that we may share the divine life of him,
> Who humbled himself to share our humanity,
> Even Jesus Christ our Lord.[57]

In the late nineteenth century, Pope Leo XIII in his encyclical *Rerum Novarum* (1891) also used the language of dignity – linking it to implicitly to Genesis 1:26 – 28. Notably however Leo does not make a direct link from this to "rights", but rather to duties:

> The soul bears the express image and likeness of God, and there resides in it that sovereignty through the medium of which man has been bidden to rule all created nature below him and to make all lands and all seas serve his interests [...] no one may with impunity outrage the dignity of man, which God himself treats with great reverence, nor impede his course to that level of perfection which accords with eternal life in heaven [...] for there is no question here of rights belonging to man, but of duties owed to God.[58]

However in another part of the encyclical in which he was seeking to engage positively with the modern world, Leo did speak about rights – although married also to duties. The encyclical sought to set out "the relative rights and mutual duties of the rich and of the poor, of capital and of labour."[59] This included the right for workers to organize themselves in associations or unions, significant, not least because it reflects the corporate and social understanding of rights, which has been a particular characteristic of Roman Catholic reflection in this area. It is notable however that though Leo spoke about the rights of particular sectors of society – such as workers, owners, the family – he did not bring

---

57 Used by different churches in various modern forms as a prayer during the Christmas season but found originally in the Sacramentarium "Leonianum" or "Veronense", Cod., Verona, Bibliotheca Capitularis LXXXV, 80.

58 Leo XIII, *Rerum Novarum: Encyclical of Pope Leo XIII on Capital and Labour*, n.p., 1891, para. 40.

59 Ibid., para. 2.

himself to speak of "the rights of man" in general, as he did not want these to usurp the place due to "duties to God".

Dignity became an increasingly prevalent motif in Roman Catholic thinking during the first decades of the twentieth century, as the Church wrestled with its response to the various totalitarian regimes, which emerged, one on its doorstep, and others in countries that proudly affirmed their Catholic credentials. The official and very public breakthrough linking dignity and rights made in Pope Pius XII's Christmas message of 1942, quoted near the beginning of this chapter, was mirrored by the writings of the Roman Catholic theologian, Jacques Maritain writing in the same year, "The dignity of the human person? The expression means nothing if it does not signify that, by virtue of the natural law, the human person has the right to be respected, is the subject of rights, possesses rights."[60] Indeed one of Maritain's great achievements was to expedite the understanding within the Roman Catholic Church that human rights, far from being hostile to natural law, should be seen as an expression of it.

Maritain was to play a significant role in the conversations that led to the promulgation of the UDHR, facilitated by the fact that after the fall of France he found himself trapped in the United States for the rest of the Second World War. But though many US liberal Catholics, both lay and clerical, welcomed the official developments in international human rights – which some of them tended to see as basically an extension of American democracy – the response of the Vatican itself to the UDHR was distinctly muted. Perhaps it was the very public roles that representatives of Protestant churches and the "Protestant" World Council of Churches had played in its formulation, perhaps it was linked to the difference of ethos between Europe and the United States, perhaps it was that some of the leadership in the Roman Catholic Church still did have to be convinced of the importance of freedom of religion, that central tenet of the UDHR – but it was notable that Pope Pius XII, who ruled the Roman Catholic Church for the next decade, never once mentioned the UDHR. It was only when Pope John XXIII ascended to the papacy in 1958 that a change of attitude came, and marked a *volte face* in the life of the Roman Catholic Church. The Church – which had previously perhaps been playing catch-up to western Protestantism – now became a peacemaker for the wider Christian community in many aspects of the field of human rights.

Even before the Second Vatican Council had produced the plethora of documents that led to a sea-change in the life of the Roman Catholic Church, Pope

---

60 Maritain, Jacques, *The Rights of Man and Natural Law*, New York: Scribner, 1943, 65.

John XXIII's personal encyclical *Pacem in Terris*[61] set out Pope John's vision in unmistakable terms. The encyclical has been described as the most widely acclaimed papal document from modern times. It was published only a few months before the Pope's death – when he was already ill with the cancer which would kill him. It therefore probably carries the weight of being Pope John's intentional "last word" to the Church and the world.

It includes a clear, though qualified, affirmation of the UDHR:

> 142. The United Nations Organization (U.N.) was established, as is well known, on June 26, 1945. To it were subsequently added lesser organizations consisting of members nominated by the public authority of the various nations and entrusted with highly important international functions in the economics, social, cultural, educational and health fields. The United Nations Organization has the special aim of maintaining and strengthening peace between nations, and of encouraging and assisting friendly relations between them, based on the principles of equality, mutual respect, and extensive cooperation in every field of human endeavor.

> 143. A clear proof of the farsightedness of this organization is provided by the Universal Declaration of Human Rights passed by the United Nations General Assembly on December 10, 1948. The preamble of this declaration affirms that the genuine recognition and complete observance of all the rights and freedoms outlined in the declaration is a goal to be sought by all peoples and all nations.

> 144. We are, of course, aware that some of the points in the declaration did not meet with unqualified approval in some quarters; and there was justification for this. Nevertheless, We think the document should be considered a step in the right direction, an approach toward the establishment of a juridical and political ordering of the world community. It is a solemn recognition of the personal dignity of every human being; an assertion of everyone's right to be free to seek out the truth, to follow moral principles, discharge the duties imposed by justice, and lead a fully human life. It also recognized other rights connected with these.

> 145. It is therefore Our earnest wish that the United Nations Organization may be able progressively to adapt its structure and methods of operation to the magnitude and nobility of its tasks. May the day be not long delayed when every human being can find in this organization an effective safeguard of his personal rights; those rights, that is, which derive directly from his dignity as a human person, and which are therefore universal, inviolable and inalienable. This is all the more desirable in that men today are taking an ever more active part in the public life of their own nations, and in doing so they are showing an increased interest in the affairs of all peoples. They are becoming more and more conscious of being living members of the universal family of mankind.

---

61 John XXIII, "Pacem in Terris," April 11, 1963, published online: *The Holy See*, http://w2.vatican.va/content/john-xxiii/en/encyclicals/documents/hf_j-xxiii_enc_11041963_pacem.html (accessed on 07.03.2022).

This affirmation comes towards the close of the encyclical, which has earlier set out in a comprehensive fashion the range of rights due to human beings:

Rights

11. But first We must speak of man's rights. Man has the right to live. He has the right to bodily integrity and to the means necessary for the proper development of life, particularly food, clothing, shelter, medical care, rest, and, finally, the necessary social services. In consequence, he has the right to be looked after in the event of illhealth; disability stemming from his work; widowhood; old age; enforced unemployment; or whenever through no fault of his own he is deprived of the means of livelihood. (8)

Rights Pertaining to Moral and Cultural Values

12. Moreover, man has a natural right to be respected. He has a right to his good name. He has a right to freedom in investigating the truth, and—within the limits of the moral order and the common good—to freedom of speech and publication, and to freedom to pursue whatever profession he may choose. He has the right, also, to be accurately informed about public events.

13. He has the natural right to share in the benefits of culture, and hence to receive a good general education, and a technical or professional training consistent with the degree of educational development in his own country. Furthermore, a system must be devised for affording gifted members of society the opportunity of engaging in more advanced studies, with a view to their occupying, as far as possible, positions of responsibility in society in keeping with their natural talent and acquired skill. (9)

The Right to Worship God According to One's Conscience

14. Also among man's rights is that of being able to worship God in accordance with the right dictates of his own conscience, and to profess his religion both in private and in public. According to the clear teaching of Lactantius, "this is the very condition of our birth, that we render to the God who made us that just homage which is His due; that we acknowledge Him alone as God, and follow Him. It is from this ligature of piety, which binds us and joins us to God, that religion derives its name." (10)[62]

Hence, too, Pope Leo XIII declared that "true freedom, freedom worthy of the sons of God, is that freedom which most truly safeguards the dignity of the human person. It is stronger than any violence or injustice. Such is the freedom which has always been desired by the Church, and which she holds most dear. It is the sort of freedom which the Apostles resolutely claimed for themselves. The apologists defended it in their writings; thousands of martyrs consecrated it with their blood." (11)[63]

---

62 *Divinae Institutiones*, lib. IV, c.28.2; PL 6.535.

63 Encyclical letter *"Libertas Praestantissimum,"* Acta Leonis XIII, VIII, 1888, 237–38. The quotation from the writings of Pope Leo XIII at this point is probably intended to be diplomatic. It is however also selective. Elsewhere Leo wrote, "Since, then, the profession of one religion is necessary in the State, that religion must be professed which alone is true, and which can

As can be seen from this extensive quotation of the document (which needs to be read in full to gain an overall impression of its expansive vision), it refers to material and physical, intellectual, moral, cultural, and spiritual rights. The detailed attention given to freedom of worship and religion marks a new era for the Roman Catholic Church; previous Popes would have found it difficult to speak in such terms.

Pacem in Terris then does move on to a discussion of "duties", which it considers as intertwined with rights, both on an individual and on a corporate basis. But it is significant that "rights" are held to come before duties ("But first We must speak of man's rights"…), as that would also not have been the case in a previous generation in the life of the Church.

Duties

28. The natural rights of which We have so far been speaking are inextricably bound up with as many duties, all applying to one and the same person. These rights and duties derive their origin, their sustenance, and their indestructibility from the natural law, which in conferring the one imposes the other.

29. Thus, for example, the right to live involves the duty to preserve one's life; the right to a decent standard of living, the duty to live in a becoming fashion; the right to be free to seek out the truth, the duty to devote oneself to an ever deeper and wider search for it.

Reciprocity of Rights and Duties Between Persons

30. Once this is admitted, it follows that in human society one man's natural right gives rise to a corresponding duty in other men; the duty, that is, of recognizing and respecting that right. Every basic human right draws its authoritative force from the natural law, which confers it and attaches to it its respective duty. Hence, to claim one's rights and ignore one's duties, or only half fulfill them, is like building a house with one hand and tearing it down with the other.

Repeated throughout the encyclical is the concept of "the universal common good": in itself a phrase, which reinforces the relational understanding of human rights, and their communal dimension. This phrase would become a major building block of later Catholic social teaching.

The groundbreaking path trodden by the encyclical of John XXIII was then reinforced by several documents promulgated at the Second Vatican Council in which the importance of human rights was restated. *Gaudium et Spes* centres on human dignity, but then considers fundamental human rights as essential to

---

be recognised without difficulty, especially in Catholic States, because the marks of truth are, as it were engraven upon it."

sustain that dignity, noting however again that there is a necessary corporate dimension, and that rights and duties cannot be separated from each other:

> Every day human interdependence grows more tightly drawn and spreads by degrees over the whole world. As a result the common good, that is, the sum of those conditions of social life which allow social groups and their individual members relatively thorough and ready access to their own fulfillment, today takes on an increasingly universal complexion and consequently involves rights and duties with respect to the whole human race. Every social group must take account of the needs and legitimate aspirations of other groups, and even of the general welfare of the entire human family.

> At the same time, however, there is a growing awareness of the exalted dignity proper to the human person, since he stands above all things, and his rights and duties are universal and inviolable. Therefore, there must be made available to all men everything necessary for leading a life truly human, such as food, clothing, and shelter; the right to choose a state of life freely and to found a family, the right to education, to employment, to a good reputation, to respect, to appropriate information, to activity in accord with the upright norm of one's own conscience, to protection of privacy and rightful freedom even in matters religious.[64]

Particular importance was given at the Second Vatican Council to religious freedom, which is seen as absolutely central to human dignity. Indeed the conciliar document that focused on religious freedom was – perhaps deliberately – called *Dignitatis Humanae* ("Of Human Dignity"), taking its name from its opening words. It then moves swiftly to its central affirmation:

> This Vatican Council declares that the human person has a right to religious freedom. [...] The council further declares that the right to religious freedom has its foundation in the very dignity of the human person as this dignity is known through the revealed word of God and by reason itself.[65]

Human dignity is thus derived both from natural law and from scriptural revelation. This central affirmation is then repeated and expanded later in the document:

> The declaration of this Vatican Council on the right of man to religious freedom has its foundation in the dignity of the person, whose exigencies have come to be are fully known to human reason through centuries of experience. What is more, this doctrine of

---

64 Paul VI, "Dignitates Humanae," 1965, para. 2, published online: *The Holy See*, http://www.vatican.va/archive/hist_councils/ii_vatican_council/documents/vat-ii_decl_19651207_dignitatis-humanae_en.html (accessed on 26.02.2022).
65 Paul VI, "Dignitates Humanae," https://www.vatican.va/archive/hist_councils/ii_vatican_council/documents/vat-ii_decl_19651207_dignitatis-humanae_en.html (accessed on 28.02.2022).

freedom has roots in divine revelation, and for this reason Christians are bound to respect it all the more conscientiously. Revelation does not indeed affirm in so many words the right of man to immunity from external coercion in matters religious. It does, however, disclose the dignity of the human person in its full dimensions. It gives evidence of the respect which Christ showed toward the freedom with which man is to fulfill his duty of belief in the word of God and it gives us lessons in the spirit which disciples of such a Master ought to adopt and continually follow. Thus further light is cast upon the general principles upon which the doctrine of this declaration on religious freedom is based. In particular, religious freedom in society is entirely consonant with the freedom of the act of Christian faith.

10. It is one of the major tenets of Catholic doctrine that man's response to God in faith must be free: no one therefore is to be forced to embrace the Christian faith against his own will. This doctrine is contained in the word of God and it was constantly proclaimed by the Fathers of the Church. The act of faith is of its very nature a free act. Man, redeemed by Christ the Savior and through Christ Jesus called to be God's adopted son, cannot give his adherence to God revealing Himself unless, under the drawing of the Father, he offers to God the reasonable and free submission of faith. It is therefore completely in accord with the nature of faith that in matters religious every manner of coercion on the part of men should be excluded. In consequence, the principle of religious freedom makes no small contribution to the creation of an environment in which men can without hindrance be invited to the Christian faith, embrace it of their own free will, and profess it effectively in their whole manner of life.[66]

What *Dignatitis Humanae* seems to be suggesting is both that the ability of human beings to make free choices, in particular concerning their relationship with the divine, constitutes the profoundest expression of their human dignity, and also that such freedom is an essential aspect of God's dealing with humanity in Christ. Thus, any coercion in religion is actually inimical to the Christian faith.

Yet as with the liberal Protestant churches and the World Council of Churches, also within Roman Catholic structures the focus of human rights was to move on, though perhaps in a less disjunctive way than the Protestant story seems to illustrate. The corporate and communal dimension of rights, as well as the link between rights and duties, which had always been a part of the Roman Catholic story from its early days, allowed for a gentler sense of transition than was the case for other parts of the Christian community. As Richard Pattee had written in 1945 "The genius of Catholicism is perhaps no better illustrated than in the subtle and profound harmony that is established between the dignity of the human

---

66 Ibid., para. 9–10.

being as a singular person, and the rights and duties of that person as a member of society."[67]

For example, there is a striking note offered in *Populorum Progressio* published by 1967, which is focusing on the fair distribution of the world's resources and the universal right of every person to take from the earth whatever he or she needs for basic sustenance:

> All other rights, whatever they may be, including the rights of property and free trade, are to be subordinated to this principle. They should in no way hinder it; in fact, they should actively facilitate its implementation. Redirecting these rights back to their original purpose must be regarded as an important and urgent social duty.[68]

A few years later the 25th anniversary of the UDHR in 1973 was marked initially by a Joint Statement from the Vatican and the World Council of Churches, to be shortly followed in 1975 by a working paper *The Church and Human Rights* produced by the Pontifical Commission on Justice and Peace.[69] A second edition of this working paper was published in 2011, which suggests that it is still seen as relevant to the discussion within the Church. Whatever its precise status within the hierarchy of Roman Catholic documents, it offers an excellent systematic reflection on the historical, practical, pastoral and theological aspects of human rights, as viewed from a Roman Catholic perspective. The theological section of the document begins by noting that human rights require us to engage with "theologies of the *imago dei,* of the Incarnation, of the Church and of liberation."[70] Much of what it then suggests relating to the *imago dei* (image of God) has already been touched upon, although the strong link that is made between the "image of God" and the "mystery" of the incarnation of Christ is a feature of the document.[71] However, some insights from the document which relate to the other key Christian theological themes include the following:
- Man's freedom to behave according to the dictates of conscience constitutes the most forceful expression of his inalienable nobility. As he preached the

---

67 Pattee, Richard, "Human Rights (June 3, 1945)," in: George N. Shuster et al. (eds.), *Problems of the Postwar World: a Catholic Hour Symposium*, 29–33, Washington, DC: National Council of Catholic Men, 1945.

68 Paul VI, *Populorum Progressio. Encyclical of Pope Paul VI on the Development of Peoples, March 26,* London: Catholic Truth Society, 1967, para. 22.

69 Pontifical Commission, "Iustitia et Pax," published online: *The Church and Human Rights. Working Paper No. 1,* Vatican City, [2]2011, http://www.clerus.org/clerus/dati/2011-07/23-13/The_Church_and_Human_Rights.pdf (accessed on 26.02.2022).

70 Ibid., para. 45.

71 Ibid., see particularly para. 40.

message of the Kingdom of God to the crowds in Palestine, Christ, himself, fully respected man's genuine freedom, not in any way forcing man but inviting him to respond freely to the Gospel message (Cf. Mk 8:34).[72]

- As he died upon the cross for all mankind and became through his resurrection the second Adam and the universal source of salvation, Jesus won for all men the power to become sons of God (Cf. Jn 1:12) and to be changed by the Holy Spirit into a new creature [...]. All men of all times and places are destined to share in this sublime equality and supernatural brotherhood.[73]

- Every person has a special relation with God, grounded in the mystery of the Incarnate Word. When the Son of God became man, he entered into the world's history as Perfect Man. He lived in a particular nation, a particular culture, even in a particular minority group, and thus raised the whole human family and all its members, which is to say human nature with all its prerogatives, to the dignity of Sons of God [...]. It is precisely this choice by our Saviour of a particular nation or people, heirs of blessings destined for all nations, which gives value and dignity to every particular people, culture or nation.[74]

- [Christ's] supreme revelation was that "God is love" (1 Jn 4:8); he therefore taught that the fundamental law of human perfection, and of the transformation of the world, is "the new commandment": "A new commandment I give unto you, that you love one another; even as I have loved you, that you also love one another" (Jn 13:34) [...]. Christ made this law of love for one's neighbour his own personal commandment and enriched it with a new meaning. For he wanted to identify himself with his brethren as the object of love. Indeed, by "taking on human nature he bound the whole human race to himself as a family through a certain supernatural solidarity and established charity as the mark of his disciples, saying, "By this will all men know that you are my disciples, if you have love for one another" (Jn 13:35). "To those therefore who believe in divine charity he gives assurance that the way of love lies open to all men and that the effort to establish a universal brotherhood is not a hopeless one." At that point Christ carried his solidarity with even "the least" of his brethren to the point of affirming: "Whatever you have done for any one of these brothers of mine, even the least, you have done it to me" (Mt 25:40) [...] But Christian love "implies an absolute demand for justice, namely a recognition of the dignity and

---

72 Ibid., para. 46.
73 Ibid., para. 46.
74 Ibid., para. 49.

rights of one's neighbour. Justice attains its inner fullness only in love. Because every man is truly a visible image of the invisible God and a brother of Christ, the Christian finds in every man God himself and God's absolute demand for justice and love." The practice of brotherly love and human and Christian solidarity to promote and defend human rights must therefore conform to the true sense of that central message of the Gospel and to the needs of men to whom it is addressed.[75]

– Although the Church with her religious role has no proper mission in the political, social or economic order, she is far from looking on religion as purely private and has always firmly stated that "out of this religious mission itself comes a function, a light and an energy which can serve to structure and consolidate the human community according to the divine law." That is why the Catholic Church has never confined her moral teaching to private or individual ethics; but on the contrary, and with ever greater insistence in modern times, she has spoken out to the world on questions of public morality such as social justice, the development of peoples, human rights, war and peace, and racism. This is part of her pastoral mission. The Church is the continuation and the presence of Christ in the world and in history. She continues the prophetic mission of Jesus, whose words and actions are all for the good of men to save, heal, liberate and assist them all [...]. In continuing the prophetic mission of her founder the Church must also preach more forcefully and realize more effectively this liberation of the poor, the oppressed and the outcast, working with others — building a world where every man, no matter what his race, religion or nationality, can live a fully human life, freed from servitude imposed on him by other men or by natural forces over which he has not sufficient control.[76]

– To imitate Christ and to be his true continuation in the world, the Church as a whole, like every Christian community, is called to work for the dignity and rights of man, both individually and collectively; to protect and promote the dignity of the human person; and to denounce and oppose every sort of human oppression. It is the risen Christ who inspires the Church in the campaign for human rights [...].[77]

– Finally, theological reflection urgently reminds us of one final aspect which is of supreme importance for the Christian – namely, the eschatological view of man and of his fundamental rights [...] even if these good fruits, which

---

75 Ibid., para. 49–52.
76 Ibid., para. 55–57.
77 Ibid., para. 58.

constitute human values, liberties and rights, will not be completely and perfectly realized except in our future homeland, this should not be an excuse for slackening our speed or effort in the struggle for justice. Rather it should impel us to even greater commitment in order to offer people a definite approximation or anticipation of the new world.[78]

The eschatological thrust with which the theological reflection concludes is also emphasised in a succinct comment made by the American Jesuit David Hollenbach in 1988. Hollenbach notes that the Roman Catholic tradition offers two complementary building blocks for the principle of human dignity, which in turn acts as the foundation stone for human rights. The first principle is one that can be owned by all people, whether or not they are religious, namely "The imperative arising from human dignity is based on the indicative of the person's transcendence over the world of things."[79] The second however is distinctly Christian, and specifically rooted in the Roman Catholic tradition. "The beliefs that all persons are created in the image of God, that they are redeemed by Jesus Christ, and that they are summoned by God to a destiny beyond history serve both to support and to interpret the fundamental significance of human existence."[80]

The theological underpinning for human rights set out here still, broadly speaking, constitutes theological orthodoxy in the Roman Catholic Church up to the present day. However, as with the ecumenical Protestant tradition discussed earlier, what exactly human rights are has been much argued about, and perhaps shifted in recent decades. In particular, the Roman Catholic Church has opposed suggestions that issues such as abortion, euthanasia, and same sex relationships should be assessed on the basis of human rights criteria. Especially during the 1990s, after the end of the Cold War, Pope John Paul II sharply critiqued the use of rights terminology for the discussion of such concerns. As far as he was concerned, they were an expression of what he described as the "culture of death", whereas human rights, as he understood them, needed to be based on the first and most fundamental right, the right to life. This critique continues within the Roman Catholic church, which is clearly very uncomfortable about some of what it refers to as "new" human rights.

The distinctive contribution offered by Pope Francis in the field of human rights is perhaps his prioritising the rights of the poor. "The dignity of the

---

78 Ibid., para. 59.
79 Hollenbach, *Claims in Conflict*, 95.
80 Ibid., 96.

human person and the common good rank higher than the comfort of those who refuse to renounce their privileges. When these values are threatened, a prophetic voice must be raised."[81] Pope Francis, and those who speak for him, believe that the Church needs to be a proactive proponent of such human rights.

But also in recent years, as with other Christian churches and organisations, political developments, especially in the Middle East, have led once again to a focus on the importance of freedom of religion, as a fundamental human right, perhaps even the human right par excellence. A 2014 address by Cardinal Turkson to the Slovak Bishops Conference notes how Pope John Paul II called religious freedom "the source and synthesis" of all the basic human rights, defining religious freedom as "the right to live in the truth of one's faith and in conformity with one's transcendent dignity as a person."[82] Significantly, Turkson's speech suggests that freedom of religion may be threatened from one of two directions, either extreme fundamentalism on the part of other religious groups, or what he called extreme secularism, in which states do not allow religions to have any sort of public role.

Before moving on from this discussion about the Roman Catholic Church and human rights there is perhaps one final thing to say. For all its profound theological reflection on human rights – which appropriately acts as a beacon for the rest of the Christian world, the Church is itself in a very ambiguous position when it comes to the practical honouring of human rights. As a quasi-State, the Vatican can sign up to the key international United Nations human rights conventions. That in most cases it has chosen not to do so is telling. For example its failure to sign up to the UN *Convention on the Elimination of All Forms of Discrimination against Women* seems likely to be connected to the understanding that the Convention constitutes a hazard to much of the current institutional life of the Church, in which clearly women and men are not equal. Indeed the very autocratic style of governance in the Roman Catholic Church sits uneasily with the ideology of human rights in which democratic forms of government are especially prized.

---

81 Francis, "Evangelii Gaudium, Apostolic Exhortation of Pope Francis," published online: *The Holy See*, http://www.vatican.va/content/francesco/en/apost_exhortations/documents/papa-francesco_esortazione-ap_20131124_evangelii-gaudium.html (accessed on 20.01.22), para. 218.
82 Turkson, Peter, "On Human Rights," published online: *Zenit*, 2014, https://zenit.org/articles/cardinal-turkson-on-human-rights/ (accessed on 18.01.2022).

5 Human Rights and the World of Orthodox Christianity

Such a hierarchal understanding of the Church is also one – though not the only – reason why Orthodox Christianity taken as a whole has, over the past seventy years, been often seemed to be very uncomfortable about human rights. There are of course a range of attitudes in the Orthodox world, and the term Orthodox encompasses both the Chalcedonian (Eastern) Orthodox churches, and the non-Chalcedonian (Oriental) Orthodox churches. In fact, if it is considered the "heart" of the Orthodox world, the Ecumenical Patriarchate located in Istanbul, but whose direct or indirect influence extends much more widely, is an example, especially under the current Patriarch Bartholomew, of a relatively open attitude to human rights, linked in part to Bartholomew's interest in the environment, and the greening of the world. It was under the auspices of the Ecumenical Patriarchate, and specifically endorsed by Patriarch Bartholomew, that in March 2020 the major document, *For the Life of the World: Toward a Social Ethos of the Orthodox Church*, was published which addresses a range of social and ethical issues, but which includes a very substantial section on human rights. Tellingly the substantial section, which is titled, *Orthodoxy and Human Rights*, includes the sub-heading, *You have created us in your image and likeness*. At the time that this current chapter was being finalised the insights of *For the Life of the World* were still being publicised and assimilated in Orthodox and ecumenical circles, but it is likely that they will become increasingly influential in the coming decade. *For the Life of the World* includes the most recent systematic statement about human rights that has been produced by any Church communion or ecumenical body. Its affirmative language about human rights stands in something of a contrast not only to the views of the Moscow Patriarchate, by far and away the most powerful and numerically largest Orthodox Church, but also to some earlier reflections on human rights by individual Greek Orthodox theologians which tended to be much more ambiguous in their assessment.

Below we will look at the views of two of these theologians, and then consider in some detail the expressed views of the Moscow Patriarchate. Its attitude to human rights has during the last 20 years or so been well documented, so it provides a useful case study about human rights and the Christian Orthodox tradition, albeit probably from the more hostile end of the spectrum. The current deep tensions in the Orthodox world between the Ecumenical Patriarch and the Moscow Patriarchate may have their presenting cause as the relationship between the Orthodox Churches in Russia and Ukraine, but in reality they are deeply embedded in different perceptions of Christian anthropology, of which the Christian understanding of human rights is a key expression.

Given the likely future importance of the section on human rights in *For the Life of the World* in ecumenical, as well as Orthodox circles, we quote its key affirmation from § 61:

> Orthodox Christians, then, may and should happily adopt the language of human rights when seeking to promote justice and peace among peoples and nations, and when seeking to defend the weak against the powerful, the oppressed against their oppressors, and the indigent against those who seek to exploit them. The language of human rights may not say all that can and should be said about the profound dignity and glory of creatures fashioned after the image and likeness of God; but it is a language that honors that reality in a way that permits international and interfaith cooperation in the work of civil rights and civil justice, and that therefore says much that should be said.

The document then continues by making the explicit link between human rights and the language of humanity as created in the image and likeness of God, and the relationship between freedom, liberty and human rights, bearing in mind a communal as well as individual dimension, and addresses in particular the question of freedom of religion. Although much more detailed it is certainly building upon earlier affirmative Orthodox reflection on human rights such as that expressed by a Pan-Orthodox conference held at Chambesy, Switzerland in 1986 which stated: "Since we continuously declare the incarnation of God and the deification of humanity, we defend human rights for every human being and every people. Since we live with the divine gift of freedom through Christ's work of redemption, we are able to reveal to the fullest the universal value that freedom has for every human being and every people."

It is interesting that this statement from the Chambesy conference makes a link between human rights and "the deification of humanity", since "deification" or *theosis* is a key theme in Orthodox theology and is itself ultimately grounded in Genesis' language of "image and likeness". It is however intriguing (and perhaps telling) how infrequently this connection is made, not even in *For the Life of the World*.

However, writing about the same time, the Orthodox theologian Anastasios Yannoulatos, originally from Greece but later to become the Archbishop of Albania, was far more cautious about the theological presuppositions on which human rights were based. It is interesting that the article, entitled *Eastern Orthodoxy and Human Rights,* was initially published in a World Council of Churches journal – the *International Review of Mission* in 1984. By the 1980s of course the Orthodox Church of Greece and several other Orthodox churches, had become members of the World Council of Churches. Presumably, the accession of these churches to membership is one substantial reason that it had become more difficult for the World Council of Churches to formulate a common theological position on human rights. Following in the tradition originally established by Irenaeus which became influential among the Greek Fathers of the Church, which distinguished between "image" and "likeness", Yannoulatos suggested that:

> likeness is offered to humankind as a possibility, not as an accomplished fact [...] the purpose of [human] existence – according to Orthodox faith and conscience – is to activate, by the grace of God, their God-given potential and move towards the realization of the likeness of God: in other words, to rise above mere biological coexistence to a genuine communion of persons, in harmony with all creatures, and with the whole creation in selfless love, after the model of the Holy Trinity, which is the supreme *koinonia agapes*.[83]

Elsewhere in the same article Yannoulatos offered a fairly radical challenge to what the late twentieth century western world had come to consider human good:

> In the Orthodox tradition, the demand for freedom of the human person is directed at a higher level: the achievement of inner freedom, which is a necessary condition for gaining fulfilment and peace and for allowing the human personality to develop to its fullest extent. The search for this kind of freedom is a central feature in the thinking and experience of Eastern Christianity. This explains the emphasis on self-restraint, askesis, fasting, limitation of needs, etc. [...].distinguish between human worth and Therefore in the Christian tradition, the model of a person with a fulfilled personality is not the successful citizen with his/her well-secured individual rights and unblemished respectability; it is the saint, the martyr, the hermit, the person who is free from desire for money, possessions, fame or recognition, the person who lives in the joy and fullness of inner freedom.[84]

Drawing attention to the central concept of the "communion of love" which is derived from the life of the Holy Trinity, Yannoulatos suggests that "the idea of 'communion' underlines the fact that the rights of each man or woman are inseparably linked with those of others."[85] Love, he suggests, is the fulfilling of freedom.

Although Yannoulatos is not hostile to the importance of religious freedom, and speaks affirmingly of the World Council of Churches declaration in 1949 which states that "religious freedom is the condition and the guardian of any

---

83 Yannoulatos, Anastasios, "Eastern Orthodoxy and Human Rights," *International Review of Mission* 73 (1984), 454.
84 Ibid., 464.
85 Ibid., 463.

other freedom", even this freedom needs to be subsumed into his vision of the inner freedom to which the Christian is called. The writer of this chapter recalls listening to Yannoulatos in November 2015 at a conference held in Albania, the country of which he is now the Orthodox Archbishop. The conference was exploring the issue of "Discrimination, Persecution, Martyrdom" in the contemporary world – a topic of course with particular resonance in Albania given its history of severe religious persecution during the communist era. For many of us who came from the west, we found the real sense of joy and privilege linked to martyrdom that the Archbishop conveyed remarkable – both admirable yet also frightening.

A rather different Orthodox theological perspective on human rights is offered by another Greek theologian Christos Yannaras. Yannaras spins connections between the world of modern Orthodoxy, the heritage of Byzantium – and the concept of the *polis* (city state) derived from Greek antiquity. The *polis* is viewed as a collective entity that is not external to the individual citizens. Thus, whoever is a member of the *polis,* and "partakes in the political and legal space of the city and is a potential bearer of political offices, is automatically a holder of rights."[86] Yannaras then draws connections between this understanding of the *polis,* and Christian Orthodox culture, which he suggests encourages "a collective and political conception of human rights and not an individual and natural rights conception."[87] It is of course interesting to reflect on this assumption and the existence of national, indeed nationalistic Orthodox churches, in several countries of Eastern Europe. Perhaps however it is also interesting to reflect that in the ancient *polis* many resident groups – including all women – were not able to participate fully in its life and enjoy the concomitant rights. Does the analogy between the *polis* and the Church extend also in this area as well?

It is also not unfair to suggest that especially in contexts such as the Middle East where the Christian churches are a minority, the human right of "freedom of religion" tends to be linked in the minds of Orthodox religious leaders to the freedom of the church as a corporate body. Freedom of religion is primarily seen as the freedom of the churches to conduct worship and maintain church buildings and charitable concerns. The freedom of individual members to decide

---

86 Yannaras, Christos, "Human Rights and the Orthodox Church," in: Emmanuel Clapsis (ed.), *The Orthodox Churches in a Pluralistic World: An Ecumenical Conversation*, Brookline, MA: WCC Publications 1989, 83 – 89.
87 Ibid.

to turn their back on the life of the church is not, on the whole, treated as a desirable priority.[88]

To turn now to the situation of the Orthodox Church in Russia, specifically the Moscow Patriarchate. A consideration of its views on human rights has become increasingly important given the role that the leadership of this Church has played in the war in Ukraine. Clearly, during the Soviet era the Church was in a very difficult situation – especially in relation to human rights. To ensure the Church's survival during the decades of state repression, the leadership of the Church had both to deny that religious persecution existed, as well as to challenge the importance of religious freedom as a human right. This was sometimes described as a "bourgeois" right, by both state and church officials.[89] There was a paradoxical irony that the concern for Christians in Eastern Europe which partly prompted the focus on religious freedom in the initial promulgation of the UDHR, was viewed in hostile terms and as potentially dangerous precisely by those it was designed to support. One example, which comes from near the close of the Soviet era, in an article by Alexei Osipov, a professor at the theological faculty of Moscow university. Osipov argued that freedom of speech should remain a human right, "only as long as it does not overstep its positive bounds", by allowing the advocacy of lies, slander, violence and other evils. When this freedom exceeds these bounds, it "can no longer be called a human right and allowed to exist in society."[90]

Of course, the Church is in a very different situation since 1991, and immensely more powerful in Russian society, yet the thought patterns and concerns of the Soviet era still linger influentially in the life of the Church, especially in relation to various manifestations of freedom. In the last twenty years or so, as well as formal or informal comments by church leaders, there have been at least three official statements issued by official church or church related bodies which have addressed the question of human rights. These are *The Basis of the Social Concept of the Russian Orthodox Church*[91] (2000) issued by the Bishops' Council, the *Declaration of Human Rights and Dignity* made by the World Russian

---

88 This is expressed, for example, in the willingness of church leaders to uphold the religiously based marriage laws in most Middle Eastern countries, in which individuals need to be members of a religious community in order to exercise their right of e. g. getting married.

89 Such views were of course raised at the WCC St Pölten consultation referred to above.

90 Osipov Alexei, "Bogoslovskie aspekty prav cheloveka," *Zhurnal Moskovskoj Patriarkhii* 5 (1984), 58, quoted in Stoeckl, Kristina, *The Russian Orthodox Church and Human Rights*, London: Routledge, 2014, 25.

91 https://old.mospat.ru/en/documents/social-concepts/ (accessed on 18.01.2022).

People's Council[92] (2006), and the *Basic Teaching on Human Dignity, Freedom and Rights*[93] adopted by the Bishops' Council in 2008. Taken as a whole they bear witness to the unease that the Church feels as regards this area. For the present purposes it is especially interesting to focus on what is said in these documents about human dignity, its link to rights, and the relationship between the individual and the community.

As one commentator put it, the Russian Orthodox Church seeks "to remind the Russian society, the Russian state (and the international community, for that matter) that the Russian Orthodox Church has been a 'formative factor' for the Russian cultural ethos, and therefore Christian anthropology, Christian vision of dignity and freedom, Christian version of rights must define – at least in a certain degree – the public discourse of values and morality."[94]

In several speeches and articles around the turn of the millennium Patriarch Kirill noted with regret that due to the prevailing international and national political circumstances in 1948 it had not been possible for Orthodox and Eastern Christians to feed their spiritual perspectives into the development of the UDHR. Intriguingly however he also, around the same period, referred to Article 29 of the UDHR which hitherto had not been given as much attention as perhaps it deserved. Article 29 states:

> Everyone has duties to the community in which alone the free and full development of his personality is possible.

> In the exercise of his rights and freedoms, everyone shall be subject only to such limitations as are determined by law solely for the purpose of securing due recognition and respect for the rights and freedoms of others and of meeting the just requirements of morality, public order and the general welfare in a democratic society.

> These rights and freedoms may in no case be exercised contrary to the purposes and principles of the United Nations.

The communitarian thrust of Article 29 – weighing the rights of the community over against the rights of individuals – was, due to both history and theology, congenial to the leadership of the Russian Orthodox Church, and has been drawn upon on a number of occasions since in Orthodox documents which ref-

---

92 http://www.pravoslavieto.com/docs/human_rights/declaration_ru_en.htm (accessed on 19.01.2022).
93 https://old.mospat.ru/en/documents/dignity-freedom-rights/ (accessed on 19.01.2022).
94 Agadjanian, Alexander, "Breakthrough to Modernity, Apologia for Traditionalism: the Russian Orthodox View of Society and Culture in Comparative Perspective," *Religion, State and Society* 31, 4 (2003), 327–46.

erence human rights. Of course, Article 29 explicitly links an individual's duties specifically to a *democratic* society, which seems to be sometimes perhaps conveniently ignored.

It is interesting to compare the three documents listed above – which of course were issued within a comparatively short space of time – less than 10 years, between 2000 and 2008. There are points where they seem to contradict each other in relation to what they say about human rights – perhaps an unintended reflection on an internal struggle for power. The first of these documents, the *The Basis of the Social Concept* promulgated by the Bishops' Council of the Church affirms the doctrine of *imago dei* but suggests that modern human rights ideology has in fact moved away from this belief:

> **IV. 7. As secularism developed, the lofty principles of inalienable human rights turned into a notion of the rights of the individual outside his relations with God. In this process, the freedom of the personality transformed into the protection of self-will** (as long as it is not detrimental to individuals) and into the demand that the state should guarantee a certain material living standard for the individual and family. In the contemporary systematic understanding of civil human rights, man is treated not as the image of God, but as a self-sufficient and self-sufficing subject. Outside God, however, there is only the fallen man, who is rather far from being the ideal of perfection aspired to by Christians and revealed in Christ (*"Ecce homo!"*). For the Christian sense of justice, the idea of human freedom and rights is bound up with the idea of service. **The Christian needs rights so that in exercising them he may first of all fulfil in the best possible way his lofty calling to be "the likeness of God", as well as his duty before God and the Church, before other people, family, state, nation and other human communities.**[95]

The World Russian People's Council, which is in effect the civil society arm of the Moscow Patriarchate with a reputation for very conservative views and a defensiveness regarding Russian culture, was responsible for the 2006 Human Rights Declaration which is startling to a western reader for the way in which it seems to deny that dignity is innate to human beings, and then continues by prioritising "traditional morality" over human rights:

> **Each person as image of God has singular unalienable worth,** which must be respected by every one of us, the society and state. It is by doing good that the human being gains

---

[95] We have printed part of this quotation in bold to reflect the fact that on the website of the Moscow Patriarchate on which this statement appears that the text is there also printed in bold – presumably for emphasis and focus, https://old.mospat.ru/en/documents/social-concepts/ (accessed on 19.01.2022).

dignity. Thus we distinguish between human worth and dignity. Worth is given, while dignity is acquired [...].

Human rights are based on the worth of the person and should have as their goal **the realization of the person's human dignity.** Therefore, human rights essentially involve morality. Any separation of these rights from morality means their profanation, for **there is no such thing as immoral dignity [...].**

Rights and liberties are inseparable from human obligations and responsibilities. The individual in pursuit of personal interests is called to relate them to those of the neighbor, family, community, nation and all humanity.

There are values no smaller than human rights. These are faith, morality, the sacred, motherland. Whenever these values come into conflict with the implementation of human rights, the task of the society, state and law is to bring both to harmony. It is unacceptable, in pursuit of human rights, to oppress faith and moral tradition, insult religious and national feelings, cause harm to revered holy objects and sites, jeopardize the motherland. **Likewise we see as dangerous the "invention" of such "rights" as to legitimize a behavior condemned by both the traditional morality and historical religions.**[96]

It has been widely suggested that one of the reasons for the adoption of the 2008 Basic Teaching on Human Dignity, Freedom and Rights[97] by the Bishops' Council was to correct the views expressed about dignity in this document issued in 2006, although even within the 2008 document ambiguity seems to remain. There is however considerable importance given to the theme of human dignity. A key opening paragraph states:

> I.2. In Orthodoxy the dignity and ultimate worth of every human person are derived from the image of God, while dignified life is related to the notion of God's likeness achieved through God's grace by efforts to overcome sin and to seek moral purity and virtue. Therefore, the human being as bearing the image of God should not exult in this lofty dignity, for it is not his own achievement but a gift of God. Nor should he use it to justify his weaknesses or vices, but rather understand his responsibility for the direction and way of his life. Clearly, the idea of responsibility is integral to the very notion of dignity. Therefore, in the Eastern Christian tradition the notion of "dignity" has first of all a moral meaning, while the ideas of what is dignified and what is not are bound up with the moral or amoral actions of a person and with the inner state of his soul.[98]

---

96 Again the text that appears in bold here is reflective of its appearance on the website of the Moscow Patriarchate, http://www.pravoslavieto.com/docs/human_rights/declaration_ru_en. htm (accessed on 19.01.2022).
97 The document is available at https://old.mospat.ru/en/documents/dignity-freedom-rights/ (accessed on 19.01.2022).
98 Ibid., 1.2.

The document then explicitly continues: "There is a direct link between human dignity and morality. Moreover, the acknowledgement of personal dignity implies the assertion of personal responsibility." Within this initial framework the document then proceeds to speak quite widely and often positively (though generally with qualifications) about a wide variety of human rights, such as the right to life, freedom of conscience and expression, creative work, education, civil and political and socio-economic rights. The standpoint from which they are set out is clearly communitarianism, however, and it is made clear that the rights of individuals cannot be exercised to the detriment of the community. This is notable in the discussion of freedom of conscience, "Freedom of conscience cannot be used to establish total control over the life and beliefs of the individual, to destroy his private, family and social morality, to insult his religious feelings, to encroach on things he holds sacred, to damage his spiritual and cultural identity as all this distorts its very essence." The document concludes by exploring the specific role of the Church in fostering human rights within the parameters that it had set out.

Tellingly however, no sooner had this document appeared – clearly intended to be the authoritative word on the subject on the part of the Russian Orthodox Church – the Bishops' Council (which had just adopted the document) issued a Pastoral Letter, which seems to contradict it:

> The idea of human rights has become one of the key concepts in politics and jurisprudence of states. This idea is often used to justify sin and to reduce the role of religion in society and to deprive people of the possibility of living their faith. *(Pastoral Letter of Bishops' Council, 2008)*[99]

It would seem likely that there is still some way to go before the Russian Orthodox Church offers a final definitive position regarding human rights!

6 Concluding Reflections

The "thread" that has run through this chapter is the role or roles that the language of *imago dei* has played consistently in Christian theological discourse on human rights. Partly as a result of its potential linkage to the foundational principle of human dignity "the image of God" has been the most wide-spread theological motif drawn upon by the great majority of Christian churches and organisations that have reflected on this topic. Its common currency has worked

---

99 Quoted in Stoeckl, *The Russian Orthodox Church*, 88.

paradoxically in two ways. On the one hand, it does help to legitimate Christian claims that the modern development in human rights is not alien to the Christian tradition and has been influenced by Christian theological insights. On the other hand the use of the idiom "image of God" to describe human beings has become so widespread within western culture that the religious origin of the expression has been almost forgotten and we could even say that it has somehow been "secularized". Ironically the expression is therefore treated by many of those who use it as though it is self-evident to human reason, rather than a religious insight derived from sacred scripture. Along with this it is important to remember that the language of "image of God" to describe humanity is not necessarily congenial to all religions: within Islam for example, it is not the most natural way of expressing the divine human relationship, although some Muslims may be prepared to allow for the use of the idiom, particularly in the context of interreligious dialogue.

We have suggested that the use of this expression has been very helpful in facilitating, at least among some Christians and at certain points in time, the privileging of freedom of religion and belief in the overall hierarchy of human rights. We have also noted the challenges that have been made to this motif by certain Christian groups and bodies. In particular there is the questioning posed by some conservative Christian groups, both Protestant and Orthodox, as to whether, as a result of the "Fall", one can talk in a real way about both the image and the likeness of God still being visibly present in humanity. Conversely the use of "image" language has also been queried by some more radical Christians, because they have regarded it as encouraging a focus on individuals and their personal rights, rather than the requirement to be members of a community and the concomitant duties this imposes. In fact, as we have sought to demonstrate in the course of this chapter, exegesis of the text of Genesis 1:26–27 does encourage a reading of the concept of "image of God" as inherently relational, requiring an individual to take seriously their relationship to God, to other human beings and to the rest of creation, and duties, or at least responsibilities, are deeply embedded into this relationship. It is no accident, that such a focus on relationships, which owes much to the influence of Karl Barth, has become increasingly stressed during the last thirty years when the language of "image of God" is used in association with human rights.

It is however interesting to reflect that the language of "image of God" is in one sense not uniquely Christian. It comes in the part of Christian scripture which is shared with another faith, Judaism. Ironically perhaps, it does seem, in relation to the theological underpinning of human rights, that Christianity may give more weight to these verses from Genesis than does Judaism.

But then we need to ask the question as to what specifically "Christian" resources – by which is meant directly related to the person and work of Jesus Christ – the Christian churches have drawn on over the last 70 years to reflect theologically on human rights? After all, the very story of Jesus Christ "born in a stable, and killed on the Cross"[100] feels as though it ought to have something to say about such aspects of human rights as poverty and torture. Indeed, the human ministry of Jesus, which, according to the Gospels privileged the vulnerable, can be seen as offering human rights (at least to others) in action. And yet of course the pattern of Jesus' own life – in which his own suffering could be described, at least to some extent, as voluntary – is sometimes used by certain Christian groups to pose a challenge to "rights" language as somehow less than Christian.

Here, I think that the Catholic and Protestant traditions have tended to diverge. Perhaps it is linked to a certain Protestant pragmatism, a less idealized understanding of the church, or a lingering assumption, even among more liberal contemporary Protestants, of the fallenness of human nature and the prevalence of sin. For a theological motif that is quite central to Roman Catholic reflection on human rights seems to be curiously absent in most Lutheran and Reformed discussion. This may be a feature that I have particularly noticed as my own ecclesiastical roots are in the Anglican tradition in which, traditionally, a considerable amount of weight is given to the incarnation of Jesus Christ, *qua* incarnation i. e. not simply as a precursor to the cross and atonement. It could be described as the difference between who Christ was and what Christ did. On the other hand, in Roman Catholic theological reflection on human rights the theme of incarnation is present, though even here it is perhaps not exploited as much as it could be. However, for example, in the 1975 report *The Church and Human Rights* near the beginning of the theological reflection section we read, "Every person has a special relation with God, grounded in the mystery of the Incarnate Word. When the Son of God became man, he entered into the world's history as Perfect Man."[101] In the New Testament, especially in the Gospel of John, and in Colossians 1:15 – 20, there is a clear connection made between what is said about Jesus Christ, God-become-human, and the language to describe humanity as "image of God" in Genesis 1:26 – 28. Christ fully and completely reveals the "image of God" in humanity, but by who he is, rather than what he does. The incarnation of God in Jesus Christ grants human beings an intrinsic dignity be-

---

100 Altmann, Walter, *Luther and Liberation: A Latin American Perspective*, trans. Mary M. Solberg, Minneapolis: Fortress, 1992, 41.
101 Pontifical Commission, "Iustitia et Pax," http://www.clerus.org/clerus/dati/2011-07/23-13/The_Church_and_Human_Rights.pdf (accessed on 26.02.2022), 49.

yond compare.[102] The language of the "cross" is not completely absent, but the work of the cross is above all to ratify the role of the incarnate Christ as a bridge between humanity and the divine and to enable human beings to participate in a corporate new humanity, for which the term "the Body of Christ" can be used, which in turn leads us towards reflection on the role of the Church. It is a language of conjunction rather than a language of disjunction. My instinct is that it would be fruitful to explore further the implications for a theology of human rights of the specifically Christological use of the theme of "image of God". For when we speak of Christ as the "image" or icon of God we find ourselves linking together in an intrinsic way both the aspect of rights and duties. It is of course also significant that in both Christian scripture and theology, it is often suggested, based on incarnational theology, that the presence of Christ can be found in others – and especially in those who are suffering or vulnerable. The vivid picture of the Parable of the Sheep and the Goats in Matthew 25:31–46 where Christ identifies himself with "one of the least of these my brethren" surely has something of importance to say about a Christian theology of human rights.

When Christians speak of "incarnation" they are suggesting that the divine can be perceived through the medium of matter and flesh: that the "image of God" is here made visible with a unique sharpness, with results that extend to encompass ultimately all humanity. This is the basis of the sacramental theology of the Christian church. So, it is interesting to suggest that the sacraments, in particular Baptism and the Eucharist, may also perhaps make a contribution to a Christian theology of human rights.[103] The language of "freedom", so often associated with human rights, is strongly linked in the writings of St Paul to baptism into Christ. This freedom in turn promises a new humanity which is marked out by a new and radical egality, "In Christ there is no longer Jew or Greek, there is no longer slave or free there is no longer male and female: for you are all one in Christ Jesus" *(Galatians 3:28)*. At its heart such a sense of participation in Christ, and in Christ's Body also breaks down the division between the individual and the communal which is the dichotomy round which discussion about human rights have often revolved. There seems to be a natural link between the sacrament of Baptism and freedom rights – including of course the right of freedom of religion itself. Correspondingly the materiality of the Eu-

---

102 So for example, "Jesus Christ vested us with human dignity. So deep are the roots of human rights." Riemeck, Renate, "The Human Rights Debate and its Historical Background," in: Erich Weingärtner/Marilyn Weingärtner (eds.), *Human Rights is More than Human Rights: A Primer for Churches on Security and Cooperation in Europe*, Rome: IDOC International, 1977, 7.
103 This suggestion was made by Prof. Hans-Christian Lehner, one of the participants in the workshop on which this chapter is based.

charist can open up some interesting reflection on social and economic rights. The discussion in 1Corinthians about the Eucharist also often some suggestive hints: the importance of generosity, the disgrace for Christians of eating in front of others who go hungry (1Corinthians 11:21), the need to forgo standing on one's "rights" if this jeopardises the wellbeing of the community (1Corinthians 10:23–29), the powerful words that speaks of being one body. The idiom of the Eucharist also transcends time:" As often as you eat this bread and drink this cup you proclaim the Lord's death until he comes." (1Corinthians 11:26). We are encouraged to take the past seriously, and yet also look for a new future, that takes account of the fact that the Body of Christ transcends the generations – and that the future also has its rights.

George Newlands, seeking to tease out what he also feels to be the rather neglected study of the relationship between Christology and human rights writes:

> Christians believe, as characterised in the incarnation of Jesus Christ. They bring the way of Jesus Christ, as an icon of humanity as God intends it, to the table for consideration. They believe that all human beings are created to be fulfilled in the image of God, and to be fulfilled with dignity and well being. They do not wish to impose this vision on others. But they offer it in the belief that it has infinite value for the human future.[104]

Bibliography

Agadjanian, Alexander, "Breakthrough to Modernity, Apologia for Traditionalism: The Russian Orthodox View of Society and Culture in Comparative Perspective," *Religion, State and Society* 31, 4 (2003), 327–46.

Altmann, Walter, *Luther and Liberation: A Latin American Perspective*, trans. Mary M. Solberg, Minneapolis: Fortress, 1992.

Barth, Karl, *Church Dogmatics III/1*, London: T&T Clark Ltd, 1958.

Barth, Karl, *Church Dogmatics III/1, First paperback edition*, London: T&T Clark International, 2004.

Bell, George, *Christianity and World Order*, Harmondsworth: Penguin, 1940.

Bell, George, "The Church in Relation to International Affairs (address at Chatham House)," *International Affairs* 25, 4 (1949), 405–14.

Brunner, Emil, "Das Menschbild und die Menschenrechte," *Universitas* 2, 3 (1947)/2, 4 (April 1947), 385–91.

Churchill, Winston S., *Letter to the Archbishop of Canterbury*, 29 October 1942.

---

104 Newlands, George, *The Transformative Imagination*, Aldershot: Ashgate, 2004, 102.

Commission of the Churches on International Affairs (ed.), *Human Rights and Christian Responsibility, Report of the Consultation, St. Pölten, Austria, 21–26 October 1974*, Geneva: Oikoumene, 1975.

Francis, "Evangelii Gaudium, Apostolic Exhortation of Pope Francis," published online: *The Holy See*, http://www.vatican.va/content/francesco/en/apost_exhortations/documents/ papa-francesco_esortazione-ap_20131124_evangelii-gaudium.html (accessed on 20.01.22).

GDR Regional Committee of the Christian Peace Conference (ed.), "The Meaning of Human Rights and the Problems They Pose," *Ecumenical Review* 27, 2 (1975), 139–46.

Harrelson, Walter, *The Ten Commandments and Human Rights*, Philadelphia: Fortress Press, 1980.

Hamilton, Alexander, *The Farmer Refuted: or, a More Impartial and Comprehensive View of the Dispute between Great-Britain and the Colonies, February 25*, New York: James Rivington, 1775.

Henkin, Louis, "Religion, Religions and Human Rights," *The Journal of Religious Ethics* 26 (1998), 229–39.

Hollenbach, David, *Claims in Conflict: Retrieving and Renewing the Catholic Human Rights Tradition*, New York: Paulist Press, 1979.

Joas, Hans, *The Sacredness of the Person: A New Genealogy of Human Rights*, Washington DC: Georgetown University Press, 2013.

John XXIII, "Pacem in Terris," April 11, 1963, published online: *The Holy See*, http://w2.vat ican.va/content/john-xxiii/en/encyclicals/documents/hf_j-xxiii_enc_11041963_pacem. html (accessed on 07.03.2022).

Kalaitzidis, Pantelis, "Individual Versus Collective Rights. The Theological Foundation of Human Rights. An Eastern Orthodox Approach," in: Elisabeth-Alexandra Diamantopoulou/Louis-Léon Christians (eds.), *Orthodox Christianity and Human Rights in Europe*, 273–96, Brussels: Peter Lang, 2018.

Leo XIII, *Rerum Novarum: Encyclical of Pope Leo XIII on Capital and Labour*, n.p., 1891.

Little, David, "Foreword," in: John Nurser (ed.), *For all Peoples and all Nations. The Ecumenical Church and Human Rights*, ix–xii, Geneva: WCC Publications, 2005.

Lutheran World Federation (ed.), *Theological Perspectives on Human Rights*, Geneva, 1977.

Maritain, Jacques, *The Rights of Man and Natural Law*, New York: Scribner, 1943.

Moltmann, Jürgen, *On Human Dignity: Political Theology and Ethics*, trans. and intro. M. Douglas Meeks, Philadelphia: Fortress Press, 2007.

Moscow Bishops' Council, "The Basis of the Social Concept of the Russian Orthodox Church," published online: The Russian Orthodox Church (ed.), https://old.mospat.ru/en/docu ments/social-concepts/ (accessed on 19.01.2022).

Moscow Bishops' Council, "Basic Teaching on Human Dignity, Freedom and Rights," published online: The Russian Orthodox Church (ed.), https://old.mospat.ru/en/docu ments/dignity-freedom-rights/ (accessed on 19.01.2022).

Moyn, Samuel, *Christian Human Rights*, Philadelphia: University of Pennsylvania Press, 2015.

Nelson, Robert J., "Human Rights in Creation and Redemption," in: Arlene Swidler (ed.), *Human Rights in Religious Traditions*, 3–12, New York: The Pilgrim Press, 1982.

Newlands, George, *The Transformative Imagination*, Aldershot: Ashgate, 2004.

The New York Times Archives (ed.), *Pope Bids Church to Guard Man's Rights*, October 13, 1938, https://www.nytimes.com/1938/10/13/archives/pope-bids-church-guard-mans-rights-tells-prelates-here-to-lead-in.html (accessed on 28.06.2022).

Nolde, O. Frederick, "The United Nations Acts for Human Rights," release by the American Committee for the World Council of Churches in the Michigan Christian Advocate, 30 December 1948 (CCIA Archives, "UN International Bill of Human Rights", 1947–48, 428.3.24, World Council of Churches, Geneva, Switzerland).

Nurser, John, *For all People and all Nations: Christian Churches and Human Rights*, Geneva: WCC Publications, 2005.

Osipov, Alexei, "Bogoslovskie aspekty prav cheloveka," *Zhurnal Moskovskoj Patriarkhii* 5 (1984), 51–58.

Pattee, Richard, "Human Rights (June 3, 1945)," in: George N. Shuster et al. (eds.), *Problems of the Postwar World: a Catholic Hour Symposium*, 29–33, Washington, DC: National Council of Catholic Men, 1945.

Paul VI, "Dignitates Humanae," 1965, para. 2, published online: *The Holy See*, http://www.vatican.va/archive/hist_councils/ii_vatican_council/documents/vat-ii_decl_19651207_dignitatis-humanae_en.html (accessed on 26.02.2022).

Paul VI, "Gaudium et Spes," 1965, published online: *The Holy See*, https://www.vatican.va/archive/hist_councils/ii_vatican_council/documents/vat-ii_const_19651207_gaudium-et-spes_en.html (accessed 18.01.2022).

Paul VI, *Populorum Progressio. Encyclical of Pope Paul VI on the Development of Peoples, March 26,* London: Catholic Truth Society, 1967.

Pontifical Commission, "Iustitia et Pax," published online: *The Church and Human Rights. Working Paper No. 1,* Vatican City, [2]2011, http://www.clerus.org/clerus/dati/2011-07/23-13/The_Church_and_Human_Rights.pdf (accessed on 26.02.2022).

Riemeck, Renate, "The Human Rights Debate and its Historical Background," in: Erich Weingärtner/Marilyn Weingärtner (eds.), *Human Rights is More than Human Rights: A Primer for Churches on Security and Cooperation in Europe*, 7–9, Rome: IDOC International, 1977.

Roosevelt, Franklin D., *The Four Freedoms, Address to Congress January 6*, 1941 (Records of the United States Senate; SEN 77 A-H1; Record Group 46; National Archives).

Russian People's Council (ed.), *The Declaration of Human Rights and Dignity*, April 6, 2006, http://www.pravoslavieto.com/docs/human_rights/declaration_ru_en.htm (accessed on 19.01.2022).

Ruston, Roger, *Human Rights and the Image of God,* London: SCM, 2004.

Stackhouse, Max L., "Public Theology, Human Rights and Mission," in: Arthur S. Dyke (ed.), *Human Rights and the Global Mission of the Church*, Boston Theological Institute Annual 1, 11–21, Cambridge, MA: Boston Theological Institute, 1985.

Stassen, Glen, "Solid Ground IV: Incarnational Discipleship and Recovery of a Historically Realistic Jesus," *Baptistic Theologies* 4, 2 (2012), 40–54.

Stoeckl, Kristina, *The Russian Orthodox Church and Human Rights*, London: Routledge, 2014.

Todt, Heinz-Eduard, "Theological Reflections on the Foundations of Human Rights," *Lutheran World* 24, 1 (1977), 45–58.

Traer, Robert, *Faith in Human Rights: Support in Religious Traditions for a Global Struggle*, Washington, D.C.: Georgetown University Press, 1991.

Turkson, Peter, "On Human Rights," published online: *Zenit*, 2014, https://zenit.org/articles/cardinal-turkson-on-human-rights/ (accessed on 18.01.2022).

Van Bueren, Geraldine, "Religion and Human Rights are a Double Lock on Dignity," published online: *The Times*, 28 April 2018, https://www.thetimes.co.uk/past-six-days/2018-04-28/register/religion-and-human-rights-are-a-double-lock-on-dignity-vxdr0326r (accessed on 26.02.2022).

Villa-Vicencio, Charles, *A Theology of Reconstruction: Nation-building and Human Rights*, Cambridge: CUP, 1992.

Weiderud, Peter, "Otto Frederick Nolde: A Human Rights Pioneer," in: Peter N. Prove/Luke Smetters (eds.), *Faith and Human Rights: Voices from the Lutheran Communion*, 13–22, Geneva: The Lutheran World Federation, 2006.

Williams, Rowan, "Lecture by Archbishop of Canterbury on Human Rights and Religious Faith," published online: World Council of Churches (ed.), https://www.oikoumene.org/resources/documents/lecture-by-archbishop-of-canterbury-on-human-rights-and-religious-faith (accessed on 18.01.2022).

Witte, John Jr., *The Reformation of Rights*, Cambridge: CUP, 2005.

World Council of Churches/Vatican City: Pontifical Council for Interreligious Dialogue/Deerfield, IL: World Evangelical Alliance (eds.), *Christian witness in a multi-religious world: Recommendations for conduct*, Geneva, 2011, https://www.oikoumene.org/en/resources/documents/wcc-programmes/interreligious-dialogue-and-cooperation/christian-identity-in-pluralistic-societies/christian-witness-in-a-multi-religious-world (accessed on 26.02.2022).

World Council of Churches (ed.), *A Declaration on Religious Liberty*, WCC First Assembly, Amsterdam, 1948.

World Council of Churches (ed.), *Statement on Universal Declaration of Human Rights*, 2008, https://www.oikoumene.org/en/resources/documents/executive-committee/2008-09/statement-on-universal-declaration-of-human-rights (accessed on 26.02.2022).

WCC First Assembly (ed.), *Report of the Church and the Disorder of Society*, Amsterdam, 1948.

Yannaras, Christos, "Human Rights and the Orthodox Church," in: Emmanuel Clapsis (ed.), *The Orthodox Churches in a Pluralistic World: An Ecumenical Conversation*, Brookline, MA: WCC Publications 1989, 83–89.

Yannoulatos, Anastasios, "Eastern Orthodoxy and Human Rights," *International Review of Mission* 73 (1984), 454–66.

Zagorin, Paul, *How the Idea of Religious Toleration Came to the West*, Princeton: Princeton University Press, 2003.

Suggestions for Further Reading

Durber, Susan, "Putting God to Rights: a Theological Reflection on Human Rights," published online: *Christian Aid*, 2016, https://www.christianaid.org.uk/sites/default/files/2017-08/putting-god-to-rights-report-june-2016_0.pdf (accessed on 26.02.2022).

Newlands, George, *Christ and Human Rights*, London: Ashgate Publishing, 2006.

Den Norske Kirke (ed.), *Set the Oppressed Free! The Church of Norway and Human Rights*, 2014,

https://kirken.no/globalassets/kirken.no/global/2014/dokumenter/menneskerettigheter_innmat_eng_korr2c.pdf (accessed on 26.02.2022).

Prove, Peter N./Smetters, Luke (eds.), *Faith and Human Rights: Voices from the Lutheran Communion*, Minneapolis: Lutheran World Federation, 2006.

Prove, Peter et al., *Strengthening Christian Perspectives on Human Dignity and Human Rights*, Geneva: WCC Publications & Globethics.net, 2022.

Witte, John Jr./Alexander, Frank S. (eds.), *Christianity and Human Rights, An Introduction*, Cambridge: Cambridge University Press, 2010.

Patricia Prentice and Abdullah Saeed
The Concept of Human Rights in Islam

Human rights as we know them today are a modern notion. They were formalized, internationally, in the 20th century in the adoption of the United Nations Declaration of Human Rights by the General Assembly. Since then, they have become an integral part of the international discourse on states' obligations and responsibilities towards their citizens, as well as providing standards to ensure human beings are treated according to their inherent human dignity.

While human rights are a relatively recent concept, it is possible to find principles and norms that serve a similar purpose, as well as the notion of "rights" in older traditions. This chapter explores these roots in Islamic tradition and, in particular, how Muslims engage with human rights today. Beginning with a discussion of the Arabic term for rights and its theological and philosophical basis, it traces the development of human rights from the sacred texts of Islam to the creation of so-called "Islamic human rights instruments" in the 20th century.

Muslim nations and scholars have not been immune from the influence of the modern preoccupation with human rights and, as a result, a great body of literature has developed, particularly in the last twenty years. Within this, two approaches can be observed. There are those scholars who take a defensive approach to human rights, rejecting compatibilities between international human rights law and Islamic law. There are also those who take a harmonistic approach, finding commonalities between the two. Today, many of those who take a harmonistic approach are engaged in the project of finding ways to reconcile Islamic law and international human rights law. These scholars, predominantly academics, living in both Muslim-majority societies and in the West, are interested in identifying places where the Islamic and international legal traditions are seemingly incompatible, and working out how to reconcile these perceived differences. The chapter identifies the protagonists involved in this project, the tools and methods they are using to address differences between the two legal systems and where the tensions lie. Finally, the chapter explores very briefly some of the commonalities between the human rights discourse in Islam and parallel discourses in other monotheistic religious traditions, particularly Judaism and Christianity.

https://doi.org/10.1515/9783110561579-005

1 Basic Terminology and the Sources of the Concept of Human Rights in the Sacred Texts and Norms of Islam

Any discussion of the compatibility (or otherwise) of Islam and international human rights law must first begin with the question of whether Islam has an equivalent notion of "rights". Legally, a "right" often means an entitlement.[1] For instance, a person may be entitled to a certain freedom or to a particular status, or they may be entitled to protection from something. If a right exists, then an individual (the right holder) may be entitled to make a claim for restitution or compensation if it has been breached or unfulfilled in some way. This is because human rights "impose duties or responsibilities on their addressees or dutybearers."[2] Legal systems define rights, although there are many debates about whether rights exist outside of legal systems, whether morally or "naturally".

An issue that commonly arises in the debates about a rights discourse in Islam is whether the Islamic conception of rights is actually founded on the idea of rights or entitlements, or whether it is really based on the notion of duties. Some Muslim scholars would agree that rights in Islam are closely connected to the obligations an individual has to God and to society at large.[3] In other words, "rights and duties are not independent legal concepts,"[4] and the two are closely intertwined. This means any right an individual has, places a corresponding duty on others via the same ruling.[5] Likewise, the rights of God place respective duties on human beings.[6] However, other Muslim scholars point out many examples can be found in Islamic tradition where rights are certainly considered entitlements in a way that is similar to international human rights law. This is not a unique debate within Islamic tradition. The relationship between rights and duties has long been the subject of disagreement beyond the Muslim world, well before the development of international human rights instruments.

---

1 Law.Com (ed.), *Right*, https://dictionary.law.com/Default.aspx?selected=1857 (accessed on 19.03.2022).
2 Nickel, James, "Human Rights," published online: *Stanford Encyclopedia of Philosophy*, 2019, https://plato.stanford.edu/entries/rights-human/#GeneIdeaHumaRigh (accessed on 19.03.2022).
3 Ali, Shaheen Sardar, "The Conceptual Foundations of Human Rights: A Comparative Perspective," *European Public Law*, 3, 2 (1997), 270.
4 Baderin, Mashood A., "Establishing Areas of Common Ground between Islamic Law and International Human Rights," *International Journal of Human Rights* 5, 2 (2001), 85.
5 Ibid.
6 Ibid., 87.

1.1 An Islamic Conception of Rights?

The Arabic term often cited for a right is *ḥaqq*. *Ḥaqq* (or the plural, *ḥuqūq*[7]) is regarded as the closest equivalent to the English word "right".[8] *Ḥaqq* can have different meanings according to the context in which it is used, such as "what is due" (to God or human beings),[9] a "right, claim, duty or truth"[10] or "certainty, justice or right".

While there are some scholars who argue it is too simplistic to equate the term *ḥaqq* with the notion of a right,[11] as the two terms come from different philosophical and conceptual frameworks,[12] there are other scholars who do so.[13] Support for this comes from the way the term is used in the Qur'ān. For example, Qur'ān 51:19 is often translated as the beggar or the outcast having a "right to",[14] the "right of"[15] or a "due share"[16] of the wealth mentioned. This implies the notion of a having a claim to it. Likewise, the Prophet Muhammad is thought to have used the term in a similar way when he said: "God has given everyone having a right his right (in the inheritance) so there shall be no bequest for (a Qur'ānic) heir."[17] There are also examples in Islamic legal tradition of the use of the word *ḥaqq* to refer to a legal norm,[18] an "interest" prescribed by the *sharī'a*[19] or an "entitlement".[20]

---

7 Ali, "The Conceptual Foundations of Human Rights," 263.
8 Anwar, Syed Mohammed, "Normative Structure of Human Rights in Islam," *Policy Perspectives* 10, 1 (2013), 81.
9 Anwar, "Normative Structure of Human Rights in Islam," 82.
10 Moosa, Ebrahim, "The Dilemma of Islamic Rights Schemes," *Journal of Law and Religion*, 15, 1, 2 (2000 – 01) 191.
11 Such as Anwar, cf. "Normative Structure of Human Rights in Islam," footnote 9.
12 Anwar, "Normative Structure of Human Rights in Islam," 81.
13 Such as, Ali, "The Conceptual Foundations of Human Rights," 263.
14 The Qur'ān: Sahih International translation.
15 The Qur'ān: Yusuf Ali's translation.
16 The Qur'ān: Pickthall's and Asad's translation
17 Baderin, "Establishing Areas of Common Ground," 84.
18 Anwar, "Normative Structure of Human Rights in Islam," 85, citing Ankawi, Shaykh al-Hakīm, *Hashia Qamar al-Aqmar 'ala Sharah al-Minar*.
19 Anwar, "Normative Structure of Human Rights in Islam," 86, citing al-Khafīf, ash-Shaykh 'Alī, *al-Haqq wa l-Zimmah*, Cairo: Maktabat Wahbah, 1945, 32.
20 Ibid., 87, citing Ibn-Nujaym, Zayn al-'Abidīn, *al-Bahr al-Ra'iq Sharḥ Kanz ad-Daqa'iq*, Cairo: Dār ash-Shurūq, 1989.

1.2 The Rights of God and the Rights of People

One distinction between the notion of a right in international human rights law and in Islamic law is that Islamic law recognizes two distinct categories of rights: the rights of God (*ḥuqūq Allah*) and the rights of people (*ḥuqūq al-ʿibād*).[21] The rights of God were recognized as those related to public well-being, such as public order or security.[22] For Muslim jurists, these rights ensured society's protection, and it was the political authority or ruler's responsibility to ensure they were maintained.[23] On the other hand, the rights of people concerned individuals' or "private rights,"[24] like the right to own property. These rights concerned private matters and aimed to protect an individual from undue state interference in their affairs.[25] *Ḥaqq al-ʿabd* (singular of *ḥuqūq al-ʿibād*) also referred to "the right of the individual Muslim." In these cases, the individual (or individuals) whose rights had been violated was free to determine whether and which legal actions should be taken against the transgressor. [26]

Through this dual system of rights the jurists aimed to "ensure that the sharīʿa as a rule of law system upholds and, when necessary, balances both society's needs (i.e., the social good) and private interests."[27] Despite this delineation of different kinds of rights, there are a number of Muslim scholars who see *ḥuqūq al-ʿibād* as an important foundation for an Islamic human rights discourse.[28] Indeed, the term has recently been incorporated into a number of Muslim-majority languages.[29]

---

21 "Human Rights," published online: John L. Esposito (ed.), *The Oxford Dictionary of Islam, Oxford Islamic Studies Online*, https://www.oxfordreference.com/view/10.1093/acref/9780195125580.001.0001/acref-9780195125580-e-893?rskey=K8e2Oq&result=893 (accessed on 05.07.2022).
22 Emon, A. M., "Huquq Allah and Huquq Al-Ibad: A Legal Heuristic for a Natural Rights Regime," *Islamic Law and Society* 13 (2006), 326.
23 Ibid., 329.
24 Ibid., 326.
25 Ibid., 331 citing Weiss, Bernard G., *Spirit of Islamic Law*, Athens, Georgia: University of George Press, 1998, 181–84.
26 Hashemi, Nader/Qureshi, Emran, "Human Rights," published online: *The Oxford Encyclopedia of the Islamic World. Oxford Islamic Studies Online*, https://www.oxfordreference.com/view/10.1093/acref/9780195305135.001.0001/acref-9780195305135-e-0325?rskey=XuSpAh&result=460 (acessed on 05.07.2022).
27 Emon, "Huquq Allah and Huquq al-Ibad," 327.
28 Hashemi/Qureshi, "Human Rights," https://www.oxfordreference.com/view/10.1093/acref/9780195305135.001.0001/acref-9780195305135-e-0325?rskey=XuSpAh&result=460 (accessed on 05.07.2022).
29 Ibid.

1.3 Islamic Legal Sources and Human Rights

In Islamic tradition[30] rights have a religious and moral framework. This may mean that "the omission of a duty or right can be subject to sanction and the upholding of a right/duty is considered virtuous."[31] Rights come from the *sharī 'a* (the Islamic legal tradition), which is based on the teachings of the Qur'ān and the Prophet's *sunna* (the traditions of the Prophet), as well as juristic concepts such as consensus and analogy.

1.3.1 The Qur'ān

The Qur'ān is the most important sacred text of Islam. It was revealed to the Prophet Muhammad over a 22–year period (610 – 632 CE). For Muslims, the Qur'ān is God's Word; it provides guidance for all areas of life. Yet the Qur'ān is not primarily a legal text. While the Prophet was alive he taught and guided the Muslim community, and the revelations that he received responded to different circumstances and events the community encountered. After his death, however, new tools and methods for interpreting the revelation had to be developed for applying its instructions, ethical teachings and guidance.

The Qur'ān was revealed in a particular socio-historical context – 7th century Mecca and Medina – two towns in the Hijaz region of Arabia, and its guidance and teachings were closely connected to that context. Historical events are mentioned in the Qur'ān, as are societal values and practices, and symbols and metaphors that its first audience could understand and relate to. As the community's situation changed, so did the Qur'ān's instructions.[32] As the society into which the Qur'ān was revealed had a different understanding of individual and collective rights to modern understandings, we will not find in the Qur'ān an articulation of human rights that is akin to international human rights law today, which only formally developed in the twentieth century. Nevertheless, much of the guidance provided in the Qur'ān can be applied to our context today, with only a very few exceptions.

---

30 This section relies heavily on the author's earlier work, Saeed, Abdullah, *Human Rights in Islam*, Cheltenham, UK: Edward Elgar Publishing, 2018, 9 – 23.
31 Moosa, "The Dilemma," 193.
32 Saeed, *Human Rights and Islam*, 9.

The Qur'ān contains concepts that provide a basis for an Islamic framework for human rights that is compatible with modern understandings. These include notions of human dignity, justice and freedom.

Like the modern human rights discourse, the Qur'ān emphasizes that people share common human dignity. According to Qur'ānic teachings, human dignity is God-granted and inherent in all human beings: it cannot be taken away by the state or by other individuals.[33] The Qur'ān says human beings were created "in the best of moulds" (Q. 95:4) and were honored and given special status in creation (Q. 17:70). God created human beings to be his vicegerent (*khalīfa*) on earth, elevating them above the angels (Q. 2:30). Since all of humanity is, according to Muslim belief, descended from Adam, every human being possesses this God-given dignity.[34]

Another concept in the Qur'ān is justice (*adl*), a major theme in the Qur'ān. Human beings are encouraged to establish justice on earth and to conduct themselves with a sense of fairness. Muslims are encouraged to be just and fair because "[justice] is next to piety" (Q. 5:9). They are also warned not to "distort" justice or to "decline to do justice" (Q. 4:135). God forbids injustice (Q. 16:90) to the extent that people will be held accountable for even a mustard seed's worth of injustice on the Day of Judgement (Q. 21:47).

The Qur'ān also acknowledges the importance of human freedom; that is, the ability and agency people have been given to make decisions. A key part of this Qur'ānic discourse is that human beings have been given freedom, even to the extent to believe or not to believe in God. Indeed, those who wish to reject God may do so. The Qur'ān says, "'The truth is from your Lord': Let him who will believe, and let him who will, reject (it)" (18:29). It also says, "Let those who wish to reject it do so [...]" (18:29). Central to texts like these is the exhortation "there is no coercion in matters of faith" (2:256). The Qur'ān also mentions other freedoms. Another freedom granted to human beings is the freedom to speak one's mind or to voice opinions. Even Satan (*Iblīs*) had the freedom to speak openly before God.

However, similar to human rights law, freedom in the Qur'ān is not unbounded. God puts limits on human freedom. The Qur'ān refers to boundaries as *ḥudūd*, a term that occurs 12 times in the Qur'ān. Often the phrase "these

---

33 Baderin, "Establishing Areas of Common Ground," 91.
34 Saeed, *Human Rights and Islam*, 10 citing al-Ahsan, Abdullah "Law, Religion and Human Dignity in the Muslim World Today: An Examination of OIC's Cairo Declaration of Human Rights," *Journal of Law and Religion* 24, 2 (2008–09), 569. Throughout this paper, the English translation of the Qur'ān by Abd al-Halim is used: Abd al-Halim, Muhammad, *The Qur'an : English Translation and Parallel Arabic Text*, Oxford: University Press, 2010.

are God's boundaries, do not transgress them" (2:187) is mentioned. Those who do not adhere to God's limits or boundaries will be chastised and punished.

In Muslim scholarship on human rights today there are often references to verses of the Qur'ān that highlight similarities or compatibilities between Islamic law and tradition and international human rights law. Since God is the primary authority in Islam and the Qur'ān is considered God's Word for Muslims, citing the Qur'ān in support of the human rights discourse or in support of a particular human right can be very persuasive for Muslims.[35]

1.3.2 Sunna or Ḥadīth (Traditions of the Prophet)

The second Islamic source of rights is the traditions of the Prophet Muhammad, also known as the *sunna*. Our knowledge of the *sunna* comes primarily from *ḥadīth*, which are narrations about what the Prophet did or said. One example of a narration that is often cited in the context of discourses on Islam and human rights is the Prophet's Farewell Sermon, which he reportedly gave in 632 CE.

> O People, just as you regard this month, this day, this city as sacred, so regard the life and property of every Muslim as a sacred trust.
> Return the goods entrusted to you to their rightful owners. Hurt no one so that no one may hurt you.
> O People, it is true that you have certain rights with regard to your women, but they also have rights over you.
> Treat your women well and be kind to them, for they are your partners and committed helpers.
> All humankind is from Adam and Eve; an Arab has no superiority over a non-Arab and a non-Arab has no superiority over an Arab; a white has no superiority over a black and a black has no superiority over a white, except by piety and good action.[36]

Given the relevance of the ideas expressed in this *ḥadīth*, the text is often cited by Muslims as evidence for Islamic concern for a number of important rights, such as equality between people of different racial, ethnic, and linguistic backgrounds.

Other *ḥadīth*-statements are also cited in support of various fundamental rights. For instance, the sanctity of human life is affirmed in this *ḥadīth:* "No

---

35 Saeed, *Human Rights and Islam*, 10.
36 Saeed, *Human Rights and Islam*, 11 citing The Prophet Muhammad, "Prophet Muhammad's Last Sermon," (Islam the Modern Religion). https://www.iium.edu.my/deed/articles/the lastsermon.html (accessed on 05.07.2022).

doubt, your blood and your properties are sacred to one another like the sanctity of this day of yours."[37]

The rights of women and orphaned children are also acknowledged by this *ḥadīth*: "I forbid you to violate the rights of two who are weak: orphans and women."[38]

1.3.3 Ijmāʿ (Consensus)

In addition to the Qurʾān and the *sunna*, *ijmāʿ* (consensus) is also considered an authoritative source of law. Q. 4:59[39] is understood to provide a basis for the authoritativeness of *ijmaʿ*; a *ḥadīth* attributed to the Prophet also affirms "my community will never agree on an error."[40] This is understood to mean that when the Muslim community or its scholars (*ʿulamāʾ*) universally agree on a point of law (in this case, a particular right), it should be considered authoritative.

1.3.4 Qiyās (Analogical Reasoning)

The final source of law relevant to our exploration of human rights is *qiyās* or analogical reasoning. As the Qurʾān only has relatively few verses that are legal in nature, *qiyās* was regularly used to develop Islamic law to help the Muslim community respond to new circumstances. It can also be used today to support particular rights.

While some of the laws developed in the past using analogical reasoning may not be relevant to our modern context today, such as those related to slavery and women, the tool itself remains useful for applying texts of the Qurʾān and *sunna* to new circumstances and contexts. Some Muslim scholars use this

---

37 al-Bukhārī (4406) and Muslim (1679), cf. az-Zuman, Sheikh Ahmad, "Human Rights in Islam," published online: *Alukah*, https://www.alukah.net/web/zoman/0/40563/# (accessed on 28.06.2022).

38 Reported by al-Ḥākim (1/63) and said to be an authentic *Ḥadīth* on the condition of Muslim.

39 "You who believe, obey God and the Messenger, and those in authority among you. If you are in dispute about any matter, refer it to God and the Messenger, if you truly believe in God and the Last Day: that is better and fairer in the end."

40 Saeed, *Human Rights and Islam*, 13 citing Ibn Mājah, *Sunan Ibn Mājah*, Kitāb al-Fitan, No. 3950; Tirmidhī, *Jāmiʾ at-Tirmidhī*, Kitāb al-Fitan, No. 2167.

form of reasoning today to argue for the compatibility between Islamic law and particular human rights.[41]

These sources of law and authority have shaped the lives of Muslims around the world for many centuries and still continue to do so. They formed the basis of Islamic law as it developed from the time of the Prophet, and shaped the jurisprudence (*fiqh*) of the major schools of law (*madhāhib*) that emerged around the 9th and 10th centuries CE. Today, many of the positions Muslims hold towards human rights, whether in support of their compatibility or incompatibility, refer to these sources of authority.

2 The Basis of Human Rights in Islam

For many Muslims, the coming of Islam represented a new emphasis on the inherent dignity of human beings.[42] Muslims consider the pre-Islamic period of Arabia to have been a time and place of moral degradation, characterized by inter-tribal in-fighting and hostility.[43] The Prophet Muhammad and the Qur'ān introduced many reforms in this context, enhancing, in some cases, the status of those who had previously few rights in society, such as orphans, women and slaves. It also introduced new social norms and rules for their protection.[44]

After his migration to Medina in 622 CE, the Prophet concluded an agreement now known as the *Constitution* or the *Charter of Medina* to govern the rights and freedoms of the various groups living in that community. Some Muslim thinkers believe this document supports "the freedom and rights of human beings irrespective of caste, color, creed, sex, religion etc."[45] While such views can be seen as reading too much into the document, there are ideas in the text that seem to support a conception of equality that many of us today can relate to, particularly equal treatment for non-Muslims (in this case, the Jews of Medina). In terms of specific rights, the charter grants social, legal and economic equality to all citizens of Medina, regardless of their religious beliefs (Article 16). It also affirms that the Jewish tribes will be "treated as one community with the Believers" (Article 30), that they will be able to keep their religion (Article 30), and they will not be discriminated against or "wronged" because of their reli-

---

41 Saeed, *Human Rights and Islam*, 14.
42 Sofi, Sartaj Ahmad, "Comparative Study of Human Rights in Islam and Universal Declaration of Human Rights," *Journal of Islamic Thought and Civilisation* 6, 1 (2016), 40.
43 Ibid.
44 See, for instance: Qur'ān 30:21; 16: 57–61; 58:1; 4:1–12; 24:32–33.
45 Ibid.

gious status (Article 17). The charter also gives equal protection to the Jewish tribes, stating, "If anyone attacks anyone who is a party to this Pact the other must come to his help" (Article 38).[46]

2.1 Classical Period

Islamic law as it emerged in the classical period did not necessarily protect human rights in the same way that human rights instruments do today. Indeed, the modern concept of human rights was only formulated and articulated in the 18th century.[47] However, we can find in Islamic law evidence of examples or references to doctrines or ideas that are compatible with modern understandings of human rights. An analysis of classical *fiqh* (Islamic jurisprudence) reveals there were values and individual rights that jurists recognized that could serve as an Islamic basis for a modern human rights discourse.[48]

The Hanafi jurist Ibn Nujaym (d. 1563)[49] is believed to have been the first Muslim scholar to provide a legal definition of rights. He described a right as *mā yastaḥiqquhu al-insān*, meaning "that to which a person is entitled."[50]

In general, the classical jurists only addressed a few of what we would consider today human rights. These included private rights such as "ownership, contractual rights, rights of parents, guardians, rights of the husband, rights of the wife, rights of children, [and the] rights of the neighbor."[51] At this time, rights were limited to those within *dār al-islām* (the abode of Islam) as, according to most legal schools, the *sharīʿa* was not applicable outside of its boundaries. As such, Muslims and non-Muslims living in *dār al-ḥarb* (the abode of war) were outside the scope of these rights on the basis that they did not share the same legal capacity as those within *dār al-islām*. Non-Muslims were granted

---

46 Lecker, Michael, *The "Constitution of Medina": Muḥammad's first legal document*, Princeton, NJ: Darwin Press, 2004; Tahir-ul-Qadri, Muhammad, *The Constitution of Medina*, published online: London: Minhaj-ul-Quran Publications, 2012, https://www.academia.edu/18365196/The_constitution_of_Medina_63_constitutional_articles_ (accessed on 19.03.2022).
47 Peters, Ruud, "Islamic law and Human Rights: A Contribution to an Ongoing Debate," *Islam and Christian-Muslim Relations,* 10, 1 (1999), 6.
48 Ibid., 8.
49 https://referenceworks.brillonline.com/entries/christian-muslim-relations-ii/ibn-nujaym-al-misri-COM_26188 (accessed on 19.03.2022).
50 Baderin, "Establishing Areas of Common Ground," 83, citing Ibn Nujaym, *al-Baḥr ar-Raʾiq,* cited in M. Tumum, *al-Ḥaqq fī sh-Sharīʿa al-Islāmīya,* Arabic), Cairo: al-Maktaba al-Maḥmūdīyah 1398AH/1978AD, 33.
51 Ibid. 85.

legal capacity inside Islamic territory or abode due to their status as protected persons. While non-Muslims were not considered equal to Muslims in classical Islamic law, there are many areas in which a non-Muslim, according to some observers, appears to have been "almost equal to that of a free Muslim."[52]

Within the abode of Islam all residents had legal protection. Their lives were protected by the law. For instance, if a person was unlawfully killed, legal action could be taken against the perpetrator. Likewise, residents' property was safeguarded by law. However, because of the different categories of legal capacity, individuals experienced different levels of freedom in practice. According to Peters, this varied according to three dichotomies: "Muslims vis-à-vis non-Muslims; men vis-à-vis women; free persons vis-à-vis slaves."[53] The person with the greatest legal capacity (and therefore rights) was a Muslim male.[54] Thus, the *sharīʿa* did not necessarily recognize the principle of equality before the law at this time.[55] So, while classical Islamic law recognized some fundamental rights, these must be viewed in light of the social and historical period in which the jurisprudence developed.[56]

2.2 Modern Period

As more and more Muslim states came under the occupying rule of colonial powers in the modern period, European ideas began to influence the legal systems and governance of Muslim states. However, this process was highly political and not all Muslim scholars or movements welcomed the influence of European ideas or models, nor what they perceived to be the encroachment of Western ideas and principles on Muslim societies. Some leading figures from this period who attempted to reconcile Islamic and Western ideas and values included the Egyptian scholar Rifāʿa Rāfiʿ aṭ-Ṭahṭāwī (d. 1871), who wrote a report on "concepts of political rights, the rule of law, liberty, equality, and the ideas of the Enlightenment"; Mirza Malkom Khan (d. 1908), the Persian diplomat, who described "European concepts of government, the rule of law, and liberty" and how they were compatible with Islam; and Namık Kemal (d. 1888), the Ottoman reformer and intellectual, who elaborated on how certain rights and freedoms

---

52 Peters, "Islamic Law and Human Rights," 8–9.
53 Ibid. 9.
54 Ibid.
55 Ibid.
56 Ibid., 13.

were compatible with Islam.[57] All of these actors contributed to the translation and spread of European ideas about issues like constitutionalism and expanded the discourse on how such modern legal principles were compatible with Islamic law.

With the drafting and adoption of key international human rights instruments occurring in parallel by the 20th century, further debates arose as to whether Islamic principles were consistent with international human rights law. Of particular concern for some members of the international community was the legal distinction between Muslims and non-Muslims and how it could be reconciled with the principle of equality before the law.[58] Many states moved to pressure Muslim regimes to remove the classical distinction between Muslim citizens and *dhimmīs* (non-Muslim protected persons).[59] Human rights non-governmental organizations, such as Amnesty International, also began to publicly condemn acts within Muslim states that were seen to contradict the aspirational goals of the *Universal Declaration of Human Rights* (UDHR),[60] such as application of the death penalty. By the end of the 20th century, most or all Muslim-majority states had incorporated at least some of the human rights principles found in international human rights law into their constitutions.[61]

2.3 Modern Islamic Human Rights Documents

Even though the UDHR is not a legally binding instrument, its adoption by the United Nations in 1948 provided Muslim majority states with a model and a vocabulary for developing their own formations of human rights.[62] These documents were, in some ways, a reaction against what they perceived as Western pressure to adopt a certain understanding of human rights, as well as a way to constructively assert Islamic values.[63]

---

57 Hashemi/Qureshi., "Human Rights," https://www.oxfordreference.com/view/10.1093/acref/9780195305135.001.0001/acref-9780195305135-e-0325?rskey=XuSpAh&result=460 (accessed on 05.07.2020).
58 Ibid.
59 Ibid.
60 Dunn, Shannon, "Islamic Law and Human Rights," in: Rumee Ahmed/Anver M. Emon (eds.), *The Oxford Handbook of Islamic Law*, Oxford: Oxford University Press, 2018. For example, the condemnation of the arbitrary arrest of political opponents, use of torture and the use of execution in Iran in 1976.
61 Hashemi/Qureshi, "Human Rights".
62 Dunn, "Islamic Law and Human Rights".
63 Ibid.

2.3.1 Universal Islamic Declaration of Human Rights

The first of these instruments – the *Universal Islamic Declaration of Human Rights (UIDHR)* – was adopted by the London-based Islamic Council of Europe in 1981 at the International Islamic Conference in Paris, hosted at the headquarters of UNESCO.[64] The document, which is non-binding, affirms that human rights have been part of Islamic tradition since its very inception. They were granted by God and therefore cannot be challenged, limited or violated by any government or authority.[65] On the contrary, Muslim governments and social organs have an obligation to uphold and implement them.[66] The purpose of human rights is to confer "honor and dignity on mankind [...] eliminating exploitation, oppression and injustice."[67] Twenty-three articles set out the substantive rights of the declaration, including the right to life, the right to freedom, the right to equality and the prohibition of impermissible discrimination, the right to a fair trial, the right to protection against torture and the rights of married women. Article 12, the right to freedom of belief, thought and speech, is set out below:

> XII. Right to Freedom of Belief, Thought and Speech
>
> a) Every person has the right to express his thoughts and beliefs so long as he remains within the limits prescribed by the Law [= *sharī'a*]. No one, however, is entitled to disseminate falsehood or to circulate reports which may outrage public decency, or to indulge in slander, innuendo or to cast defamatory aspersions on other persons.
>
> b) Pursuit of knowledge and search after truth is not only a right but a duty of every Muslim.
>
> c) It is the right and duty of every Muslim to protest and strive (within the limits set out by the Law)[= *sharī'a*] against oppression even if it involves challenging the highest authority in the state.
>
> d) There shall be no bar on the dissemination of information provided it does not endanger the security of the society or the state and is confined within the limits imposed by the Law. [= *sharī'a*]

---

64 Saeed, *Human Rights and Islam*, 52 citing Koraytem, Tabet, "Arab Islamic Developments on Human Rights," *Arab Law Quarterly* 16, 3 (2001), 260.
65 University of Minnesota Human Rights Library (ed.), *Universal Islamic Declaration of Human Rights, Adopted by the Islamic Council of Europe on 19 September 1981/21 Dhul Qaidah 1401*, http://hrlibrary.umn.edu/instree/islamic_declaration_HR.html (accessed on 19.03.2022), preamble.
66 Ibid.
67 Ibid.

e) No one shall hold in contempt or ridicule the religious beliefs of others or incite public hostility against them; respect for the religious feelings of others is obligatory on all Muslims.

While the UIDHR's articles share some similarities with the UDHR, commentators have pointed out there are substantial differences between the two instruments. Ebrahim Moosa (2000), for example, argues that the UIDHR's clear reference to the priority of duties and obligations to God over rights puts it fundamentally at odds with "secular" human rights instruments because "rights mean certain fundamental and unconditional entitlements simply on the grounds of being human."[68] He also criticizes the repeated reference to the *sharīʿa* as a "statutory limitation" to qualify the rights set out in the instrument.[69] Ann Elizabeth Mayer (2013) identifies 11 rights in the UIDHR that are subject to the provisions of the *sharīʿa*.[70] She uses the example of Article 11 to illustrate how the *sharīʿa* serves to limit the rights elaborated in the declaration: "Article 11 provides for a right to participate in public life, but the provision is qualified in a way that ensures that it will have discriminatory impact on non-Muslims."[71]

2.3.2 Cairo Declaration on Human Rights in Islam

The second Islamic human rights instrument, for our purposes, was the *Cairo Declaration on Human Rights in Islam*, adopted by the 57 states of the Organization of the Islamic Conference (OIC) in 1990. Like the UIDHR, the document is not legally binding. The Cairo Declaration states that human rights are "binding divine commands" that come from the Prophet and the sacred texts of Islam.[72] These fundamental rights must be protected because to not do so would be a sin. Therefore, safeguarding human rights is both an individual and a collective community responsibility.[73]

---

68 Moosa, "The Dilemma," 196.
69 Ibid., 197.
70 Mayer, Ann Elizabeth, *Islam and Human Rights: Tradition and Politics,* New York: Westview Press, 2013, 78.
71 Ibid.
72 University of Minnesota Human Rights Library (ed.), *Cairo Declaration on Human Rights in Islam,* Aug. 5, 1990, U.N. GAOR, World Conf. on Hum. Rts., 4th Sess., Agenda Item 5, U.N. Doc. A/CONF.157/PC/62/Add.18, 1993, [English translation], http://hrlibrary.umn.edu/instree/cairodeclaration.html (accessed on 19.03.2022).
73 Ibid.

The Declaration sets out 22 substantive rights, including the right to freedom of opinion, the right to equality before the law, the right to security, the right to own property, the right to freedom of movement, the rights of women and children and the right to life. The right to freedom of expression and opinion, for example, is set out below:

ARTICLE 22:

(a) Everyone shall have the right to express his opinion freely in such manner as would not be contrary to the principles of the Shari'ah.

(b) Everyone shall have the right to advocate what is right, and propagate what is good, and warn against what is wrong and evil according to the norms of Islamic Shari'ah.

(c) Information is a vital necessity to society. It may not be exploited or misused in such a way as may violate sanctities and the dignity of Prophets, undermine moral and ethical Values or disintegrate, corrupt or harm society or weaken its faith.

(d) It is not permitted to excite nationalistic or doctrinal hatred or to do anything that may be an incitement to any form or racial discrimination.

Analysts point out there are quite a few differences between the UDHR and the Cairo Declaration in the provisions addressing "gender, the family, religious freedom, and importantly, self-determination."[74] Moreover, "[a]bsent from these categories is religion, which is included in UDHR Article 16." [75] Articles 24 and 25 also make it clear that all rights in the document are subject to "the Islamic Sharī'a"[76] and can only be explained or clarified with reference to it.[77]

2.3.3 Covenant on the Rights of the Child in Islam

Another example of an attempt to develop an Islamic version of an international human rights convent is the *Covenant on the Rights of the Child in Islam*, which was adopted at the 32nd Islamic Conference of Foreign Ministers in 2005.[78] It is an

---

74 Dunn, "Islamic Law and Human Rights".
75 Ibid.
76 University of Minnesota Human Rights Library (ed.), *Cairo Declaration on Human Rights*, http://hrlibrary.umn.edu/instree/cairodeclaration.html, Article 24.
77 Ibid., Article 25.
78 Saeed, *Human Rights and Islam*, 152 citing Rajabi-Ardeshiri, "The Rights of the Child," 484; Organisation of Islamic Cooperation (ed.), *Resolutions on Islamic and Cultural Affairs Adopted by the Twenty-Second Islamic Conference of Foreign Ministers*, Casablanca, Kingdom of Morocco, 8 – 10 Rajab, 1415 H (10 – 12 December, 1994), Resolution No. 16/22-C on *Child Care and Protection*

important document because it represents the OIC's first attempt to create a binding human rights instrument.[79] In 2017, the OIC held a thematic discussion on the Covenant, noting "all the OIC Member States have signed and ratified the UN CRC [Convention on the Rights of the Child]." It was therefore proposed that the Covenant on the Rights of the Child in Islam should be reviewed to "bring it in conformity with the international human rights instruments and make it more representative, broad based and implementable."[80]

The *Covenant on the Rights of the Child in Islam* represents the cumulative efforts of Muslim majority states to provide formal protections for children, recognizing the responsibility of Muslim communities to protect children due to their vulnerable nature. Children also suffer greatly in the face of natural and human disasters, violence and conflict.[81] It further recognizes "Islamic efforts" to contribute to the drafting of the 1989 UN Convention on the *Rights of the Child.*[82] In terms of its content, it tries to follow the UN Convention on the *Rights of the Child* (CRC) as a model. However, like other Islamic human rights instruments, the document has been criticized for failing to provide adequate protections in comparison to those set out in international human rights standards.[83]

2.4 Reflections on the Islamic Human Rights Instruments

Many observers have pointed out the shortcomings of these instruments vis-à-vis the human rights protections found in international instruments. In some instances, a broader range of rights are protected by the international documents. In others, the same rights are covered by both legal regimes, yet the scope of the rights contained in the Islamic instruments is much narrower or governed by provisos that limit the circumstances under which the protections apply. Instru-

---

in the Islamic World. Available http://ww1.oic-oci.org/english/conf/fm/22/Resolution22-C.htm (accessed on 05.07.2022).
79 Mosaffa, N., "Does the Covenant on the Rights of the Child in Islam Provide Adequate Protection for Children Affected by Armed Conflicts," *Muslim World Journal of Human Rights, 8,* 1 (2011), 14.
80 *Outcome Document of Thematic Debate on Revisiting the OIC Covenant on the Rights of Child in Islam,* 2017, https://oic-iphrc.org/en/data/docs/session_reports/13th/Outcome%20Document%20%20for%2013th%20%20Session.pdf (accessed on 19.03.2022).
81 Organization of the Islamic Conference (OIC), *Covenant on the Rights of the Child in Islam,* June 2005, OIC/9-IGGE/HRI/2004/Rep.Final, https://www.refworld.org/docid/44eaf0e4a.html (accessed on 28.06.2022), preamble.
82 Ibid.
83 See, for instance, Mosaffa, "Does the Covenant on the Rights of the Child in Islam".

ments like the UIDHR or Cairo Declaration, particularly in the English translations of such documents, seem to apply many of the rights associated with international human rights law, yet limit their scope by saying they are subject to "law". This essentially means they are subject to *sharīʿa* or classical Islamic law. Such a statement often renders the instrument meaningless or, at the very least, weak compared to international human rights law. This has been a significant criticism of these instruments. However, there are scholars who see the very fact that such instruments have been drafted a positive development. They believe they show "a desire of Islamist leaders to participate in international human rights discourse" and a way to express grievances regarding "European colonization of traditionally Muslim lands, and the ensuing imposition of European legal structures; the impact of European law on Muslim family law; and the European Christian missionaries who converted, or attempted to convert, Muslims."[84]

3 Relevant Islamic Legal Concepts and Human Rights

Literature on Islam and human rights increased significantly from the 1980s onwards. Muslim scholars interested in exploring such issues often attempt to find the basis for an Islamic conception of human rights in Islamic tradition, particularly within the Islamic legal and theological literature. Here we provide some basic concepts that are relevant to this interest.

3.1 A Key Purpose of Sharīʿa: Enhancing Human Dignity

Scholars such as Mashood Baderin argue that one of the key purposes of the *sharīʿa*[85] is the protection and preservation of human dignity. He states: "[r]espect for justice, protection of human life and dignity, are central principles inher-

---

84 Dunn, "Islamic Law and Human Rights".
85 *Sharīʿa* is often translated as "Islamic law". The term *sharīʿa* itself occurs once in the Qur'an (the primary religious text of Islam), where it designates a divinely appointed path: "We have set you on a *sharīʿa* of command, so follow it" (45:19). The term is linguistically associated with terms such as "the path", "the way", or "the road". These words indicate that *sharīʿa* is considered to be the path set by God for Muslims to follow for them to achieve salvation, and that it refers to the totality of guidance contained in the Qur'an and Sunnah.

ent in the sharīʿa which no differences of opinion can exclude. They are the over-all purpose of the sharīʿa, to which the Qurʾān refers."[86] As alluded to earlier in our discussion of the rights of God and the rights of human beings, one of the reasons for the distinction Muslim jurists made between these different catego-ries of rights was to ensure that the *sharīʿa* balanced the rights and freedoms of individuals, on the one hand, and the maintenance of public order in a way that was compatible with the Islamic values of society, on the other. Too strong an emphasis on the rights of individuals could have negative implications for broad-er society.[87] Likewise, an emphasis on maintaining social order could quash the rights of individuals. Indeed, this tension between the rights of individuals and those of the collective is still something that many societies around the world grapple with today.

The effort to balance the needs of the individual and the collective can be seen in the way the *sharīʿa* approaches the notion of human dignity. The legal texts that affirm the dignity of human beings and protect it from being affronted are articulated in a way that refers to the individual. However, "[t]he individual is not [...] addressed as an isolated entity but as part [...] of the community."[88]

Muhammad Shahrur emphasizes humanity has been granted honor and dig-nity. The Qurʾān, according to Shahrur, emphasizes "the preservation of human dignity" and "individual autonomy".[89] Shahrur refers to the Qurʾānic teaching that human beings were created from a single soul and no one is superior to an-other based on his or her gender, color, race or nationality.[90] The only criteria by which God may consider someone more exalted than others is his or her level of piety.[91] Amina Wadud emphasizes that "since God is the highest conceptual as-pect of all, then no person can be greater than another person, especially for mere reasons of gender, race, class, nationality, etc." People should therefore be considered equal, regardless of their gender, race or nationality. Indeed, they should "occupy a relationship of horizontal reciprocity, maintaining the highest place for God in His/Her/Its uniqueness."[92]

---

86 Baderin, Mashood A., *International Human Rights and Islamic law*, Oxford: Oxford University Press, 2005, 13.
87 Ibid., 103.
88 Ibid.
89 Shahrur, Muhammad, *The Qurʾan, Morality and Critical Reason: The Essential Muhammad Shahrur*, trans. Andreas Christmann, Leiden: Brill, 2009, 451.
90 Ibid., 382.
91 Ibid., 390.
92 Wadud, Amina, "Foreword: Engaging Tawhid in Islam and Feminisms," *International Feminist Journal of Politics* 10 (2008), 437.

Mohsen Kadivar says the Qur'ān emphasizes human dignity in many of its verses and this forms the basis of their inherent human rights: "human beings are similar in dignity and in human spirit [...] The basis for equality in rights is the [common] essence of all human beings; humans have equal rights because they share this divine essence."[93] Kadivar notes that the Qur'ān says human beings were created equally from a single man and woman: no superiority of race or gender is evident from the creation of human beings. The Qur'ān says: "People, We created you all from a single man and a single woman, and made you into races and tribes so that you should recognize one another" (Q 49:13) and "People, be mindful of your Lord, who created you from a single soul" (Q 4:1).[94] According to Kadivar, the notion of "fundamental equality" is more consistent with "the spirit of the Qur'ān and Islamic standards" because, according to Islamic teaching, "God is addressing the self or human spirit, which accepted the divine covenant and carries the "trust" (*amāna*)."[95] Hassan Yousefi-Eshkevari agrees, stating, "[i]n Qur'ānic ontology, no human is distinct from other humans; neither race, nor color, nor status brings distinction, as clearly stated in a famous verse (49:13)."[96] Therefore, human beings "are equal in humanity (i.e. none is more human than the other)."[97]

3.2 Objectives of Islamic Law and the Five Necessities

In the Islamic tradition, the purposes of the *sharī'a* are addressed under the broader legal discourse of *maqāṣid ash-sharī'a*, which refers to the goals and objectives of the *sharī'a* either generally or with reference to its particular themes and subjects.[98] While the *maqāṣid* of the *sharī'a* were strictly defined and limited to a particular number under classical Islamic law, some contemporary Muslim

---

93 Kadivar, Mohsen, "Revisiting Women's Rights in Islam: 'Egalitarian Justice' in Lieu of 'Deserts-Based Justice'," in: Ziba Mir-Hosseini et al. (eds.) *Gender and Equality in Muslim Family Law: Justice and Ethics in the Islamic Legal Tradition*, 213–34, London: I.B. Tauris, 2013, 225.
94 Ibid., 215.
95 Ibid., 226.
96 Yousefi-Eshkevari, Hassan, "Rethinking Men's Authority Over Women: Qiwama, Wilaya and Their Underlying Assumptions," in: Ziba Mir-Hosseini et al. (eds.), *Gender and Equality in Muslim Family Law: Justice and Ethics in Islamic Legal Tradition*, trans. Ziba Mir Hosseini, 191–211, New York, NY: I. B. Tauris & Co Ltd, 2013, 194.
97 Ibid., 195.
98 Kamali, Mohammad Hashim, "Maqasid al-Shariah and Ijtihad as Instruments of Civilisational Renewal: A Methodological Perspective," *Islam and Civilisational Renewal* 2, 2 (2011), 248.

scholars are finding ways to expand the scope and number of *maqāṣid* to include specific human rights.

Early jurists identified five essential goals (*ḍarurīyāt*) of the *sharī'a*: the protection of life, intellect, religion, property and family.[99] A key proponent of these goals – the jurist and theologian al-Ghazālī (d. 505/1111) – argued the purpose of the *sharī'a* is to promote and protect these five goals because they are essential to human life and society. In fact, "[the] necessity is such that no community can exist without them."[100] This is why they are given such a prominent place in the *sharī'a*.

After al-Ghazālī, the jurist ash-Shāṭibī (d. 1388) elaborated further on the idea of the essential goals of the *sharī'a*. Like al-Ghazālī, he identified five main objectives of the *sharī'a* that were critical, "not only to the proper functioning of the religious-spiritual and mundane affairs of human life, but also to the very existence of human society."[101] His list consisted of "religion, life, mind, offspring and property/wealth."[102]

Recently, scholars have revisited the notion of the objectives of the *sharī'a* and considered whether they could be expanded beyond the five essentials identified by scholars like al-Ghazālī and ash-Shāṭibī. Yusuf al-Qaraḍāwī (b. 1926), for example, identifies further objectives to the five identified by al-Ghazālī, including justice, human dignity and human rights, especially the rights of freedom for the oppressed and social welfare assistance. For him, key objectives of the *sharī'a* include "preserving true faith, maintaining human dignity and rights, calling people to worship God, purifying the soul, restoring moral values, building good families, treating women fairly, building a strong Islamic nation and calling for a cooperative world."[103]

Kamali is also one scholar who argues that the *maqāṣid* cannot be limited to a certain number of essentials. He points out that the *sharī'a* is not limited in that sense because Muslims understand it to have ongoing relevance, even centuries after the original revelation. Therefore, its objectives must be allowed to grow and develop through independent reasoning (*ijtihād*).[104] Kamali proposes that several tools should be employed for this purpose, including induction (*istiqrā'*),

---

99 Kamali, "Maqasid al-Shariah and Ijtihad," 246.
100 El-Mesawi, Mohamed El-Tahir, "From al-Shāṭibī's Legal Hermeneutics to Thematic Exegesis of the Qur'ān," *Intellectual Discourse* 20, 2 (2012), 194.
101 El-Mesawi, "From al-Shāṭibī's Legal Hermeneutics," 197.
102 Ibid.
103 Auda, Jasser, "Realizing *Maqasid* in the *Shariah*," in: Idris Nassery et al. (eds.), *The Objectives of Islamic Law*, London: Lexington Books, 2018, 39.
104 Kamali, "Maqasid al-Shariah and Ijtihad," 266.

unrestricted reasoning (*istidlāl*), human intellect (*'aql*), and recognition of our innate human nature (*fiṭra*). These, along with the primary texts of Islam (the Qur'ān and the *sunna*), should be used to "identify the *maqāṣid* according to an open-ended scale of values[105] focused on realizing benefits for human beings on both individual and societal levels."[106] The key point is that through an expansion of *maqāṣid*, it may be possible to support a wide range of fundamental human rights.

3.3 Natural Rights and Natural Law

The history of contemporary human rights law is often traced back to the discourses around natural law that emerged in Europe around the 17th and 18th centuries. Natural law theory argues that "the moral standards that govern human behavior are, in some sense, objectively derived from the nature of human beings."[107] Philosophers such as Thomas Aquinas, before the modern period, elaborated further, arguing that "reason [...] is the first principle of human acts."[108] "[S]ince human beings are by nature rational beings, it is morally appropriate that they should behave in a way that conforms to their rational nature."[109] If this is, as is sometimes suggested, the source of modern-day human rights law, is there an equivalent discourse in Islam that would suggest Islam and international human rights law are compatible at this conceptual level?

The debate about whether there is an equivalent notion of natural rights in Islam surfaces in relation to discussions about the use of reason to determine God's will in the absence of a direct teaching or instruction from the Qur'ān.[110] The relationship between the *sharī'a* and reason is a debate that has been of interest to Muslim scholars since the early years of Islam.[111] Muslims believe the Qur'ān is God's word and it contains guidance for attaining salvation

---

105 Ibid., 266.

106 Ibid., 249.

107 Himma, Kenneth Einar, "Natural Law," published online: *Internet Encyclopedia of Philosophy: A Peer-Reviewed Academic Resource* (online) *The Internet Encyclopedia of Philosophy*, https://www.iep.utm.edu/ (accessed on 19.03.2022).

108 Ibid.

109 Ibid.

110 Emon, Anver M., "Introduction," published online: Anver M. Emon, *Islamic Natural Law Theories*, Oxford: Oxford University Press, 2010, https://oxford.universitypressscholarship.com/view/10.1093/acprof:oso/9780199579006.001.0001/acprof-9780199579006-chapter-1 (accessed on 19.03.2022), 13.

111 Ibid.

and for living in a way that satisfies God's commands. However, the Qur'ān does not explicitly address every situation a Muslim will encounter. Muslim jurists, therefore, had to develop tools and methodology for expanding the scope of the Qur'ān's instruction to address new situations. In this context debates developed about whether and how reason should be used to build upon the Qur'ān's teaching.

Some scholars argue there is no natural law discourse in Islamic tradition. Since God is the ultimate legislator, "reason cannot be an authoritative source for divine injunctions."[112] Reason can only confirm what is contained in the texts of the Qur'ān.[113] Yet other scholars, such as Muḥammad 'Abduh and Rashid Riḍa, saw no difficulty using reason to "develop the Sharī'a in light of changed historical realities."[114] They argued there was, in fact, a natural law discourse in Islam that opened the door for the use of reason to interpret the Qur'ān. For example, Muḥammad 'Abduh (d. 1905) "equated the *Sharī'a* with natural law [...]." Rashid Riḍa, who was influenced by 'Abduh's teachings, was a strong advocate of using reason to expand the *sharī'a*, using the doctrine of *"maṣlaḥa* [public interest] as a source for legal and political reform."[115]

4 Modern Perceptions of the Concept of Human Rights within Different Islamic Schools of Thought

In general, Muslim discourses on human rights fall into two broad categories: defensive and harmonistic.

4.1 Defensive Approaches

Defensive approaches argue that Islam and international human rights law cannot be reconciled. They either perceive no common ground between the two systems or disregard any commonalities that can be found. Defensive approaches

---

112 Ibid.
113 Ibid.
114 Ibid 15.
115 Ibid 16, citing Khadduri, Majid, "Maṣlaḥa," published online: *EI*², Leiden: Brill Online, http://dx.doi.org/10.1163/1573-3912_islam_SIM_5019 (accessed 30.06.2022).

consider international human rights law to be a Western, anti-Islamic agenda,[116] being imposed from the outside. Those who take this position are suspicious of human rights and perceive them as either some form of colonial or imperialist agenda[117] or as a yardstick to criticize Islam and challenge its foundational place in Muslim societies. Some defensive approaches reject human rights absolutely, seeing them as entirely incompatible with Islamic law and teachings, while other approaches emphasize "Islamic" formulations or instruments they believe to be more acceptable for Muslims or true to Islamic teachings. The *Universal Islamic Declaration on Human Rights* and the *Cairo Declaration on Human Rights in Islam* are two examples of this latter approach.

From the perspective of Muslim states, a defensive approach takes the form of entering reservations against certain articles when they ratify the UN human rights treaties. The reservations against the *Convention on the Elimination of All Forms of Discrimination Against Women (CEDAW)* are a good example of this practice. Twenty-one Muslim-majority states have lodged qualifications or objections against one or more of its articles.[118] Many states have simply stated they will not be bound by any obligations that are contrary to Islamic law or which do not conform with the *sharīʿa*. *Sharīʿa*-based objections can also be found in the reservations made by Muslim-majority countries against the articles of other human rights treaties as well.[119]

Underlying many defensive approaches is the belief that classical Islamic legal positions must be maintained in the modern period, although they were set down in a very different socio-historical era to today. For those who adhere to this position it is unacceptable to challenge classical legal scholarship because it carries almost the same status as divine revelation.[120] To consider con-

---

116 Baderin, Mashood A., "Islam and the Realization of Human Rights in the Muslim World: a Reflection on Two Essential Approaches and Two Divergent Perspectives," *Muslim World Journal of Human Rights*, 4, 1 (2007), 10.

117 an-Naʿim, Abdullahi Ahmed, "The Contingent Universality of Human Rights: The Case of Freedom of Expression in African and Islamic Contexts," *Emory International Law Review* 11, 1 (1997), 29, 32.

118 United Nations/Office of the High Commissioner for Human Rights (ed.), *Status of Reservations and Declarations,* https://treaties.un.org/Pages/Treaties.aspx?id=4&subid=A&lang=en (accessed on 09.06.2022)

119 See, for example, Egypt's reservation to the ICCPR: https://treaties.un.org/Pages/ViewDetails.aspx?chapter=4&clang=_en&mtdsg_no=IV-4&src=IND (accessed on 05.07.2022).

120 Farrag, Ahmad, "Human Rights and Liberties in Islam," in: Jan Berting et al. (eds.), *Human Rights in a Pluralist World: Individuals and Collectivities,* 137– 53, Westport, CN: Meckler, 1990, 141, cited in Bielefeldt, Heiner, "Muslim Voices in the Human Rights Debate," *Human Rights Quarterly* 17, 4 (1995), 604.

textualizing or reinterpreting it is therefore perceived as equivalent to attempting to change the revelation itself or the teachings of Prophet Muhammad.

Another approach that falls into this category is Sultanhussein Tabandeh's *Muslim Commentary on the Universal Declaration of Human Rights*. Where he sees inconsistencies between the UDHR and the *sharīʿa*, Tabandeh simply states that Muslims do not need to be bound by these provisions.[121] Another approach emphasizes that Islamic and "Western" conceptions of human rights cannot be reconciled because they are fundamentally different. Syed Mohammed Anwar from Pakistan is one scholar to takes this view. He argues:

> Islam is an altogether different paradigm [...]. The fundamental difference lies in the origin of rights as Islam seeks its guidance from Divine sources while the West acknowledges lessons learnt through human experience. Thus the approach and objectives lie far apart and this lead to differences in outlook and behaviors in all areas and aspects of life.[122]

A further approach is represented by those Muslims who argue that Islamic conceptions of human rights are "superior" to that of the West. Perhaps, one of the early and most prominent Muslim thinkers of the 20th century to focus on human rights from this perspective was the Pakistani political Islamist Abū l-Aʿlā Mawdūdī (d. 1979). Mawdūdī argued that human rights did not emerge in the West, as was commonly assumed, but was given to mankind by God through the sacred law of Islam. [123] As human rights are God-given: "No legislative assembly in the world, or any government on earth has the right or authority to make any amendment or change in the rights conferred by God. No one has the right to abrogate them or withdraw them."[124] On this basis all Muslims and Muslim authorities must "accept, recognize and enforce them"[125] as part of the Islamic faith. If they don't, the Qurʾān is clear about the consequences.[126] For Mawdūdī, the Islamic notion of human rights is far superior than the understanding that emerged in Western thought as late as the 18th century, which culminated in the Universal Declaration.[127] This document, he declares, is merely

---

121 Tabandeh, Sultanhussein, *A Muslim Commentary on the Universal Declaration of Human Rights*, London: F. T. Goulding & Co., 1970, cited in Abdullahi Ahmed An-Naʿim, *Toward an Islamic Reformation: Civil Liberties, Human Rights and International Law* (2001), 171.

122 Anwar, "Normative Structure of Human Rights in Islam," 81.

123 Mawdudi, Abu Aʿla, *Human Rights in Islam*, Islamic Publications Limited: Lahore, 1977/1995, 39.

124 Ibid., 12.

125 Ibid.

126 Ibid.

127 Ibid., 11.

"an expression of pious hope"[128] that cannot be enforced and is only "for the sake of show and exhibition [...] [but] denied in actual life when the show is over".[129] On the other hand, human rights violations, according to Islam, have very clear sanctions and are associated with more just and "equitable laws".[130]

Mawdūdī goes on to describe some of the human rights enshrined by Islam, including "the right to live and respect human life",[131] the importance of respecting and protecting a woman's chastity,[132] the right of the needy and destitute to receive help from the property or wealth of Muslims,[133] the prohibition against slavery[134] and the equality of all human beings regardless of "color, race or nationality."[135] These human rights, according to Mawdūdī, are safeguarded regardless of whether the person is a believer or an unbeliever.[136]

4.2 Harmonistic Approaches

Apart from the defensive approaches to Islam and human rights outlined above, there are those that take a "harmonistic perspective",[137] arguing that while there are conflicts between the two, they can be reconciled or harmonized using certain doctrines or tools of interpretation from Islamic tradition. Those who adopt these approaches are at the forefront of the discourse on reconciling international human rights with Islamic norms today.

Several strategies have been put forward to reconcile Islamic law and international human rights law in this way, including procedural devices to prevent laws that are seen as contrary to human rights standards being applied; emphasizing Islamic doctrines, principles or values that are compatible with international human rights law; the reinterpretation of texts of the Qur'ān or *sunna* that are no longer seen as applicable in the modern period (using, for example, contextualization); and emphasizing the jurisprudence of the courts in Muslim-

---

128 Ibid., 12.
129 Ibid.
130 Ibid., 39.
131 Ibid., 14.
132 Ibid., 16.
133 Ibid., 17.
134 Ibid.
135 Ibid., 20.
136 Ibid., 14
137 On this terminology and related concepts, cf. Baderin, Mashood A., "Islam and the Realization of Human Rights in the Muslim World: A Reflection on Two Essential Approaches and Two Divergent Perspectives," *Muslim World Journal of Human Rights* 41 (2007), 12.

majority states that take into account or apply international human rights standards in their decision making.[138]

For example, Mashood Baderin argues the Qur'ān and the *sunna* (*ḥadīth*) contain commands that support many of the substantive rights that can be found in international human rights law. These include: "the right to life, to property, to privacy, to justice, to personal freedom, to freedom of expression, to freedom of religion and conscience, to freedom of association, to freedom of movement, to equality, to education, to housing, to sustenance, to asylum, to basic needs, to freedom of assembly, to protest etc."[139] Scholars such as Norani Othman and Zainah Anwar from Malaysia propose that many classical legal doctrines misrepresent the intentions of the Qur'ān's teachings, particularly concerning women.[140] They believe that as Islamic law developed in the 8th to 10th centuries CE, it incorporated many of the assumptions, values and social norms of the time. These became embedded in classical Islamic law through *taqlīd*[141] – the uncritical following of earlier rulings by Muslim jurists – and continue to be applied today.[142] To remove their influence, these scholars argue, Muslims must go back to the Qur'ān and *sunna* to determine what these primary texts say about men and women. Verses that appear to condone discrimination or inequality between the sexes should not be taken literally but viewed in their historical situation and context.[143]

4.2.1 Sunnī-Shīʿa Harmonistic Thinkers and Convergence

Among the scholars who adopt a harmonistic approach there is much consensus between *Sunnī* and *Shīʿa* schools of thought, particularly concerning the founda-

---

138 Arzt, Donna E., "The Application of International Human Rights Law in Islamic States," *Human Rights Quarterly*, 12, 2 (1990), 202, 228 with reference to Anderson, "Modern Trends in Islam: Legal Reform and Modernisation in the Middle East," *The International and Comparative Law Quaterly* 20, 1 (1971), 12 – 15.
139 Baderin, "Establishing Areas of Common Ground," 95.
140 See, for example, Sisters in Islam, *Reforming Family Law in the Muslim World*, https://sistersinislam.org/muslim-family-law (accessed on 09.06.2022), and Othman, Norani, "Grounding Human Rights Arguments in Non-Western Culture: Shari'a and the Citizenship Rights of Women in a Modern Islamic State," in: Joanne R. Bauer (ed.), *The East Asian Challenge for Human Rights*, 169 – 92, Cambridge: Cambridge University Press, 1999.
141 Sisters in Islam, *Reforming Family Law in the Muslim World*, https://sistersinislam.org/muslim-family-law/ (accessed on 09.06.2022).
142 Ibid.
143 Ibid.

tional principles that give rise to a human rights discourse in Islam. Here we provide some examples of such principles and how both *Sunnī* and *Shī'a* scholars see them.

a Emphasis on the Qur'ānic Concept of Justice

The UDHR makes an explicit connection between human dignity and justice, emphasizing that: "recognition of the inherent dignity and of the equal and inalienable rights of all members of the human family is the foundation of freedom, justice and peace in the world."[144] Like the UDHR, Islamic law is concerned with justice, a principle emphasized by both *Sunnī* and *Shī'a* scholars. Fazlur Rahman, for example, argues social justice is central to the Qur'ān and Muḥammad's prophetic mission.[145] The message of socioeconomic justice and egalitarianism is central to the Qur'ān's basic message, Rahman says.[146] Nurcholish Madjid agrees that the Qur'ān emphasizes social justice and the public good. He affirms, "[t]he principal teachings of Islam [include] social justice and the care and protection of the weak, the poor, and the oppressed, as contained in many passages of the Quran."[147] Likewise, Amina Wadud argues that the underlying spirit of Qur'ān is embodied in principles such as justice, equity, harmony and moral responsibility.[148]

This same emphasis on justice can be found in *Shī'a* human rights scholarship. Mohammad Mojtahed Shabestari notes that the theme of justice is constantly highlighted in the Qur'ān; therefore Muslims today should strive to "move in the direction of justice" in accordance with contemporary understandings.[149] Yusuf Sanei also sees justice and equality as principles that underlie the spirit of the Qur'ān.[150] Likewise, Hassan Yousefi-Eshkevari observes that the theme of justice is emphasized in numerous Qur'ānic verses, as well as the *ḥadīth* literature.

---

144 https://www.ohchr.org/sites/default/files/UDHR/Documents/UDHR_Translations/eng.pdf (accessed on 19.03.2022).
145 Rahman, Fazlur, *Major Themes of the Qur'an*, Chicago et al.: University of Chicago Press, ²2010, 37.
146 Rahman, Fazlur, *Islam and modernity*, Chicago et al.: University of Chicago Press, 1984, 19.
147 Madjid, "The Necessity of Renewing Islamic Thought and Reinvigorating Religious Understanding," 287.
148 Wadud, *Qur'an and Woman*, 3.
149 Shabestari, Muḥammad Mujtahed, *Explanation of the Basis for the Debate with the Muslim Lawyers*, http://mohammadmojtahedShabestari.com/ (accessed on 05.07.2022).
150 Akbar, Ali , "Ayatollah Yusuf Sanei's Contribution to the Discourse of Women's Rights", *Religions* 12 (2021) 3, 10.

Mohammad Arkoun uses the Qur'ān's emphasis on justice in support of Islam's compatibility with the international human rights discourse. He states:

> Islam gave humanity an ideal code of human rights 1400 years ago. The purpose of these rights is to confer honour and dignity on humanity and to eliminate exploitation, oppression and injustice [...].[151]

Abdulaziz Sachedina further argues that the concept of justice in the Qur'ān could be used to advance human rights from an Islamic perspective:

> Justice [is] a comprehensive notion that specifies an entire program for the spiritual and moral development of an individual in society that reflects God's will and especially God's purposes for humanity. Accordingly, God's purposes for humanity include providing necessary guidance to all human beings, without exception, to achieve the stated goal of establishing a just society.[152]

b Distinguishing Between the Mutable and Immutable Aspects of Religion

Both *Sunnī* and *Shī'a* scholars have debated which ethico-legal precepts of the Qur'ān should be considered immutable and which might be subject to reinterpretation in light of the norms and values of the modern period. Shahrur frames the issue in this way: "Just as in the seventh-century people understood Allah's *Book* with the help of what was *then* contemporary knowledge, in the twenty-first century we must understand it with what is *now* contemporary knowledge."[153] He argues, "[o]nly through such a truly contemporary rereading of Allah's *Book* can we succeed in achieving real reform."[154] Shahrur's methodology for doing this is to divide verses into the categories of "eternal, absolute and objectively valid," or "relative, temporal and subjectively conditioned."[155] For Shahrur, legal rulings of the Qur'ān can be legitimately changed "as a result of epistemological and scientific developments that take place in our societies."[156]

---

151 Arkoun, Mohammed, *Rethinking Islam: Common Questions, Uncommon Answers,* Boulder: Westview Press, 2003, 106.
152 Sachedina, Abdulaziz, *Islam and Challenge of Human Rights,* New York: Oxford University Press, 2008, 60.
153 Shahrur, *The Qur'an,* 2.
154 Ibid.
155 Christmann, Andreas, "'The Form is Permanent, but the Content Moves': The Qur'anic Text and its Interpretation(s) in Mohamad Shahrour's *al-Kitab wal-Qur'an*," in: Suha Taji-Farouki (ed.), *Modern Muslim Intellectuals and the Qur'an,* Oxford/New York: Oxford University Press, 2004, 271–72.
156 Shahrur, *The Qur'an,* 496.

Distinguishing between the mutable and immutable teachings of the Qur'ān, *Shī'a* scholar Shabestari argues: "The only everlasting messages pertaining to the commands or instructions addressed to humans are found in those passages which focus on morality and are known as ethical verses (*āyāt-e akhlāqī*) and in those which deal with the issues of the religious worship (*āyāt-e ebādatī*)."[157]

4.2.2 Reflections on the Harmonistic Approaches

Harmonistic approaches have in common their use of independent reasoning to reconcile Islam and human rights, emphasizing principles and approaches that go back to the foundational texts of Islam. In doing so they seek to understand the fundamental meaning or "spirit" of the text and take into account contemporary norms and values. These scholars argue that legal rulings and doctrines that are incompatible with the modern period should be set aside or brought into line with the perspectives of the 21st century. Classical Islamic law itself may have to be reformed so it remains relevant to the experiences and concerns of Muslims today.

At the heart of discussions about whether Islam and international human rights laws are compatible is the debate about whether classical Islamic legal positions should continue to be applied today. Again, scholars are divided over this question. On the one hand, those who argue that classical rulings and positions should be maintained tend to conclude that human rights law and the *sharī'a* are incompatible.[158] On the other hand there are scholars who see Islamic law as flexible and able to evolve[159] and have no difficulty putting aside some of the classical positions. Bielefeldt, an observer of this discourse on Islam and human rights, suggests that the perceived incompatibilities between Islam and human rights are not because of Islam itself but related to certain interpretations of Islamic law.[160]

The tension between those who advocate for new ideas, approaches and methodology to interpreting the Qur'ān and the *sunna* and those who uphold the classical approaches to interpreting the Qur'ān, particularly its emphasis

---

157 Rodziewicz, Magdalena, "The End of Traditional Islamic Jurisprudence in Hermeneutics of Moḥammad Mojtahed Shabestarī," *Journal of Shi'a Islamic Studies* 10, 2 (2017), 212.
158 Baderin, "Islam and the Realization of Human Rights in the Muslim world," 3.
159 Ibid., 22.
160 Bielefeldt, Heiner, "'Western' Versus 'Islamic' Human Rights Conceptions? A Critique of Cultural Essentialism in the Discussion on Human Rights," *Political Theory* 28, 1 (2000), 103.

on a literal reading of ethico-legal texts, is very much a part of the discourse on Islam and human rights today.

5 Current Muslim Thinking and Human Rights: Examples of Areas of Difficulty and Possible Ideas for Reconciliation

The difficulty in reconciling Islamic law and norms with international human rights law is most challenging when it comes to reconciling Islamic law with certain substantive rights; for example, with the rights concerning women, the rights of the child, freedom of expression and freedom of religion. Here we provide some examples of this.

5.1 Islamic Law and Women

Human rights treaty bodies have expressed concern about several incompatibilities between Islamic law and international human rights law when it comes to the rights of women. One of these is in relation to the practice of polygamy, which clashes with Article 23(4) of the *ICCPR (International Covenant on Civil and Political Rights)* and Article 16(1) of *CEDAW (Convention on the Elimination of all Forms of Discrimination Against Women)*. Both these articles state that men and women must have equal rights in marriage.[161] Polygamous marriages are not commensurate with this expectation of equality, and therefore such marriages should not be tolerated.[162]

Despite the acceptance of polygamous marriages in classical Islamic law, many reformist Muslim scholars today argue such marriages should not be seen as a right for Muslim men. These relationships were permissible in early Islam because of a particular set of issues related to the historical context of Mecca and Medina. Part of this was about protecting a range of vulnerable women in society at the time. For these scholars, there is therefore no particular reason why polygamous marriages cannot be significantly restricted or even

---

161 Saeed, *Human Rights and Islam*, 133.
162 Comm CEDAW, "General Recommendation 21 on Equality in Marriage and Family Relations," 1994, UN Doc A/47/38, [14].

abolished, if need be, thereby making it possible to accept the notion of equality expressed in such articles.

In relation to divorce, classical Islamic law gives more rights to men. This can again conflict with Article 16(1)(c) of CEDAW, which states that women should have equal rights with men not just in marriage but at the point of its dissolution.

Muslim scholars who support equal rights for men and women in divorce argue that the rights given to men in early Islam reflected the practices that existed in pre-Islamic times and are therefore related to the historical context of that time. For them, there is no requirement in the Qur'ān or in the traditions of the Prophet that Muslims must continue with these arrangements thereafter. The unilateral right to repudiation that exists in classical Islamic law for men, for instance, can be discontinued, making it possible to support equal rights for men and women.[163] Venkatraman (2008) notes that even in classical Islamic law different schools of law had somewhat different ideas about divorce and the rights of both parties. The *Mālikī* school of law, for example, tended to be more favorable to women in the case of divorce.[164] So the argument is that even if we look to Islamic legal tradition, we can find arguments that seem to be in favor of some degree of equal rights for both men and women. If what is provided in classical Islamic law is not meant to be immutable, they argue, Islamic law in the modern period can accommodate equal rights for both men and women in marriage and divorce.

Inheritance is another example that is often cited as evidence of the inequality between men and women under classical Islamic law. Based on the Qur'ānic verse "Concerning your children, God commands you that a son should have the equivalent share of two daughters" (Q. 4:11), classical Islamic law adopted the view that a son should have double that of a daughter. This verse clearly prescribes a different amount of inheritance based on a person's gender. Given that this text is in the Qur'ān, it is difficult for many Muslims to argue that the inheritance rules may be changed to accommodate the idea of equal rights for both men and women in inheritance today. However, various ways of equalizing what a son and a daughter receive are often used to soften the Qur'ānic prescription in relation to inheritance. Such tools include the doctrine of *hiba* (gift), which permits a person to bequeath (while they are still alive) part of their estate

---

163 See, for instance, Ali, Kecia, *Marriage and Slavery in Early Islam*, Cambridge, US: Harvard University Press, 2010, 3; Scott, Rachel M., A Contextual Approach to Women's Rights in the Qur'an: Readings of 4:34," *The Muslim World* 99 (2009), 73.
164 Venkatraman, Bharati Anandhi, "Islamic States and the United Nations Convention on the Elimination of all Forms of Discrimination against Women: Are the Shari'a and the Convention Compatible?," *The American University Law Review* 44, 5 (1995), 2008.

to another person. However, the issue of inheritance remains a difficult one for Islamic law and international human rights law because of the clear Qur'ānic texts on this.

5.2 The Rights of the Child

While many of the rights of the child under Islamic law are seen as compatible with international human rights law, there are still some areas where incompatibility can be found. One of these is the age of maturity or adulthood, which determines the legal capacity of the child. For example, the age of maturity defines when a child may marry or if they can be held legally responsible for certain criminal acts. In some Muslim-majority states, the legal age for marriage and/ or criminal responsibility are set at younger than 18 years old, often based on the definitions provided in classical Islamic law.[165] This causes tensions with international human rights law, which defines adulthood as from 18 years of age.

In classical Islamic law the age of maturity (*bulūgh*) is not linked to a particular age and can vary from person to person.[166] When a girl or a boy reaches puberty then they are an adult from a classical Islamic legal perspective. This idea of an age of maturity conflicts with international human rights law, which defines a set age for adulthood. This is the legal age for marriage. If a person under 18 enters into a marriage contract it can be considered unacceptable— as a form of child marriage. Both *CEDAW* and the *Convention on the Rights of the Child (CRC)* take the view that those under 18 may not have the capacity to express full, free and informed consent to a marriage.

This can be a difficult issue from a classical Islamic legal point of view. However, Muslim scholars who argue for adjusting the classical Islamic legal position to what is acceptable today argue that even in this area it is possible for Islamic law to redefine what an adult is. For them, there is nothing in the Qur'ān or in

---

165 For instance, the age of criminal responsibility is specified as at "the age of maturity" in Iran. For girls this is around 8 years old and for boys, it is around 14 years. Cf. *Islamic Penal Code of Iran*, Article 147, https://iranhrdc.org/wp-content/uploads/pdf_en/Iranian_Codes/Islamic_Penal_Code_of_the_Islamic_Republic_of_Iran_212133839.pdf (accessed on 04.07.2022).
166 Hashemi, Kamran, "Religious Legal Traditions, Muslim States and the Convention on the Rights of the Child: An Essay on the Relevant UN Documentation," *Human Rights Quarterly* 29, 1 (2007), 199.

the traditions of the Prophet to suggest that the classical Islamic legal position on the definition of adulthood is an immutable one.[167]

Related to this is the idea that the death penalty cannot be applied to anyone under 18 years old. For classical Islamic law, a person who has reached maturity can be held responsible for their crimes. Where this leads to the death penalty, this can also be applied. This is another area where reconciliation with international human rights law is challenging, but if we look at the actual practice of Muslim majority countries around the world, many have adopted the definition of a child provided by the *Convention on the Rights of the Child*. In a sense, this reconciliation has already taken place, at least for the vast majority of Muslim states.

5.3 Freedom of Expression

Freedom of expression is considered a fundamental human right according to international human rights law and it is enshrined in various articles, including Article 19 of the ICCPR. According to this provision, freedom of opinion and expression may only be restricted for the purposes of: "the rights or reputations of others, for the protection of national security, public order, or public health or morals."[168] However, the *sharīʿa* permits a broader range of limitations to the right. One of these is blasphemy, which aims to "[protect] the sensibilities and beliefs of the Muslim community in particular and that of other faiths in general."[169]

There are several ways Islamic law and international human rights law might be reconciled in this regard. First, by Muslim states putting aside the death penalty for blasphemy. The death penalty can be set aside because there is no Qur'ānic instruction or hadith which suggest this should be its punishment. Moreover, there is no clear definition of blasphemy in the Qur'ān or hadith. Existing definitions of blasphemy (and its associated punishment) were the product of *ijtihād* or interpretation. This therefore creates room for states to set aside the penalty, allowing blasphemy laws to still be applied in a way that is consistent with Article 19 of the ICCPR. Second, Muslims scholars could use *ij-*

---

167 For instance Hashemi argues that understandings of maturity stem from tribal traditions in the pre-Islamic tradition, cf. Hashemi, "Religious Legal Traditions," 200.

168 Australian Human Rights Commission, *Permissible Limitations of the ICCPR Right to Freedom of Expression*, https://humanrights.gov.au/our-work/4-permissible-limitations-iccpr-right-freedom-expression (accessed on 19.03.2022).

169 Baderin, *International Human Rights*, 128.

tihād to reinterpret classical notions of blasphemy in a way that is compatible with international human rights law.[170]

5.4 Freedom of Religion

Article 18 of the ICCPR states that "Everyone shall have the right to freedom of thought, conscience and religion."[171] It is widely recognized that the right includes an individual's freedom to adopt a religion or belief system of their choice (or none at all) and protection from being compelled to adopt a certain religion or belief system. Article 18(2) of the ICCPR prohibits any action that may curtail an individual's freedom in this regard.[172]

For Muslims, the largest obstacle to adopting this understanding of religious freedom is the issue of apostasy. There is nearly unanimous agreement among classical Muslim jurists that apostasy – leaving Islam – should be punished with death.[173] While only a few Muslim-majority states still apply the death penalty for apostasy, it remains "politically and legally salient".[174] Such cases often become extremely "high profile". They are given prominence (and condemnation) by news agencies, human rights organizations and commentators alike, and often feature in political and legal discussions about the country where the penalty has been imposed. From the perspective of the HRC, apostasy laws and the application of the death penalty for apostasy are incompatible with Article 18 of the ICCPR.[175]

In the modern period, many reformist Muslim scholars have argued that the classical laws of apostasy do not need to be applied in the same way today. According to them, the death penalty for apostasy came from certain traditions attributed to the Prophet which seem to suggest that converts from Islam should be punished with death. These narrations were used in the emerging period of Islamic law to develop what is now known as the law of apostasy and its associ-

---

170 Saeed, *Human Rights and Islam*, 185.
171 https://www.ohchr.org/en/instruments-mechanisms/instruments/international-covenant-civil-and-political-rights (accessed on 21.06.2022).
172 Saeed, *Human Rights and Islam*, 195
173 Ibid., 202
174 Ibid., 207 citing Mohammad H. Fadel, "Public Reason as a Strategy for Principled Reconciliation: The Case of Islamic Law and International Human Rights Law," *Chicago Journal of International Law* 8, 1 (2007), 18.
175 See, for instance, the Committee's concluding remarks with respect to the fourth periodic report of Sudan (9 July 2014), http://www.ohchr.org/EN/NewsEvents/Pages/DisplayNews.aspx?NewsID=14841&LangID=E (accessed on 09.12.2017).

ated punishment – the death penalty. Muslim jurists supported their view that apostasy should be punished by death by referring to several hadith attributed to the Prophet. Perhaps the most important in this regard is: "Whoever changes his religion, kill him,"[176] which seems to give explicit permission for Muslims to kill anyone who changes their religion from Islam. However, although widely considered reliable, *hadīth* such as this do not reach the level of certainty that is required from textual evidence to justify the death penalty.[177] Moreover, not all Muslims hold this position. Those Muslims who more readily accept the ICCPR's articulation of religious freedom claim there is nothing in the Qur'ān or hadith that clearly supports apostasy or blasphemy laws. Accordingly, these laws are not part of the fundamentals of Islam; they were developed from legal or political interpretations that are not inherent to the religion and which do not carry enough authority in themselves to justify such restrictions to religious freedom. Given the absence of clear instructions in both the Qur'ān and hadith, it is possible to develop an understanding of religious freedom that is both in line with the Qur'ān and compatible with international human rights standards.

What this means is that the apostasy laws developed in classical Islamic law should not be considered immutable. For these scholars, both the Qur'ān and the Prophet strongly support the idea of freedom of belief and religion for all people, including Muslims. A Muslim should have the right to adopt whatever religion he or she wants to, according to this view. Therefore, for them, there is no reason why reconciliation is not possible between Islamic law and international human rights law in the area of freedom of religion.

6 Possible Dialogical Elements, Differences and Overlaps of the Concept in Relation to the Other Two Monotheistic Religions (Judaism and Christianity)

The three Abrahamic traditions, Judaism, Christianity and Islam, appear to have much in common in their discourses on human rights. So far in this paper we have been exploring the way Muslims have attempted to engage with interna-

---

176 *Ṣaḥīḥ al-Bukhārī* 9:84:57, Translation of Ṣaḥīḥ al-Bukhārī's Book 84 (undated), http://www. islamicity.com/mosque/sunnah/bukhari/084.sbt.html (accessed on 19.03.2022).
177 See discussion in Saeed, *Freedom of Religion*, 59.

tional human rights law and how they see the close connection between human rights today and what exists in Islamic tradition, in particular, Islamic law. In this section, we can see there are many similar ideas at work in both Judaism and Christianity. Here, we are not interested in outlining Jewish and Christian conceptions of human rights as such, but rather to point out one or two examples of shared concepts among the three traditions when it comes to discourses on human rights.

6.1 Judaism

The actual term "human rights" may not exist in the Jewish scriptures. However, ideas, values and resources that are compatible with human rights or which represent certain rights can be found in important religious texts. Many contemporary Jewish movements and groups also affirm human rights. Indeed, the *Declaration on Judaism and Human Rights* (1974)[178] affirms that "Human rights are an integral part of the faith and tradition of Judaism."[179]

Similar to the notion in the Christian tradition, the doctrine of creation, which affirms human beings were created in God's image, is the basis of human rights in Judaism.[180] From this, all human beings are regarded as having inherent dignity,[181] can be considered one human family[182] and have the right to life.[183] Supporting this, it is considered that any act of disrespect towards another person is an act of disrespect towards God Himself because in the image of God He made (the human person)."[184]

Based on human beings' inherent dignity, the Torah emphasizes that the vulnerable in society – strangers, widows, orphans, and the poor – should be

---

178 Human Rights Resource Center: McGill International Colloquium on Judaism and Human Rights (ed.), *Declaration on Judaism and Human Rights*, Adopted in Montreal on April 23, 1974, by The Jacob Blaustein Institute for the Advancement of Human Rights of the American Jewish Committee; Canadian Jewish Congress; Consultative Council of Jewish Organisations, http://www.ajcarchives.org/AJC_DATA/Files/7A6.PDF (accessed on 09.06.2022).
179 Ibid.
180 Ibid.
181 Rosen, David, *Judaism and Human Rights*, https://www.rabbidavidrosen.net/wp-content/uploads/2016/02/Judaism-and-Human-Rights.pdf (accessed on 19.03.2022).
182 Human Rights Resource Center, *Declaration on Judaism and Human Rights*, http://www.hrusa.org/advocacy/community-faith/judaism1.shtm (accessed on 09.06.2022).
183 Rosen, *Judaism and Human Rights*, https://www.rabbidavidrosen.net/wp-content/uploads/2016/02/Judaism-and-Human-Rights.pdf (accessed on 19.03.2022).
184 Ibid.

protected.[185] There are specific laws that instruct people to respect the "underprivileged's dignity"[186], as well as "laws for the socially weak, the Levite, the alien, the orphan, and the widow [...] to be satisfactorily fed every three years".[187] Slaves also have the right to be released "with dignity and provision after six-year debt servitude."[188]

The rights of the poor are also acknowledged in other passages of the Torah. For instance, "the poor have the rights to be freed from their debts, avoid usury, and to be loaned again whenever they have needs."[189] Flowing on from this is the principle of justice. Isaiah 1:17 states, "[d]evote yourselves to justice; aid the wronged. Uphold the rights of the orphan; defend the cause of the widow."[190] Justice is emphasized "because [the] human is created in the image of God."[191]

According to Daisy Tsai, "biblical laws deem all human beings [...] [a] person and intend to preserve human life with ethical considerations." This means those who were commonly perceived as having no value at the time, who were treated as "things" rather than "persons", were perceived by the Torah as human beings and rights bearers.[192] The verse which states that humans are created in the likeliness of God has another consequence: all human beings are considered equal before God. As a result, "equality before the law for all social groups, including aliens and immigrants, is made explicit in Exodus 12:49, Leviticus 19:34 and Numbers 15:16."[193]

Jewish texts also affirm the following rights: the right to health;[194] the right to freedom (encompassing a ban on slavery);[195] the right to earn a livelihood;[196]

---

185 Tsai, Daisy Yulin, *Human Rights in Deuteronomy: With Special Focus on Slave Laws*, Berlin et al.: De Gruyter, 2014, 179.
186 See Deut. 24:6, 10 – 13, 14 – 15,17 – 18, 19 – 21; 25:3.
187 Deut 14:28 – 29; 26:12 – 13.
188 Referring to Deut 15:12 – 15. See Tsai, *Human Rights in Deuteronomy*, 79.
189 Ibid.
190 Ibid.
191 Novak, David, "A Jewish Theory of Human Rights," in: Christian M. Green/John Witte (eds.), *Religion and Human Rights: An Introduction*, 27 – 41, Oxford: Oxford University Press, 2012, 31.
192 Tsai, *Human Rights in Deuteronomy*, 179.
193 Wright, Christopher, *Old Testament Ethics for the People of God*, Downers Grove: InterVarsity Press, 2004, 310.
194 Belkin, Samuel, *In His Image: The Jewish Philosophy of Man as Expressed in Rabbinic Tradition*, Westport: Greenwood Press, 1979, 112, cf. Rosen, "Judaism and Human Rights," https://www.rabbidavidrosen.net/wp-content/uploads/2016/02/Judaism-and-Human-Rights.pdf (accessed on 19.03.2022).
195 Ibid.
196 Rosen, "Judaism and Human Rights".

and the right to equality before the law,[197] as well as various property and environmental rights.[198]

6.2 Christianity

For many Christians, the notion of human rights is drawn from biblical teachings.[199] The Bible describes human beings as created in the image of God. Gen 1:26 – 27 says:

> Let us make man in our image, after our likeness: and let them have dominion over the fish of the sea, and over the fowl of the air, and over the cattle, and over all the earth, and over every creeping thing that creepeth upon the earth. So God created man in his own image, in the image of God created he him; male and female created he them.[200]

Being created in the image of God gives human beings an essential dignity that is not shared by other aspects of creation. Richard Harries says, "God creates and at once recognizes the value of what He has created."[201] The Bible emphasizes that God loves human beings and is patient with them, recognizing that each individual is uniquely God's creation. The fact that "God desires [...] the wellbeing and flourishing of individual human beings" leads us to see the value in other human beings for themselves.[202] These ideas form the basis of a Christian human rights discourse.

The inherent dignity of human beings is the foundation for many biblical teachings. As all human beings are made in God's image, all are regarded as equal before God. Gal 3:28 says, "There is neither Jew nor Gentile, neither slave nor free, nor is there male and female, for you are all one in Christ

---

197 S. Belkin, *In His Image*, 87, cf. Rosen, "Judaism and Human Rights," 9.

198 Rosen, "Judaism and Human Rights".

199 Schirrmacher, Thomas P., "Human Rights and Christian Faith," published online: *Global Journal of Classical Theology* 3,2 (2002), https://www.galaxie.com/article/gjct03-2-05 (accessed on 19.03.2022).

200 New International Version (NIV).

201 Harries, Richard, "The Complementarity between Secular and Religious Perspectives of Human Rights," in: Nazila Ghanea et al. (eds.), *Does God Believe in Human Rights? Essays on Religion and Human Rights*, 17 – 28, Boston/Leiden: Martinus Nijhoff Publishers, 2007, 23.

202 Ibid.

Jesus."[203] Jesus dies on the cross for all people, demonstrating the value of all human beings. Indeed, through this act he "demonstrates the value of every single human being."[204]

The creation of human beings in God's image has important ramifications for how human beings perceive and relate to each other.[205] Unbelievers too are created in God's image, and Christians are encouraged to see them as "brothers and sisters."[206] The taking of human life devalues the image of God and, therefore, must be punished. This is affirmed in Genesis 9:6, which requires the taking of the perpetrator's life as a consequence of injuring the image of God.[207] Christians are encouraged to "love your neighbor as yourself" (Matt 22:39) and to provide for the poor because this "honors God".[208] Even thieves have the right to life.[209] There is also a strong emphasis on human freedom in the Bible,[210] with many verses rejecting the practice of slavery and its various forms.

On the basis of their inherent dignity as bearers of the divine image, human beings are given a degree of authority over and responsibility for the animals.[211] Moltmann describes the relationship between creation and rights in this way:

> In the identification of our humanity as created in the image of God, we affirm: the equal dignity and interdependence of man and woman; the equal validity and interdependence of personal rights (freedom and dignity) and social rights (justice and community). As humanity stands in a covenant relationship to God, that relationship carries with it covenant

203 Wolterstorff, Nicholas P., "Christianity and Human Rights," in: Christian M. Green/John Witte (eds.), *Religion and Human Rights: An Introduction*, Oxford: Oxford University Press, 2012, 53.

204 CELAM (Episcopal Conference of Latin America), *Nueva Evangelización, Promoción Humana, Cultura Cristiana, "Jesucristo Ayer, Hoy y Siempre*, IV conferencia General del Episcopado Latinoamericano, Santo Domingo, Republica Dominicana, 12–28 Octubre 1992, Santo Domingo: Ediciones MSC, 1993, cited in: Fortman, Bas de Gaay, "Religion and Human Rights: A Dialectical Relationship," published online: *E-International Relations*, https://www.e-ir.info/2011/12/05/religion-and-human-rights-a-dialectical-relationship/ (accessed on 19.03.2022).

205 Schirrmacher, "Human Rights and Christian Faith," https://www.galaxie.com/article/gjct03-2-05 (accessed on 05.07.2022).

206 Ruston, "Religious Truths and Human Coexistence," 35.

207 Schirrmacher, "Human Rights and Christian Faith".

208 Wolterstorff, "Christianity and Human Rights," 53.

209 Ibid.

210 Ibid.

211 Ibid.

responsibilities in our stewardship of creation. This means "my rights" and "the rights of my neighbor" are equally valid and interdependent [...].[212]

According to a number of Christian scholars, biblical teachings support a number of rights, including equality, economic rights such as the right to "a just share in life, nourishment, work, shelter, and personal possessions",[213] the right to access to justice and to fair judicial proceedings,[214] the right to equality before the law for "the wealthy, the poor, as well as to both nationals and for foreign residents",[215] protection from torture and the prohibition of slavery.[216]

Even though human rights have a divine origin according to Christian teachings, it is the state's role to uphold and protect them. [217]

6.3 Points in Common Between the Approaches of Different Religious Traditions and Dialogical Elements

As this brief overview suggests, there are many points of overlap between Judaism, Christianity, and Islam. Firstly, within each tradition there is support for a notion of human rights that stems from the inherent dignity of all human beings, a dignity they were endowed with at the point of creation. On this basis, commands and laws were established in each tradition to encourage people to treat the vulnerable in society, such as widows, orphans and the poor, in a way that recognizes this dignity, protects them and provides for them. Human life is considered valuable, and the taking of a life is considered an affront to God. Moreover, human beings are considered fundamentally equal because they share the same status in creation, one above all other created beings.[218]

Second, each tradition agrees that human rights have a divine origin and find support for both the concept of human rights and for particular substantive rights within the scriptures of the tradition. Thus, within each tradition, human

---

212 Moltmann, Jürgen, "A Definitive Study Paper: A Christian Declaration on Human Rights," in: Allen O. Miller (ed.), *A Christian Declaration on Human Rights: Theological Studies of the World Alliance of Reformed Churches*, 25–34, Grand Rapids, MI: Eerdmans, 1977.
213 Ibid.
214 Schirrmacher, "Human Rights and Christian Faith".
215 Ibid.
216 Ibid.
217 Ibid.
218 Quran 2:30 says, "And [mention, O Muḥammad], when your Lord said to the angels, "Indeed, I will make upon the earth a successive authority [...]"

rights come from a religious and moral framework, although they differ with respect to what this framework entails.

Within each tradition there are also doctrines and historical practices that are not easily reconciled with contemporary international human rights standards. Many of the tensions concern how people who are not members of their communities are defined and treated[219] and the specific rights and freedoms granted to non-believers – those who do not follow orthodox beliefs or practices – and others who traditionally had a lesser status within the community, such as women or slaves.[220] Each tradition appears to be undergoing a similar process of determining in what circumstances such doctrines and rulings were laid down, whether they are in fact mutable or immutable aspects of the tradition, and how core beliefs concerning human beings may be applied in the different circumstances of the 21st century.

These commonalities provide a basis for dialogue between the three religious communities. Each tradition recognizes that human beings share inherent human dignity that is God-granted and cannot be taken away by human authorities. Each tradition upholds the belief that human beings were created by God and share fundamental equality with each other on this basis. Each tradition recognizes the sanctity of life and that there should be penalties for the taking of a life. On this basis, there is great scope for solidarity concerning the promotion and protection of human rights around the world and potential for joint action to address human rights violations that threaten human beings' inherent, God-given dignity. J. Paul Martin argues that engagement with the international human rights system is useful in this regard because it provides common "standards, language and institutions" that can assist "religiously and culturally diverse societies to deal with common [...] social problems."[221] Thus international human rights standards provide an important framework for dialogue and action that can bring together the three monotheistic religious traditions.

6.4 Concluding Remarks

Islam, like the other monotheistic religious traditions, recognizes a concept of human rights. While the notion of *ḥaqq* is not as developed, nor as expansive as its equivalent within international human rights law (primarily because it

---

219 Martin, J. P., "The Three Monotheistic World Religions and International Human Rights," *Journal of Social Issues* 61, 4 (2005), 831.
220 Ibid.
221 Ibid., 829.

evolved in a very different historical context), there are elements that the two concepts share that can form a basis for a common discourse around rights. In addition, the Qur'ān upholds the inherent dignity of human beings and strongly emphasizes the pursuit of social justice as a divine mandate. Islamic law, like international human rights law, places the onus on governments to ensure the safety, security and rights of their citizens, while at the same time acknowledging that state power may be legitimately curtailed. Indeed, no ruler may act with impunity if they exercise power in a way that is outside their mandate or in a way that violates their covenant with their citizens.

Muslim-majority states' engagement with the international human rights system has, at times, been fraught with difficulties. Many states have been criticized by human rights treaty monitoring bodies, such as the HRC and CEDAW, for failing to promote and protect human rights standards in their jurisdictions. Some commentators also perceive attempts to create so-called Islamic human rights instruments as further evidence that some Muslim states are unwilling to engage with the international human rights system or to uphold its standards. Yet attempts to create a binding Islamic human rights treaty under the auspices of the Organization of the Islamic Cooperation have been met with little enthusiasm by its member states.

Muslim states' engagement with the international human rights system, at least in the case of some states, is likely to remain ambivalent for the foreseeable future. However, most Muslim states are continuing to engage with the international human rights system. There are many examples of states reforming their domestic laws to take into account human rights standards in particular areas or of national courts referring to international human rights law in their decision making. Moreover, emerging Muslim scholarship on human rights is finding ways to reinterpret or put aside aspects of classical Islamic law that are contrary to international human rights law, removing further obstacles that may prevent Muslim states' engagement with the international system. The work of scholars such as An-Na'im, Baderin, Wadud, Kamali and others demonstrates that there are compatibilities between Islamic and international human rights law and that incompatibilities can be addressed in a way that is both authentic to Islamic legal tradition and cognizant of international standards.

The concept of rights within Islamic tradition and the resources that can be found in the Qur'ān and the traditions of the Prophet Muḥammad that are compatible with the contemporary notion of rights also form a basis upon which Muslims can engage with other religious traditions around human rights issues. Like Islam, both Judaism and Christianity recognize the inherent dignity of human beings. They recognize that all human beings were created by God and come from the same human family and are all equal at a fundamental level.

All three traditions recognize the sanctity of life; that effort must be made to protect life and that those who take away life must be appropriately and lawfully punished. These commonalities provide important scope for mutual engagement around human rights issues and the potential for joint initiatives involving the three traditions.

Bibliography

Akbar, Ali, "Ayatollah Yusuf Sanei's Contribution to the Discourse of Women's Rights," *Religions* 12 (2021), 1–13.

Ali, Kecia, *Marriage and Slavery in Early Islam,* Cambridge, US: Harvard University Press, 2010.

Ali, Shaheen Sardar, "The Conceptual Foundations of Human Rights: A Comparative Perspective," *European Public Law* 3, 2 (1997), 261–82.

An-Na'im, Abdullahi Ahmed, "The Contingent Universality of Human Rights: The Case of Freedom of Expression in African and Islamic Contexts," *Emory International Law Review* 11, 1 (1997), 29–66.

Anwar, Syed Mohammed, "Normative Structure of Human Rights in Islam," *Policy Perspectives* 10, 1 (2013), 79–104.

Arkoun, Mohammed, *Rethinking Islam: Common Questions, Uncommon Answers,* Boulder: Westview Press, 2003.

Arzt, Donna E., "The Application of International Human Rights Law in Islamic States," *Human Rights Quarterly* 12, 2 (1990), 202–30.

Auda, Jasser, "Realizing *Maqasid* in the *Shariah*," in: Idris Nassery et al. (eds.), *The Objectives of Islamic Law,* 35–56, London: Lexington Books, 2018.

Australian Human Rights Commission, *Permissible Limitations of the ICCPR Right to Freedom of Expression,* https://humanrights.gov.au/our-work/4-permissible-limitations-iccpr-right-freedom-expression (accessed on 19.03.2022).

Baderin, Mashood A., "Establishing Areas of Common Ground between Islamic Law and International Human Rights," *International Journal of Human Rights* 5, 2 (2001), 72–113.

Baderin, Mashood A., *International Human Rights and Islamic Law,* Oxford: Oxford University Press, 2005.

Baderin, Mashood A., "Islam and the Realization of Human Rights in the Muslim World: A Reflection on Two Essential Approaches and Two Divergent Perspectives," *Muslim World Journal of Human Rights* 4, 1 (2007), 1–25.

Bielefeldt, Heiner, "'Western' Versus 'Islamic' Human Rights Conceptions?: A Critique of Cultural Essentialism in the Discussion on Human Rights" *Political Theory* 28, 1 (2000), 90–121.

University of Minnesota Human Rights Library (ed.), *Cairo Declaration on Human Rights in Islam,* Aug. 5, 1990, U.N. GAOR, World Conf. on Hum. Rts., 4th Sess., Agenda Item 5, U.N. Doc. A/CONF.157/PC/62/Add.18, 1993, [English translation], http://hrlibrary.umn.edu/instree/cairodeclaration.html (accessed on 19.03.2022).

CELAM (Episcopal Conference of Latin America), *Nueva Evangelización, Promoción Humana, Cultura Cristiana, "Jesucristo Ayer, Hoy y Siempre,* IV conferencia General del Episcopado

Latinoamericano, Santo Domingo, Republica Dominicana, 12–28 Octubre 1992, Santo Domingo: Ediciones MSC, 1993, cited in: Fortman, Bas de Gaay, "Religion and Human Rights: A Dialectical Relationship," published online: *E-International Relations*, https://www.e-ir.info/2011/12/05/religion-and-human-rights-a-dialectical-relationship/ (accessed on 19.03.2022).
Committee on the Elimination of Discrimination against Women (CEDAW), *General Recommendation 21 on Equality in Marriage and Family Relations, Adopted by the Committee on the Elimination of Discrimination Against Women at its Thirteenth Session nin 1994.*, 1994, UN Doc A/47/38, https://original.religlaw.org/content/religlaw/documents/cedawgenrec21_1994.htm (accessed on 09.06.2022).
Dunn, Shannon, "Islamic Law and Human Rights," in: Rumee Ahmed/Anver M. Emon (eds.), *The Oxford Handbook of Islamic Law,* 819–41, Oxford: Oxford University Press, 2015.
El-Mesawi, Mohamed El-Tahir, "From al-Shāṭibī's Legal Hermeneutics to Thematic Exegesis of the Qurʾān," *Intellectual Discourse* 20, 2 (2012), 99–149.
Emon, Anver M., "Introduction," published online: anver M. Emon, *Islamic Natural Law Theories,* Oxford: Oxford University Press, 2010, https://oxford.universitypressscholarship.com/view/10.1093/acprof:oso/9780199579006.001.0001/acprof-9780199579006-chapter-1 (accessed on 19.03.2022).
Emon, Anver M. "Huquq Allah and Huquq Al-Ibad: A Legal Heuristic for a Natural Rights Regime," *Islamic Law and Society* 13 (2006), 325–91.
Farrag, Ahmad, "Human Rights and Liberties in Islam," in: Jan Berting et al. (eds.), *Human Rights in a Pluralist World: Individuals and Collectivities,* 137–53, Westport, CN: Meckler, 1990.
Harries, Richard, "The Complementarity between Secular and Religious Perspectives of Human Rights," in: Nazila Ghanea et al. (eds.), *Does God Believe in Human Rights? Essays on Religion and Human Rights*, 17–28, Boston/Leiden: Martinus Nijhoff Publishers, 2007.
Hashemi, Kamran, "Religious Legal Traditions, Muslim States and the Convention on the Rights of the Child: An Essay on the Relevant UN Documentation," *Human Rights Quarterly* 29, 1 (2007), 194–227.
Hashemi, Nader/Qureshi, Emran, "Human Rights," published online: *The Oxford Encyclopedia of the Islamic World. Oxford Islamic Studies Online,* https://www.oxfordreference.com/view/10.1093/acref/9780195305135.001.0001/acref-9780195305135-e-0325?rskey=XuSpAh&result=460 (accessed on 19.03.2022).
Himma, Kenneth Einar, "Natural Law," published online: *Internet Encyclopedia of Philosophy: A Peer-Reviewed Academic Resource,* https://iep.utm.edu/ (accessed on 19.03.2022).
"Human Rights," published online: Esposito, John L. (ed.), *The Oxford Dictionary of Islam, Oxford Islamic Studies Online,* https://www.oxfordreference.com/view/10.1093/acref/9780195125580.001.0001/acref-9780195125580-e-893?rskey=K8e2Oq&result=893 (accessed on 19.03.2022).
Human Rights Resource Center: McGill International Colloquium on Judaism and Human Rights, *Declaration on Judaism and Human Rights*, Adopted in Montreal on April 23, 1974 by the Jacob Blaustein Institute for the Advancement of Human Rights of the American Jewish Committee; Canadian Jewish Congress; Consultative Council of Jewish Organisations, http://www.ajcarchives.org/AJC_DATA/Files/7A6.PDF (accessed on 09.06.2022).

Kadivar, Mohsen, "Revisiting Women's Rights in Islam: 'Egalitarian Justice' in Lieu of 'Deserts-Based Justice'," in: Ziba Mir-Hosseini et al. (eds.) *Gender and Equality in Muslim Family Law: Justice and Ethics in the Islamic Legal Tradition*, 213 – 34, London: I.B Tauris, 2013, 225.

Kamali, Mohammad Hashim, "Maqasid al-Shariah and Ijtihad as Instruments of Civilisational Renewal: A Methodological Perspective," *Islam and Civilisational Renewal* 2, 2 (2011), 245 – 71.

Law.Com (ed.), *Right*, https://dictionary.law.com/Default.aspx?selected=1857 (accessed on 19.03.2022).

Lecker, Michael, *The "Constitution of Medina": Muḥammad's First Legal Document*, Princeton, NJ: Darwin Press, 2004.

Martin, J. P., "The Three Monotheistic World Religions and International Human Rights," *Journal of Social Issues* 61, 4 (2005), 827 – 45.

Mawdudi, Abu A'la, *Human Rights in Islam*, Lahore: Islamic Publications Limited, 1977/1995.

Mayer, Ann Elizabeth, *Islam and Human Rights: Tradition and Politics,* Colorado: Westview Press, 2013.

Moltmann, Jürgen, "A Definitive Study Paper: A Christian Declaration on Human Rights," in: Allen O. Miller (ed.), *A Christian Declaration on Human Rights: Theological Studies of the World Alliance of Reformed Churches*, 25 – 34, Grand Rapids, MI: Eerdmans, 1977.

Moosa, Ebrahim, "The Dilemma of Islamic Rights Schemes," *Journal of Law and Religion* 15, 1/2 (2000 – 01), 185 – 215.

Mosaffa, N., "Does the Covenant on the Rights of the Child in Islam Provide Adequate Protection for Children Affected by Armed Conflicts," *Muslim World Journal of Human Rights* 8, 1 (2011), 1 – 18.

Nickel, James, "Human Rights," published online: *Standford Enclyclopedia of Philosophy*, 2019, https://plato.stanford.edu/entries/rights-human/#GeneIdeaHumaRigh (accessed on 19.03.2022).

Novak, David, "A Jewish Theory of Human Rights," in: Christian M. Green/John Witte (eds.), *Religion and Human Rights: An Introduction,* 27 – 41, Oxford: Oxford University Press, 2012.

Othman, Norani, "Grounding Human Rights Arguments in Non-Western Culture: Shari'a and the Citizenship Rights of Women in a Modern Islamic State," in: Joanne R. Bauer (ed.), *The East Asian Challenge for Human Rights*, 169 – 92, Cambridge: Cambridge University Press, 1999.

Organization of the Islamic Conference (OIC), *Covenant on the Rights of the Child in Islam*, June 2005, OIC/9-IGGE/HRI/2004/Rep.Final, https://www.refworld.org/docid/44eaf0e4a.html (accessed on 28.06.2022).

Organisation of the Islamic Conference (ed.), *Outcome Document of Thematic Debate on "Revisiting the OIC Covenant on the Rights of Child in Islam,* 2017, https://www.oic-iphrc.org/en/data/docs/session_reports/13th/Outcome%20Document%20%20for%2013th%20%20Session.pdf (accessed on 19.03.2022).

Peters, Ruud, "Islamic Law and Human Rights: A Contribution to an Ongoing Debate," *Islam and Christian-Muslim Relations* 10, 1 (1999), 5 – 14.

Rahman, Fazlur, *Major Themes of the Qur'an*, Chicago et al.: University of Chicago Press, [2]2010.

Rahman, Fazlur, *Islam and Modernity*, Chicago et al.: University of Chicago Press, 1984.

Rodziewicz, Magdalena, "The End of Traditional Islamic Jurisprudence in Hermeneutics of Moḥammad Mojtahed Shabestari," *Journal of Shiʿa Islamic Studies* 10, 2 (2017), 207 – 30.

Rosen, David, *Judaism and Human Rights*, https://www.rabbidavidrosen.net/wp-content/up loads/2016/02/Judaism-and-Human-Rights.pdf (accessed on 19.03.2022).

Sachedina, Abdulaziz, *Islam and Challenge of Human Rights*, New York: Oxford University Press, 2008.

Saeed, Abdullah, *Human Rights and Islam: An Introduction to Key Debates Between Islamic Law and International Human Rights Law*, Cheltenham: Edward Elgar Publishing Limited, 2018.

Scott, Rachel M., "A Contextual Approach to Women's Rights in the Qurʾān: Readings of 4:34," *The Muslim World* 99 (2009), 60 – 85.

Schirrmacher, Thomas P., "Human Rights and Christian Faith," *Global Journal of Classical Theology* 3, 2 (2002), https://www.galaxie.com/article/gjct03-2-05 (acessed on 19.03.2022).

Shabestari, Muḥammad Mujtahed, *Explanation of the Basis for the Debate with the Muslim Lawyers*, http://mohammadmojtahedShabestari.com/ (accessed on 19.03.2022).

Shahrur, Muhammad, *The Qurʾān, Morality and Critical Reason: The Essential Muhammad Shahrur*, trans. Andreas Christmann, Leiden: Brill, 2009.

Sisters in Islam (ed.), *Reforming Family Law in the Muslim World*, https://sistersinislam.org/ muslim-family-law/ (accessed on 09.06.2022).

Sofi, Sartaj Ahmad, "Comparative Study of Human Rights in Islam and Universal Declaration of Human Rights," *Journal of Islamic Thought and Civilisation* 6, 1 (2016), 37 – 46.

Tabandeh, Sultanhussein, *A Muslim Commentary on the Universal Declaration of Human Rights*, London: F. T. Goulding & Co., 1970.

Tahir-ul-Qadri, Muhammad, *The Constitution of Medina*, published online: London: Minhaj-ul-Quran Publications, 2012, https://www.academia.edu/18365196/The_con stitution_of_Medina_63_constitutional_articles (accessed on 19.03.2022).

Tsai, Daisy Yulin, *Human Rights in Deuteronomy: With Special Focus on Slave Laws*, Berlin et al.: De Gruyter, 2014.

University of Minnesota Human Rights Library (ed.), *Universal Islamic Declaration of Human Rights, Adopted by the Islamic Council of Europe on 19 September 1981/21 Dhul Qaidah 1401*, http://hrlibrary.umn.edu/instree/islamic_declaration_HR.html (accessed on 19.03.2022).

United Nations/Office of the High Commissioner for Human Rights (ed.), *Status of Reservations and Declarations*, https://treaties.un.org/Pages/Treaties.aspx?id=4&subid= A&lang=en (accessed on 09.06.2022).

Venkatraman, Bharati Anandhi, "Islamic States and the United Nations Convention on the Elimination of all Forms of Discrimination against Women: Are the Shariʾa and the Convention Compatible?," *The American University Law Review* 44, 5 (1995), 1949 – 2014.

Wadud, Amina, "Foreword: Engaging Tawhid in Islam and Feminisms," *International Feminist Journal of Politics* 10 (2008), 435 – 38.

Wright, Christopher, *Old Testament Ethics for the People of God*, Downers Grove: InterVarsity Press, 2004.

Wolterstorff, Nicholas P., "Christianity and Human Rights," in: Christian M. Green/John Witte (eds.), *Religion and Human Rights: An Introduction*, 42–55, Oxford: Oxford University Press, 2012.

Yousefi-Eshkevari, Hassan, "Rethinking Men's Authority Over Women: Qiwama, Wilaya and Their Underlying Assumptions," in: Ziba Mir-Hosseini et al. (eds.), *Gender and Equality in Muslim Family Law: Justice and Ethics in Islamic Legal Tradition*, trans. Ziba Mir Hosseini, 191–212, New York, NY: I. B. Tauris & Co Ltd, 2013.

Suggestions for Further Reading

Baderin, Mashood A., "Establishing Areas of Common Ground between Islamic Law and International Human Rights," *International Journal of Human Rights* 5, 2 (2001), 72–113.

Baderin, Mashood A., *International Human Rights and Islamic law*, Oxford: Oxford University Press, 2005.

Bielefeldt, Heiner, "'Western' Versus 'Islamic' Human Rights Conceptions?: A Critique of Cultural Essentialism in the Discussion on Human Rights," *Political Theory* 28, 1 (2000), 90–121.

Eslami, R. A., "System of Human Rights in Islam?" *Journal of Human Rights* 15, 2 (2020), 19–36.

Mayer, Ann Elizabeth, *Islam and Human Rights: Tradition and Politics*, New York: Westview Press, 2013.

Moosa, Ebrahim, "The Dilemma of Islamic Rights Schemes," *Journal of Law and Religion* 15, 1, 2 (2000–01), 185–215.

Ruud, Peters, "Islamic Law and Human Rights: A Contribution to an Ongoing Debate," *Islam and Christian-Muslim Relations* 10, 1 (1999), 5–14.

Emon, Anver M/Ahmed, Rumee (eds.), *The Oxford Handbook of Islamic Law*, New York: Oxford University Press, 2018.

Saeed, Abdullah, *Human Rights and Islam: An Introduction to Key Debates Between Islamic Law and International Human Rights Law*, Cheltenham: Edward Elgar Publishing Limited, 2018.

Souaiaia, A. E., *Human Rights in Islamic Societies: Muslims and the Western Conception of Rights*, London, NY: Routledge, 2021.

Georges Tamer and Catharina Rachik
Epilogue

1 Introduction

As Heiner Bielefeldt states in his introduction to this volume, human rights en-compass the inherent dignity, equality and freedom of all humans and form a normative consensus on the international stage. They also include the right to religious freedom and belief, which entails the right to change one's religion or belief, as well as to manifest one's religion or belief in teaching, practice, wor-ship, and observance. Especially the right to religious freedom shapes the rela-tionship between religions and human rights.

The *Universal Declaration of Human Rights* (UDHR) of 1948 issued by the General Assembly became the major reference for subsequent developments of human rights conventions. Since human rights are immediately binding upon states as their formal guarantors under international law, religious communities must formulate their attitude towards them. The liberating spirit of human rights as a modern concept has posed a major challenge to religions and their tradi-tional ethical teaching.

In regard to the relationship between human rights and religion, affinities as well as conflicts can be observed. The language of human rights is enriched with religious ideas, metaphors, and concepts. Formulations and terms of human rights documents, like "inviolability" exhibit a religious reference. The closeness of religious language and human rights is not a coincidence: human rights go beyond the sphere of rights for they touch upon existential questions of man. Human dignity, human responsibility and the moral framework are topics of var-ious religious traditions as well as of the modern human rights discussion. The ethos that underlies the modern concept of human dignity is also to be found in the Tanakh, Bible and the Qur'ān.

Through these various examples, which postulate a harmony between both human rights and religion, the assumption could be made that both follow the same goals and are built upon equal normative aspirations. Both acknowledge human dignity and inviolability. This motivated various agents of different reli-gious communities to state that human rights are born out of religious traditions. At the same time, representatives of the human rights approach are interested in emphasizing overlaps of both concepts as they underline the extent of the nor-mative consensus of human rights.

https://doi.org/10.1515/9783110561579-006

But we have to acknowledge that these affinities are basic and that there are conflicts between the religions relevant in the present context and human rights. The dichotomy arises out of questions and claims in regard to gender equality, gender identity, sexual orientation as well as religious freedom and belief. Especially these emancipatory aspects of the human rights approach clash with traditional religious values. In this context, critics of the human rights approach hold it to be an anthropocentric ideology, in which the human would be the measure of all things and would stand above religious systems. This contradicts traditional religious thinking in which humans are subordinate to their creator. Reservations against human rights are still noticed especially in some circles of the orthodox churches as well as Islamic contexts.

The core function of the human rights approach is the empowerment of human beings for shaping peaceful coexistence between various religions and belief systems. History has shown that human rights developed in circumstances of conflict-driven pluralization processes. In this way, they represent a paradigm shift towards the *recognition of pluralism*. For human rights, it is not only to tolerate other religions but to recognize the inherent value of religious pluralism. But human rights are more than a device to enforce diversity because they recognize the potential responsible agency and dignity of all humans, so they are the beginning point of any normative interaction.

This empowerment function shows the specific normative authority claimed by human rights, but also the existing limitations of the human rights approach. Therefore, the question here is where the concept of human rights is to be located towards religious systems. It cannot be a one-dimensional view. One problem would be the perception of human rights as a part of religious or belief systems, because it would mean to tie them to a specific belief, hence they would lose their universal claim. But the placement of human rights at the same level of other religions or above them would cause problems as well. It would mean that they add to religious pluralism and not *shape* it. This means that we should not perceive the concept of human rights as a belief-system or ideology, but rather as a normative framework, in which the human is located in the center granting him freedom and dignity independently from his religious affiliation. Institutionalizing human rights also means granting them a specific authority and since humans are located in the center, it involves everybody, also religious communities. Human rights as a normative framework also limits their specific authority because they are not at the same level as the Tanakh, Bible or the Qur'ān. They do not provide answers for existential questions of human life. The underlining of human rights not being a crypto-religion or religious belief system also hints at the modesty of their function. They are limited to the necessary aim to normatively shape pluralistic coexistence.

Tracing the relationship between religion and human rights in the three monotheistic faiths, the following questions arise: To what extent do the holy scriptures and classical (antique and medieval) sources in Judaism, Christianity and Islam deal with human rights and what language do they use? What kind of discourse has emerged in the three traditions and how did they engage in actively shaping a human rights concept? What kind of rejections and reservations are there towards the human rights concept? Which exegetical and theological methods were developed in the respective traditions for further discourse?

In the following, we deal with these and other questions concerning the relationship between human rights and the three monotheistic religions to discover commonalities and differences within their traditions.

2 Human Rights and Judaism

In Judaism we can observe that there are a variety of concepts which can be derived from traditional sources suggesting acknowledgement of a broad range of human rights. While many scholars have pointed to the emphasis on duties and obligations in Judaism, these are intertwined with protections and entitlements similar to modern human rights discourses. In some cases, the Rabbinic tradition goes even further because it built a strong basis of protection and respect for human life, health, property, and dignity.

Concepts of human dignity and equality are found in the book Genesis of the Torah. Here it is the Creation Narrative which serves as a starting point for a discussion of human rights. The most famous verse hinting at innate human dignity is that God created humans – both man and woman – in his image (Gen 1:26 – 28). This passage also affirms the special rank of humans which, in turn, corelates to certain fundamental rights and duties they have towards each other. It invokes not only the dignity of humans but also their equality. The Mishna reflects this by the teaching of Rabbi Tanḥuma, that if humans would mistreat each other, they would mistreat God, since humans reflect the divine. The creation narrative also includes a passage reflecting the descending of all humans from just a single human. Already, Jewish texts of Late Antiquity are asking for the reason, why the human population derived from just one human and not an entire race. The answer by the Rabbis was that this way humans would have one common ancestor and nobody would be entitled to more respect or rights than the other. In other words, this passage underlines human equality further. This is enforced by another biblical teaching which became a Golden Rule in Judaism: to love one's neighbor as one loves oneself.

Among these basic concepts of dignity and equality some concepts are closely connected to human rights in Jewish law: Thus, the inviolability of human life is affirmed early in the Torah and is reinforced by a strict prohibition on murder. Jewish law prescribes that a Jew must passively allow him or herself to be killed rather than kill another without just cause. Most rights can be deduced from positive obligations, for example the expansive obligations the Torah prescribes towards the poor speak for the right to life and dignity. Rabbinic law formulated obligations to establish communal charity and welfare funds to provide for the poor, and developed a broad range of duties in this sense to exercise equal treatment. This conception includes the provision of material needs for every person in the community: It starts with the protection of vulnerable groups, the protection of immigrants and non-citizens over to the duty of paying wages to workers on time. These duties also hint at the strong conception of justice in Judaism.

In Jewish law there is a basic guarantee and protection of one's autonomy. In Jewish thought the restriction of this autonomy requires the consent of the individual citizen. That means that no legislation can be imposed on the people without their majority consent. The status of natural liberty is illustrated by the interpretation of the acceptance of the Torah: Without the human consent the law could not have been imposed on them, according to Rabbinic teaching.

However, when it comes to rights related to religious freedom, gender or association, the matter becomes more complex and complicated. This is due to the strong normative claims about correct practice and observance of religious rules. There may be tolerance towards practice of other religions, but within religious communities that kind of tolerance is usually not extended when members deviate from certain norms. The Torah asks for observance of ritualistic norms from its community: It thus prohibits work on Sabbath, prohibits idolatry and includes regulations for animal sacrifices. Many regulations affect the relationship between the individual and God as well as the religious observance in the private sphere and prescribe punishments for breaking these rules.

But by critically examining classical Rabbinic sources analysis shows that Rabbis carved out significant space within Jewish communities for individual freedom. A broad range of examples from Antiquity to the Middle Ages show, that this kind of religious freedom was acknowledged in its general refusal to coerce Jews to conform to ritual norms. Even if the Rabbis had the power and authority to enforce punishment in cases where ritual law by individuals was not observed, they decided not to do so. Jewish law was more concerned with policing good relations between people than ensuring proper human relationships with God. Even if the Torah prescribed punishments for these transgressions, the Rabbis decided not to exercise punishment in cases, where there was no harm to others or the community, since law prescriptions gave them the flexibility.

In conclusion, this means that there was individual freedom of religion and conscience within a normative Jewish framework because sinful acts by humans were not prosecuted. Examples of these can be shown in relation to Rabbinic law enforcement in civil matters, like in cases of the practice of usury or private sexual offenses if all parties involved consented. Although it is strictly forbidden by the Torah and severe punishments are prescribed for such cases, Rabbis decided not to act upon them. Things were different when religious sins affected others. An example would be the adequate education of children, especially of religious contents to be able as an adult to function in a Jewish community, but also to be able to live his or her life in a secular environment. Since this has an impact on others, the Rabbis chose not to leave much freedom for parents and enforced education for children. Despite these examples, observation of religious law by individuals was important to the Rabbis. Even though they did not choose severe corporal punishments, they had other means like distancing the sinners socially, using economic restrictions or at last banishing them from the community. But these means applied only when people sinned in a public manner.

This analysis can serve as a basis for further discussion in modernity about individual religious freedom. Especially when it comes to the topic of living a dignified life within a community, Jewish law provides a strong basis, because it demands from its members good treatment of each other, charity, and responsibility. In the private sphere, individuals were free to observe religious rules or ignore them. One could state that this reflects a caring community with enough individual freedom. How Jewish communities cope with that complex tradition shows the example of modern Israel. Here, the challenge is the balance between democratic values and traditional religious values. When it comes to rights of religious freedom in Israel, there are still many challenges: the recognition of pluralistic Jewish faith in the diaspora; the question of religious prayer at and on the Temple Mount; the recognition of conversion to Judaism and being Jewish, and the confrontation of anti-Semitism in diasporic communities. Especially the last point will have a significant impact on the relationship of Judaism and religious freedom and its presence in future discourses.

3 Human Rights and Christianity

The relationship between Christianity and human rights has two faces: On the one hand, there are many examples from the Constantine era until the present where "rights" were not observed, a circumstance rooted in the concept of the self-sacrificial suffering of Christ. On the other hand, the development of the human rights concept in the 20th century was actively shaped by Christian theologians of both protestant and catholic origin. Though their work was characterized by religious commitment and motivation, they aimed at implementing a universal or secular basis of human rights thinking for all humanity, and not a distinctively Christian basis. But when it comes to "new" human rights, like gender equality, same sex relationships, rights of women, or abortion, these topics remain a challenge for a lot of Christian communities, especially in Roman Catholic and Orthodox circles.

The important contribution Christianity made to the development of human rights is the linkage between human rights and human dignity, which is reflected in human rights documents. This linkage was a result of global political circumstances, especially during and after the time of totalitarian regimes and the horrors of the second world war and was made by Roman Catholic and Protestant activists and representatives. When it comes to the question of the extent that Christianity played in the modern international reflection on human rights, views differ. The question here is whether the human rights language can be completely detached from the religious sphere.

The theological underpinning of the connection between human rights and human dignity is drawn directly from the biblical account of the creation narrative in Genesis 1:26 – 28. The central motif hinting at innate human dignity is that humans were "created in the image and likeness of God". It also underlines the special rank of humans as God's representatives. In turn, to ignore this status of humans and their dignity would also mean to ignore God's goal of creation and his dominion. Even if this passage has motivated different interpretations as regarding rights and duties connected to it, it has been the primary cornerstone of the engagement of Christians in the human rights debate. But the human rights debate has motivated theologians to explore that passage in more broader terms. In relation to women's rights Genesis 1:26 – 28 has been recently drawn on to underline that it is both male and female who are created in God's likeness and image and that they are equal. Furthermore, the statement that humans are acting as God's representatives on earth not only gives them rights but also responsibilities, for the creation as well as for each other. From a Christian point of view this means that people have the duty of expressing justice, compassion, faithfulness and love. But the understanding of the human being as the likeness and image of God is likewise a commandment and a legal principle, as well as a right and responsibility. This becomes apparent in Genesis 9:6 with the prohibition of murder and bloodshed, which is linked to the principle of right to life.

The engagement of different churches in the human rights development and discourse, as well as the theological contributions made for this reason, must be seen in the context of global political and social changes on the one hand, and on the other hand in regard to the historical development of these respective movements. For the Protestant representatives their initial focus on religious freedom can be best explained from the fight for rights and freedom which is deeply anchored in these movements themselves historically. Freedom of religion played a major role in the involvement of the ecumenical movement in the human rights discourse, but this focus shifted due to international circumstances like Socialism or the struggle against racism and became rather a means by which other rights could be promoted, and not the center. On theological terms the motif of *imago dei* still was in the center of the engagement with human rights, but the theological question on how "the Fall" influenced the rank of humans remained. It was mainly answered through the person of Christ, who was viewed to have restored human dignity through his actions. The Christological underpinning of human rights became the center of the theological debate. Human rights were seen as being strongly connected with human duties and responsibilities. Recently, the topic of religious freedom was given more attention due to the situation of Christians in the Middle East. But a systematical theological reflection on human rights is still to be expected.

Within the Roman Catholic Church there has been a major change towards the attitude of human rights since the 19th century. Although the language of human dignity is already to be found in theological texts from the 7th century onwards, its linkage to human rights was made in 1942 by Pope Pius XII's as a reaction to historical events. It mirrored the theological thinking of the Roman Catholic theologian Jacques Maritain who held the view that human rights are anchored in natural law. A broad change in the attitude towards human rights came with the writing *Pacem in terris* 1958 by Pope John XXIII which includes a qualified affirmation of the UDHR. It also contains the right to freedom of worship and religion which shows a clear change in Catholic thinking. But rights were seen always in connection with duties. Subsequent documents of the Second Vatican Council reinforce this view and further promote the importance of human rights, especially of religious freedom as being central to human dignity. Here, human dignity is deduced from natural law as well as scriptural revelation. The document *Dignitatis Humanae* includes the statement that freedom is an essential aspect of God's dealing with humanity in Christ, so any coercion in religion would be inimical to the Christian faith. Also, in the Roman Catholic church there has been a shift in emphasis of certain rights. In the present, Pope Francis especially focusses and promotes the rights of the poor, and the importance of religious freedom is emphasized particularly due to the situation of churches in the Middle East. The theological discussion connected to human rights revolves around the motif *imago dei*, the incarnation, the redemption by Jesus and the connection of eschatology and human rights. In general, the view towards human rights of the Roman Catholic Church is still traditional. When it comes to rights of women, abortion, or same sex relationships there is still resistance and unease.

Within Orthodox Christianity (Chalcedonian and non-Chalcedonian churches), sources show that different views are being held towards human rights with various theological underpinnings. There are affirmations as well as reservations. The Ecumenical Patriarchate located in Istanbul has recently shown an open attitude towards human rights. It released the document *For the Life of the World* which is affirmative of the language of human rights, especially of the "creation of humanity in Gods likeness and image" and its relationship between freedom, liberty and human rights. A cautious attitude towards the basis of human rights is apparent in the writings of the Archbishop of Albania, Anastasios. Here, the motif *imago dei* is interpreted differently because there is a difference between likeness and image. The likeness is not a fact but a possibility for humans. According to this view, freedom means something different since it is about the achievement of inner freedom. In general, especially in contexts such as the Middle East where the Christian churches are a minority, the human right of "freedom of religion" seems to be linked in the minds of Orthodox religious leaders to the freedom of the church as a corporate body rather than the individual. Regarding the orthodox Church of Russia, recent documents dealing with human rights show ambiguity towards them and in some points contradict each other. Here, the central motif is *imago dei* as well, but with different interpretations. The last of these documents puts the theme human dignity in the center but underlining the connection to responsibility. A wide variety of human rights are acknowledged, but the focus lies on the need of the community. A clear human rights-statement of the church is still missing.

4 Human Rights and Islam

Traditional sources of Islam demonstrate that there is acknowledgement of a broad range of human rights in Islam. A fundamental basis is provided by the Qur'ān acknowledging and emphasizing the inherent dignity of all humans. Moreover, a special rank of humans is underlined because God created humans to be his vice-regent on earth and the angels were asked to bow before Adam (Q 17:70; 2:30). This human dignity is interconnected with human equality which is also found in the Creation-narrative of the Qur'ān. Since all humans descended from Adam as a common ancestor, they are seen as equal. This human image serves as a basis in connection to other more particular rights granted to humans: The Qur'ān establishes a broad concept of justice between humans including the prohibition of unjust bloodshed and prohibition of murder. Humans are asked to establish justice on earth, justice is placed right next to piety (Q 5:9), and God forbids injustice (Q 16:90). Interconnected with the theme of justice is the protection of the poor which is emphasized throughout the scripture encompassing the right of individuals of a due share of wealth (Q 51:19). Also, the theme of human freedom is addressed by the Qur'ān to the extent that humans can make their own decisions and even have the right refusing to believe in God (Q 18:29). Moreover, the Qur'ān underlines that there is no coercion in faith (Q 2:256) and humans are free to voice their opinion. Of course, this freedom is bounded by several duties the Qur'ān imposes on humans. Additional documents referring to the historical circumstances of the Qur'ānic revelation, like the farewell-sermon of Muhammad, show that equality is further emphasized. According to these sources, humans must be granted equality regardless of their racial, ethnic, or linguistic backgrounds. Believers of other monotheistic faiths, like Jews, were granted protection and keeping their religion in the constitution of Medina.

Like Judaism, rights and duties in Islam are closely connected and cannot be regarded as independent legal concepts. Any right an individual has corresponds to a religious duty. In classical Islamic law (fiqh) various concepts were developed not only to impose duties on the community, but scholars like Ibn Nujaym (d. 1563) developed a pre-modern concept of human rights. The formulated rights were the right to ownership, contractual rights, rights of parents, guardians, rights of the husband, rights of the wife, rights of children, and the rights of the neighbor. These principles can serve as an important basis for modern human rights debates in Islam. Another legal source for a discussion on human rights are the formulations of the five necessities in classical texts which comprise protection of life, intellect, religion, property, and family. But all these rights were limited to Islamic lands and the applicability of the sharī'a. Inside the abode of Islam all residents enjoyed legal protection. Non-Muslims within the abode of Islam enjoyed a protected status, but historical sources show that their treatment varied in different eras and under different historical circumstances and that they were not regarded as fully equal to Muslims in that they had to pay a poll tax.

Engaging with different methods formulated by Islamic law led to fruitful discourse on human rights in modernity. The first is the distinction in classical law between the rights of God and the rights of people, which balances private and societal interests and granting individuals freedom. Second, through the formulation of purposes of sharī'a (maqāṣid) the list of protected rights can be expanded. The use of reason has been another fruitful tool to analyze sources in this regard. Scholars like Mashood Baderin defined justice and the protection of human dignity and life as the key principles of the *sharīʿa*.

In the modern era, the history of many majority Muslim countries is connected to the experience of colonialism and their struggle to develop their own identity after gaining independence. A variety of Muslim scholars and thinkers engaged in discussions about European ideas, enlightenment, and Islamic reform. But in this historical framework, Muslims felt pressured to accept Western ideas and perceived them as something foreign and as part of the colonial agenda. Moreover, when it came to the discussion of human rights there was and still is an ongoing debate as to what extent these ideas are compatible with Islamic rules and concepts. By the end of the 20th century all Muslim majority states had at least incorporated some basic human rights into their constitutions. But the content of Islamic human rights documents shows a clear reaction to the outside pressure which most Muslim majority states felt of incorporating Western ideas of human rights.

Documents of Islamic human rights formulations show acceptance and the importance of human rights and even declare them to be part of the Islamic religion from its very beginnings, as in the case of the *Universal Islamic Declaration of Human Rights* (UIDHR) and *Cairo Declaration on Human Rights in Islam*. In conclusion, Islamic states and organs have to protect and uphold them. But the same documents show concentration on duties and obligations and moreover, a limitation of the scope of human rights by binding them to the *sharīʿa*. Rights of children received extra attention by the Islamic Conference of Foreign Ministers in 2005, but the document was criticized for failing to conform with international human rights standards. Despite this criticism it shows the efforts of Muslim majority countries to participate in the international human rights discourse. The problem remains of exercising and including human rights in these states in reality.

In a broader sense the engagement of different Muslim representatives and scholars in the human rights debate can be categorized into two approaches: One is a defensive approach, which rejects the human rights approach as such, because it is perceived as a Western concept which cannot be reconciled with Islamic values. Moreover, human rights are deemed to be part of a colonial and anti-Islamic agenda. Some advocates of this approach simply favor Islamic formulations of human rights over Western formulations, or hold the view that Islam already supplied humanity with the necessary human rights. One example of this on a state level is the refusal to accept women rights conventions by explaining these conventions would be contrary to the *sharīʿa*. Others argue that Islamic values stand above Western secular concepts or that classical Islamic law cannot be reinterpreted in modernity.

Furthermore, there is a harmonistic approach arguing that Islam and human rights are very different but can be reconciled by using different methods of interpretation such as independent reasoning. Especially when it comes to rights of women, sources must be reinterpreted because they emerged in a different historical context. Representatives of this approach underline certain qualities of Qur'ānic concepts, for example that the Qur'ān emphasizes social justice, human dignity and equality.

In the contemporary Islamic debate on human rights, problematic areas such as rights concerning women, the rights of the child, freedom of expression and freedom of religion, can be identified. One matter for debate remains polygamy in Islam, and there are many efforts constraining this practice by the reinterpretation of classical sources. When it comes to religious freedom, the issue of apostasy is the most complicated one since traditional Islamic thinking doesn't usually entail such a practice. But because norms regarding apostasy are not solely based on the Qur'ān and Sunna, they are not immutable and there is room for interpretation, according to some scholars. Moreover, it is pointed out that the Qur'ān and Muhammad advocated freedom of belief and religion, so also Muslims in contemporary states should have the possibility to freely choose their religion.

5 Commonalities and Differences

Judaism, Christianity and Islam share a basic concept of the human being as the zenith of creation. In all three religions, the Creation Narrative serves as a starting point. Although the stories in the Bible and in the Qur'ān differ, it comes to the same basic idea: humans possess inherent dignity because they are "created in the image and likeness of God", according to the Bible, and declared God's vice-regent on earth, according to the Qur'ān. Here, the angels are asked to bow before Adam, which reminds of statements in the Letter to the Hebrews (Heb 1:6) granting man a higher rank than the angels. That God created the humans in his image is reported in a ḥadīth and, thus, became part of the Islamic conception of man.[1] Furthermore, equality among humans is secured, according to the three traditions, because the human race stems just from one human.

From a religious point of view, the special state of the humans can be considered as the foundation of the modern concept of human rights. However, all

---

[1] Al-Bukhārī, al-Jāmi' aṣ-Ṣaḥīḥ, Isti'dhān 1, Bāb ba'd as-Salām, no 6, 227, cf. Melchert, Christopher, "God Created Adam in his Image," *Journal of Qur'anic Studies* 13, 1 (2011), 113–24.

three religions agree that with rights come duties and responsibilities. These duties require, primarily, from the believer religious observance, which is intrinsi-
cally connected to founding and living in a good and just community, where
members take care of each other. Giving charity and protecting the poor is an important cornerstone of the monotheistic religions. The prohibition of bloodshed
and murder further underlines this point. Here also, the monotheistic traditions
are closely connected: Surah 5:52 states that if someone kills another human
being it would be as if he or she would have killed the whole world. This
verse echoes the Talmud, where a similar statement is found.[2] The interconnect-
edness of rights and duties is also emphasized in non-religious discourses. Just
recently, Aleida Assmann pointed to the importance of the connection of human
rights and duties as a reminder that rights cannot exist without duties and that
this point is inevitable for shaping a pluralistic society in modernity.[3]

The contributions included in this volume show clearly that human rights
are intensely debated within each one of the three religions, which led to the pro-
duction of documents on human rights from the perspective of the respective religious communities. But one must critically ask to what extent these documents
are regarded as binding when it comes to political decisions which affect the
rights of individuals or communities. In reality, human rights are not observed
in many countries, which is mostly due to unfavorable political circumstances.
However, what role do religious leaders play in such cases in order to enforce
respect for and implementation of human rights? What, rather, can be observed
is that religious authorities, based on theological convictions, strive to elaborate
particularities of human rights that are appropriate to them and to implement
them in their respective contexts.

Although all three religions offer a common basis for human rights, as mentioned above, they include at the same time restrictions of individual rights concerning gender, sexuality and children, to name just a few examples. Especially
religious freedom or women rights remain in all three religions a matter of debate. Even if one can state that Rabbinic law offers a certain individual freedom
in the private sphere – the same could be said about Islamic law – this freedom
is very narrow and doesn't necessarily agree with the modern idea of freedom.
Even if religious authorities would choose not to prosecute certain ritual transgressions, religious obligations remain and collide with the modern principle
of individual freedom. Another point of dissent between the modern concept

---

2 bSanhedrin 37a.
3 Assmann, Aleida, *Menschenrechte und Menschenpflichten. Schlüsselbegriffe für eine humane
Gesellschaft*, Wien: Picus, 2018.

of human rights and traditional religious views is that the sinner is usually deprived of certain rights and has, in some societies, still to expect societal exclusion, which in pre-modern societies had a huge impact on one's life.

In addition to the Creation Narrative, in Christianity the Incarnation Doctrine offers a further theological foundation of human dignity, which is also basic for the development of the concept of human rights. From a traditional Christian point of view, the question arises here whether non-Christians, who do not believe in the incarnation and, thus, in the human dignity restored by it, could enjoy the same restored state which Christians enjoy, according to that view. An inclusivist position, according to which Christ's redemption has a universal effect, would certainly affirm this. However, the Creation Narrative in Genesis remains the cornerstone of the human rights debate in Christianity. In that way, a common basis for further discussion on human dignity and equality is given across the three religions. Nevertheless, theological differences emerge when one dives deeper into the Narrative of Creation and the Fall of Adam and Eve: For Christians, this was a challenge to the question, if humans in some sense have to earn their dignity back. In the Qur'ān, the Fall does not have the severe theological consequences developed in Christianity.

The prominent position of the human beings in the created world remains the firm basis, common to the three religions, for the development of human rights. This is also the foundation of interreligious discourses on it, in order to discuss many still open questions. This remains relevant, especially when looking at the historical development of human rights. The history of the emergence of human rights documents shows that especially Protestant and Roman Catholic Christians participated in developing them. Because of global political circumstances, other religious communities, like the Russian church, were not able to do the same. Moreover, Islamic countries deem them as something Western. As a consequence, these communities tend to hold a rather defensive view towards the *Universal Declaration of Human Rights* and prefer to formulate human rights based on their own cultural and religious traditions. This shows the need for a new interreligious discourse which cannot be bound to religious issues themselves.

Although each of the three religions has developed its own conception of man with specific nuances, the shared basis in the discourse makes it possible to discuss the fundamental question of how the emancipatory concept of human rights can be reconciled with religious profound views of man, whereby the latter subordinates the individual to the community and speaks of man's duties to God and fellow human beings rather than of human rights. In addition to this tension, the universality of human rights across cultures and religions presents another problematic area that can only be addressed discursively if solutions to the difficulties it raises should be sought. One of these difficulties is that the desired implementation of human rights in the world must suffer serious disruptions if, in the process of implementation, cutbacks would have to be made in favor of religious and cultural particularities. Is it possible to formulate a human rights charter which is not anchored in certain basic cultural and religious belief? Would different interpretations of human rights have to be permitted in the various religious communities and cultural circles, leading to different practices? Or should the same human rights – not reshaped by the religions according to particular interests – apply across regions and religions to one humanity, so that they can have a universally valid guiding function that moves societies to be shaped according to them?[4] In order to make progress on these and other questions towards a better world, Judaism, Christianity and Islam, in discourse with one another, must come up with constructive proposals which appeal not only to their followers but also to secular people. This should be possible, not in order to eradicate religious and cultural particularities, but to create a humane basis on which diversity and difference can grow and flourish in a peaceful world.

Finally, the overview of the engagement of the three faiths showed that there is still much work to do from an exegetical and theological point of view. Human rights in the New Testament are not fully explored yet, and the same could be said about the Qur'ān and the Hebrew Bible. Since each one of the three religions demonstrates that there is much room for the interpretation of the traditional sources, fruitful discourse can, thus, revolve around the development of hermeneutical methods which can be utilized in a useful human rights debate currently and in the future.

---

4 For a discussion on these questions see Amesbury, Richard, "Inter-Religious Declarations of Human Rights: Grounding Rights or Constructing 'Religion'?," *Religion and Human Rights* 5 (2010), 43–64; Twiss, Summer/Grelle, Bruce (eds.), *Explorations in Global Ethics: Comparative Religious Ethics and Interreligious Dialogue*, New York: Routledge, 2000; Schreiner, Peter, "European Institutions, Human Rights and Interreligious Education," in: Manfred L. Pirner/Johannes Lähnemann/Heiner Bielefeldt (eds.), *Human Rights and Religion in Educational Contexts. Interdisciplinary Studies in Human Rights*, vol. 1, 273–83, Switzerland: Springer, 2016; Lehmann, Karsten B., "Construction of the Concept of Religion in the United Nations' General Assembly: From Human Rights to Dialogue and Harmony," in: Stanley D. Brunn/Roland Kehrein (eds.), *Handbook of the Changing World Language Map*, vol. 1, 2761–76, Switzerland: Springer, 2020.

List of Contributors

Clare Amos was head of the interreligious office at the World Council of Churches, Geneva, specialising in relations with Judaism and Islam, until her retirement in 2018. She has an academic background in both interreligious concerns and biblical studies, and before moving to Geneva in 2011 was Director of Theological Studies at the Anglican Communion Office in London. Currently she holds the honorary role of Director of Lay Discipleship in the Church of England Diocese in Europe. Her commentary on Genesis, *Birthpangs and Blessings: A Commentary on the Book of Genesis* (Sacristy Press, Durham) was published in 2022 and she has contributed a chapter to the forthcoming publication *The Covid Pandemic and the World's Religions: Challenges and Responses* edited by Dan Cohn-Sherbok and George Chryssides (Bloomsbury Press).

Heiner Bielefeldt has been Full Professor of Human Rights and Human Rights Politics at the University of Erlangen-Nuremberg since October 2009. Before taking the newly established chair for Human Rights, he was Director of the German Institute for Human Rights (based in Berlin) which is the officially accredited national human rights institution of Germany. Bielefeldt's research interests, above all, include different interdisciplinary facets of human rights theory and practice. Between 2010 and 2016, he also served as the United Nations Special Rapporteur on freedom of religion or belief.

Michael J. Broyde is professor of law at Emory University School of Law, the director of the SJD Program, and Berman Projects Director at the Center for the Study of Law and Religion at Emory University. He is also a core faculty member at the Tam Institute of Jewish Studies at Emory. His most recent books include *Setting the Table: An Introduction to the Jurisprudence of Rabbi Yechiel Mikhel Epstein's Arukh HaShulhan* (Academic Studies Press, 2021, co-authored with Shlomo Pill of the Center for the Study of Law and Religion*)*, *Sex in the Garden: Consensual Encounters Gone Bad in Genesis* (Wifpf & Stock, 2019), and *Sharia Tribunals, Rabbinical Courts, and Christian Panels: Religious Arbitration in America and the West* (Oxford Press, 2017).

Shlomo C. Pill is senior lecturer at Emory University School of Law and the Paul and Marion Kuntz Scholar in Law and Religion at the Center for the Study of Law and Religion at Emory University. His work focuses on Jewish and Islamic law, jurisprudence, and American constitutional law with a focus on religious liberty issues. Pill's articles have been published in the Buffalo Law Review, Mississippi Law Journal, Harvard Journal of Racial and Ethnic Justice, Pepperdine Dispute Resolution Journal, Touro Law Review, and other academic and popular outlets. His recent book, *Setting the Table: An Introduction to the Jurisprudence of Rabbi Yechiel Mikhel Epstein's Arukh Hashulhan* (with Michael J. Broyde) was published by Academic Studies Press in January 2021.

Patricia Prentice is a researcher with a particular interest in social cohesion and religious communities. She has worked in Australia and overseas in the government, academic and not-for profit sectors, including in Cairo, Egypt, working for an organisation specialising in Arab-West Understanding and in Geneva, Switzerland for a human rights advocacy group. Pat-

https://doi.org/10.1515/9783110561579-007

ricia has managed research projects in Indonesia, Singapore and Pakistan and written on various topics, including Islam and human rights, intercultural marriage, Islamophobia, Islam and Australian values, and stories of resilience from Australia's religious communities during the COVID-19 crisis. She is a researcher at the National Centre for Contemporary Islamic Studies at the University of Melbourne.

Catharina Rachik is currently research associate at the Friedrich-Alexander-Universität Erlangen-Nürnberg (FAU) where she coordinates the book-series "Key Concepts in Interreligious Discourse". Before she joined the "Bavarian Research Center for Interreligious Discourses" she has been research associate and coordinator in the "Center for Islamic Theology" at the University of Münster. She gained her M.A. in Islamic Studies at the University of Münster. She is writing her dissertation about "Moses in the Qur'ān". Her research focuses on Qur'ānic Studies and Tafsīr (Classical and Modern), the Qur'ān in Late Antiquity, Prophet stories in the Qur'ān, as well as on the field of Islamic art.

Abdullah Saeed is currently the Sultan of Oman Professor of Arab and Islamic Studies and Redmond Barry Distinguished Professor at the University of Melbourne. Among his key publications are *Human Rights and Islam* (Edward Elgar, 2018). *Reading the Qur'an in the Twentieth Century: Towards a Contextualist Approach* (Routledge, 2014), *The Qur'an: an introduction,* (Routledge 2008), *Approaches to the Qur'an in Contemporary Indonesia* (edited, Oxford, 2005); *Islamic Banking and Interest: A Study of the Prohibition of Riba and its Contemporary Interpretation* (EJ Brill, 1996).

Georges Tamer holds the Chair of Oriental Philology and Islamic Studies and is founding director of the Bavarian Research Center for Interreligious Discourses at the Friedrich-Alexander-Universität of Erlangen-Nürnberg. He received his Ph.D. in Philosophy from the Free University Berlin in 2000 and completed his habilitation in Islamic Studies in Erlangen in 2007. His research focuses on Qur'ānic hermeneutics, philosophy in the Islamic world, Arabic literature and interreligious discourses. His publications include: *Zeit und Gott: Hellenistische Zeitvorstellungen in der altarabischen Dichtung und im Koran*, 2008; the edited volumes *Islam and Rationality. The Impact of al-Ghazālī* (2015); *Hermeneutical Crossroads: Understanding Scripture in Judaism, Christianity and Islam in the Pre-Modern Orient* (2017). He is the editor of the *Erlanger Jahrbuch für Interreligiöse Diskurse*.

Index of Persons

https://doi.org/10.1515/9783110561579-008

Index of Subjects

https://doi.org/10.1515/9783110561579-009

www.ingramcontent.com/pod-product-compliance
Lightning Source LLC
Chambersburg PA
CBHW052007270326
41929CB00015B/2823